THE
Female Fear

The Social Cost of Rape

Margaret T. Gordon

AND

Stephanie Riger

UNIVERSITY OF ILLINOIS PRESS

Urbana and Chicago

This book is printed on acid-free paper.

Library of Congress Cataloging-in-Publication Data

Gordon, Margaret T., 1939-
   The female fear : the social cost of rape / Margaret T. Gordon,
Stephanie Riger.
      p. cm.
   Reprint. Originally published: New York : Free Press, c1989.
   Includes bibliographical references and index.
   ISBN 0-252-06169-1 (alk. paper)
   1. Rape—United States—Psychological aspects. 2. Women—United
States—Attitudes—Case studies. 3. Fear of crime—United States—
Case studies. 4. Rape—United States—Public opinion. 5. Public
opinion—United States. I. Riger, Stephanie. II. Title.
HV6561.G67 1991
362.88'3—dc20   90-45161
                                                            CIP

To the Susans of our Cities
and
to Sarah and Seth, Matthew and Jake, our children

Contents

List of Tables and Figures

Preface to the
Paperback Edition

WE are gratified at the response our book has provided—from the eighty-four-year-old man who told us it had helped him understand for the first time the fears of his wife of sixty years, to the twenty-year-old receptionist who, as she stood in the aisle of a bookstore reading it, found her paralysis and fear turning to energizing anger.

Talk show hosts have proclaimed it is "must reading" for "all men," and women law students are using it as a resource in their efforts to reform teaching about rape law

Women journalists have found themselves surprised at their own reactions as they were led to consider the role of the press and other institutions in creating and sustaining the female fear and the terrible costs of that fear to our society. Therapists have found it useful to consider the relationship between institutional responses to rape and individual responses.

We are pleased and excited that this new paperback edition will make our book more easily accessible, especially to students and others who may become leaders of agencies, organizations, institutions, and even movements that have the opportunity to change realities for women, and hence our society.

Margaret T. Gordon
University of Washington
Seattle, WA

Stephanie Riger
University of Illinois at Chicago
Chicago, IL

Preface

In the late 1970s, women throughout the country marched through city streets chanting "Take back the night!" They were protesting the fear that has increasingly restricted women's lives, a fear shared by women of all ages, yet until recently rarely articulated—a fear of rape. This fear, its sources, and the ways that women cope with it are the subjects of this book.

Our connection with this topic is both professional and personal since we, too, experience this female fear. We began our studies of women's fear several years ago, when we were both participating in a large, federally funded research project on the impact of crime on cities. The central question of that research was how the tremendous rise in crime since 1964 has affected urban neighborhoods. Did it cause neighbors to cower behind armed fortresses out of fear, or did it cause them to organize and unite against a common threat? As that research progressed, we both felt that a central piece of the story was being overlooked. While the impact of crime on neighborhoods was certainly important, the fear of crime seemed to be experienced primarily by women, and that research project had no plans specifically to examine women's fear. The male members of the research team either did not think this topic was sufficiently important, or were afraid that asking questions about rape and other sources of women's fear would offend participants and cause them to drop out of the study. As is so often the case in academia, issues of concern to women had to be pushed forward by women researchers. Because we believed that fear of rape has a profound effect on women's lives, we began our own separate study to investigate it.

We were fortunate that the federal government, under pressure from feminist groups, had just established the National Center for the Prevention and Control of Rape within the National Institute of Mental Health. With the support of a research grant from that Center, we were able to interview women in three cities: Chicago, Philadelphia, and San Francisco. Our project staff interviewed 299 women and 68 men in these cities. Insofar as possible, in-person interviews were conducted in respondents' homes by interviewers matched with them by race and language. In each city, there was a project office where some interviews were conducted; this office was used when the respondent requested that the interview not be at home or when the interviewers were fearful of going to certain areas. Most in-person interviews lasted approximately 90 to 100 minutes, but some ran as long as three hours.

Our typical respondent is a woman of thirty-five with a high school education and an income between $10,000 and $15,000 from part-time employment. About half (53 percent) of the women were white, and slightly more than half (54.5 percent) were not married at the time of the interview. While the sample is not representative of the whole population in these cities (we deliberately interviewed more women than men and we concentrated our interviews in two neighborhoods in each city), the responses people gave let us explore in depth the sources of fear and how women cope with it in their daily lives.

Our project worked cooperatively with the Reactions to Crime Project (also at the Center for Urban Affairs and Policy Research at Northwestern University). Together, the two projects interviewed by telephone a citywide sample of 540 women and men in each of three cities and an additional 3,533 women and men living in selected neighborhoods in those three cities. The telephone interviews let us look at citywide levels of fear of crime, as well as the impact of crime on urban neighborhoods. The samples in the telephone surveys are representative of the cities from which they were drawn, and they provide a context for understanding the responses about sexual assault given by the people interviewed in person in the six neighborhoods.

In asking questions about fear, we wanted to know whether all women were afraid, or only some women. What were some of the factors that made some women more fearful than others? And, most important, how did women cope with that fear? Did fear of crime, especially fear of rape, hold all women captive, dependent on men for protection, as some feminists claimed? Or had women evolved strategies of their own to keep themselves safe? And what was the overall impact of fear of rape on the quality of women's lives?

Over the course of this research, we found it difficult at times to separate ourselves from the topic. Constantly reading about and discussing rape and other forms of violence against women often left us anxious and depressed. Staff working with us also found themselves disturbed. When news about our project appeared in the newspaper, we received many calls from women who had been raped or otherwise victimized, wanting to do something—anything— to help so that others wouldn't have to suffer the same abuse. But most frequently, when we would happen to mention to friends or casual acquaintances that we were doing research on fear of crime, women would respond with great enthusiasm, eager to share with us their own experience of fear of victimization. It was as if they had never told these stories before. Publicly considered too trivial for discussion, this taboo topic is nonetheless a matter of great private concern. Women's immediate, enthusiastic reaction to the topic of fear of rape convinced us to share our research findings not only with the academic community in scientific journals (as is typical with the findings of research projects), but also with the general public.

Acknowledgments

SINCE we began this project, our lives have changed. Our personalities, our careers, and our friendship have all been affected by what we've learned about how fear impacts on women's lives. We are grateful to have been able to do this work together, and to have done it when we did.

Many people have contributed to our thinking and to our successfully completing this project. We would like to give special thanks to Elizabeth Kutzke, Gloria Levin, and Mary Lystad—all at various times of the National Center for the Prevention and Control of Rape at the National Institute for Mental Health* —for their faith and support. Paul J. Lavrakas, Robert LeBailly, and Mary Rogel graciously gave us competent research assistance. Linda Heath, now Associate Professor of Psychology at Loyola University in Chicago, made significant contributions to the chapter on media and is co-author of that chapter. Shirley Dvorin, co-author of the chapter on the law, is now an attorney in the Chicago area. We are grateful to friends and colleagues. The late Fred DuBow generously gave time and wisdom to us during the early days of the project. Wesley Skogan, Arlene Kaplan Daniels and Howard Becker never faltered

*This work was partially supported by grant #1 RO1 MH 29620 from the National Institute of Mental Health and the Center for Urban Affairs and Policy Research at Northwestern University. In addition, the chapter on rape and the media was written while Gordon was on leave from Northwestern as a Senior Fellow at the Gannett Center for Media Studies at Columbia University. Riger's work was partially supported by sabbatical and research leave from Lake Forest College.

in their encouragement and willingness to read and comment on drafts. And of course we owe a great debt to the people who cheerfully typed numerous versions of this manuscript—especially Kathryn McCord and Janet S. Soule. We are grateful, too, to Joyce Seltzer of The Free Press for helping us translate academic jargon into English. Finally, we want to thank our husbands, Andrew Gordon and Dan Lewis, and children, Sarah, Seth, Matthew, and Jake, for being understanding not only of our absences, but also of our occasional depression and sometimes despair prompted by the nature of this topic.

Perhaps most of all, we are grateful to the women who shared their thoughts and feelings and experiences with us. We hope our work justifies the time and faith they gave us.

In the end, it is we who take the responsibility for our conclusions. We have tried to put the issues in perspective. We hope we have succeeded.

Margaret T. Gordon
Northwestern University
Evanston, IL

Stephanie Riger
Lake Forest College
Lake Forest, IL

1

Learning to Fear

I emerged from the warmth and conviviality of a group of friends at a restaurant into the darkness and emptiness of a city street late at night. My car was just around the corner, but getting to it meant walking under an unlit viaduct. As I approached the viaduct, I saw a man starting toward me from the other end of the block. My heart began to pound. I held my breath, and began to calculate: Does he have bad intentions? Is he bigger than I am? Should I scream? Where can I run if he attacks? The bar on the corner is open, but is that a source of safety or of greater danger? My anxiety increased as the man got closer. I tightened, and the calculations continued: Should I look him directly in the eye, or will that be interpreted as a come-on? Should I walk briskly, or will that convey fear? The man approached, walked past me, and continued down the street. I was unharmed. Did he know how frightened I was? If I had been raped, would I have been blamed for being out alone in a dark, dangerous place? Would I have blamed myself?

—Jane

INCIDENTS like this one happen to countless numbers of women hundreds of times over the course of their lives. Each incident, taken by itself, may seem trivial. But the sum of these incidents exacts a heavy toll for women who live in cities—and for women who avoid cities because of the possibility of such occurrences. The fear, the anxiety, the distress are all a daily part of urban life for many women.

Why is it that most women nod knowingly at the mention of "fear of rape," although many neither have been victimized nor know a victim? Why do two-thirds of this nation's women say they do not feel safe walking in their own neighborhoods at night, and that if they were attacked, even their friends would blame them for being out alone? How does it happen that fear of rape is experienced privately by so many women, yet is rarely discussed?

The fear experienced by the average American woman, the centrality of rape to that fear, and the impact of that fear on the way she conducts her day-to-day life is a subject that, strangely, has been confined to private discourse. The fact that women's fear is generally misunderstood, and is seriously eroding individual lives as well as the fabric of community and social life, argues for a more public discussion.

The only crime women fear more than rape is murder.[1] And while rape is not often uppermost in the minds of most women, it is ever present. Most women experience fear of rape as a nagging, gnawing sense that something awful could happen, an angst that keeps them from doing things they want or need to do, or from doing them at the time or in the way they might otherwise do. Women's fear of rape is a sense that one must always be on guard, vigilant and alert, a feeling that causes a woman to tighten with anxiety if someone is walking too closely behind her, especially at night. It is a fear that calls up admonitions women have heard from childhood through adolescence and into maturity. It evokes visions of horrifying experiences of women known or heard about, and of women portrayed on TV and movie screens and in the newspapers. It makes women reflect on the often devastating consequences for victims and their families and friends.

This fear is more than a fear of being mugged or robbed; it is the fear of being sexually violated. This special fear, this added burden, is part of the contemporary experience of being a woman in the United States. It is related to sexual taboos and myths that are woven throughout the fabric of our society and which make it difficult to confront. It is worse than fear of other crimes because women know they are held responsible for avoiding rape, and should they be victimized, they know they are likely to be blamed.

Fear of sexual assault is not the only fear driving women's lives, or even the major one; most women worry more about losing their jobs, getting a divorce, or getting cancer. Fear of rape is, however, a feeling women are never totally free of, and it can, from time to time, terrorize them. As one feminist says, "I have never been free of the fear of rape. From a very early age, I, like most women, have thought of rape as part of my natural environment—something to be feared and prayed against like fire or lightning. I never asked why men raped. I simply thought it one of the mysteries of human nature."[2]

How widespread is this fear? Every woman has it to a degree, and all women are affected by it. It "keeps women off the streets at nights. Keeps them home. Keeps women passive and modest for fear they be thought provocative."[3] It influences where they go and when, and the routes they take. For some women, this fear is so deeply felt that it totally controls their day-to-day activities. For others, it is like a nagging background noise, coming to the forefront of awareness only when they sense danger. Some women deny fear, but take precautions—such as carrying Mace—which would seem to belie their words. Some, like one young woman interviewed, admit to having "moments of being afraid" but are "determined to push them down" because they "don't want to stay in all the time" as fear would dictate. There are other women who deal with the issue by simply refusing to think about it. For still other women, a habitual caution blossoms into fear after some triggering event, as if they had stepped forever over some invisible threshold.

One woman, Anne, now a therapist, was not conscious of any fear of rape until she was about forty years old. She grew up in a midsize Minnesota town and learned to trust most people. When she moved to Chicago, she thought it was sensible to take some additional precautions, such as locking the doors to protect her material goods, but she was not afraid for her personal safety. Anne's fear for herself and her teenage daughter arose when she worked as a therapist-in-training in a hospital in a high-crime neighborhood. Every patient she was assigned over the course of a year had been the victim of rape or childhood sexual abuse, and Anne could see the devastation wrought by those victimizations in their lives and in the lives of people close to them. Her newly found fear prompted her to behave differently, to take more precautions than she had ever before, and to worry more about her daughter's safety.

Anne's fear was a result of adjusting to a new environment. It came relatively late in life. The level of fear women experience is rooted in both individual psychological and social determinants. The former vary greatly and thus have varying impact. The latter seem to have more uniform consequences.

Personal experiences women have as young girls are especially influential in forming their attitudes toward sexual assault and in initiating female fear. Most American women, especially those living in large cities, have been confronted in their youth by adult men (either within the home or outside) who make sexual advances either directly, or indirectly through gestures or humor.

One middle-aged professional woman recalled an incident from her childhood:

> One hot summer day when I was about eleven my dad sent me to the store to get a pack of cigarettes for him. As the clerk returned the change, he reached over the counter and grabbed my breasts! Shocked and embarrassed, I dropped everything and ran home and told my dad. Enraged, he ran out of the house without even putting his shirt on, yelling at me to stay put. Twenty or thirty minutes later, he came back. He was sweating and told me never to go back to that store. I didn't think I had done anything wrong, but I felt that he was angry at me. Then he got himself a drink, something alcoholic. Finally, he picked me up and sat me on his lap, and said he loved me. A little while later, he got up and went over to the couch. Lying down on his stomach, he asked me if I would rub his back. I began with his neck which always seemed tight, and worked down his spine to the top of his shorts. Then I lightly pounded his back with my fists. Next he asked me to rub his legs, explaining that since he was so tall his leg muscles were always tight, too. After a few minutes, without saying a word, he abruptly got up and went to the bathroom. When he came back, he told me to go to my room for a while. Nothing else was said, but I felt that I was being punished for the incident at the store. Years later, I realized he had been sexually aroused.
>
> —Nancy

Another woman, now in her seventies, remembers being dragged into an alley by a man when she was ten or twelve years old. He pushed her to the ground and groped under her dress, pulling at her panties. Terrified, she just lay there, praying that someone would walk by and he would leave. Someone did, and he left. She got up, brushed herself off, and walked home in a daze.

Such early experiences together with vague warnings from their fathers and mothers not to talk to strangers, or get into strangers' cars because "something bad could happen," leave young adult women with a sense of danger and vulnerability related to sexual organs, to adult men, and a confusion about the appropriate way to behave. These experiences are often reinforced by pressures and problems young women experience during their dating years. Junior high and high school boys often make sexual jokes about parts of young girls' bodies, and many young women are pushed to "go all the way," or further than they want to, on dates.

One high school sophomore, Melissa, came home crying because she had overheard the boy she liked, P. J., saying he didn't care which of two girls he went out with, Melissa or Nancy, because they both had big breasts. This experience taught Melissa to be embarrassed by her body, and to wonder from then on just why men were interested in being with her.

Another teenager, Alice, was pressured to "go all the way" by her boyfriend of two years. Alice came from a churchgoing family, and her mother had told her she should "save herself" for the man she married. Alice felt torn between her love for Gary and the admonitions of her mother. One night she came home sobbing, with her blouse ripped, saying that Gary had gotten angry when she resisted having sex with him, shouting that she must not really love him. Two days later, Gary broke up with Alice. This not only left Alice feeling unhappy and confused, but affected her sexual behavior on dates for the next several years.

A college professor used to resent the admonitions of her mother, until she learned why her mother felt as she did.

> My mother is a fearful woman. Much of our relationship is colored by her fear—she warning me of the dangers in daily living, and I resenting her filling me with fears. In particular, she had always warned me against men: they only want one thing, all the standard clichés. I had always dismissed her fears as exaggerations—after all, she lived a comfortable middle-class existence in a safe suburb. When I was forty, and she in her late sixties, we were driving down an urban street lined with high-rise apartment buildings. My mother said she could never live there because of the elevators. I had my typical reaction of annoyance—she's being paranoid again, exaggerating the danger of fire or some such rare event. No, she said—it was because of what had happened when she was little, stating that as if I knew the story. What happened? She had been attacked, nearly raped in an elevator when she was little, and ever after had feared elevators (and, I might add, men) and had done her best to protect her children by frequent warnings. My vision of her shifted from that of a paranoid, fearful woman to that of a victim whose scars live on, not only in herself but also in the fears she passed on to her children.
>
> —Jane

The discomfort and confusion young women feel with respect to their sexuality is exacerbated by the role of sexual coercion and seduction as displayed in advertising, films, and other media. They seem to advise women to be sexy and alluring if they want to be happy. Then there are wolf whistles, unwanted hugs and pinches—what the authors of one book call "mini-rapes"[4]—which continually remind women they are vulnerable, sexual objects. And there are the stories about how badly victims are treated by police, medical personnel, and the courts. In addition, there are the ever-present stories in the news describing new rapes, reminding women that in this country, rape is a common event.

The result of all these forces is widespread, multidimensional, confusing female fear, with important consequences for women and for society.

Female fear feeds on misinformation about rape. Because for so many years rape has been a taboo topic shrouded in mystery and shame,[5] many people know little about the crime except the myths pervasive in our culture. Some of the more common are:

- Victims are young, careless, beautiful women who invite rape.
- Victims are "loose" women who provoke rapists.
- No healthy woman can be raped, and any woman can avoid it.
- A woman who goes to a man's house on the first date implies she is willing to have sex and if she refuses, is inviting rape.
- Women charge rape to cover accidental pregnancies or to take revenge.
- No woman can do much about rape, so she might as well lie back and enjoy it.
- Rapists are sex-starved men.
- All rapists are sick, or had crazy or sick mothers.
- Otherwise decent men are spurred to rape by the clothing or behavior of women.
- Rapists act on uncontrollable sexual impulses.
- Victims are to blame for rape.

Most adults grew up during times when such beliefs were an accepted part of the common culture and went both unchallenged and unchecked. Although they are not based in reality, they are still widely believed, even by women themselves. Research indicates that myths shape people's attitudes about rape,[6] concerning both beliefs about victims (such as a woman's responsibility for causing or preventing rape, a woman's expected behavior during a rape attack, and attitudes toward women who have been raped) and beliefs about rapists (the mental state of rapists, motivations of rapists, and appropriate punishments for rapists). A person's sex, race, and general attitudes toward women are related to her/his attitudes on these different dimensions. Men, blacks, and persons favoring traditional rather than liberal views of women's roles tend to believe to a greater extent that women are responsible for causing, and therefore preventing, rape; that women are less desirable following rape; that rapists are mentally abnormal, motivated by sexual desire; and that punishments for rapists should be harsh. Other analyses indicate that the higher the tolerance for violence and sex-role stereotyping, the greater is the rape myth acceptance.[7] The more educated seem to question the myths. In one study, college students who had factual knowledge about rape rejected rape myths,[8] suggesting that a policy of public education may help to dispel these myths.

The widespread acceptance of myths about rape reinforces women's early experiences, heightening fear and fueling the idea that they are responsible for attacks.

2

The Pervasiveness
of Female Fear

FEMALE fear is the result of the interaction of social, sexual, and psychological forces. Perhaps its strongest component is ultimately the fear of death. The fundamental anxiety about dying, and the certainty of it, are the sources of *all* fears experienced by human beings.[1] Yet it is rarely in the forefront of people's minds because, if it were, people would find it too difficult to cope with day-to-day life.[2]

People are said to fear death for several reasons: fear of physical suffering; fear of humiliation over being unable to cope with it; interruption of goals, especially for younger people; impact on survivors; fear of punishment for past wrongs; and fear of simply not existing.[3] Many of these death-related anxieties are the same or similar to what women say they fear about rape.

Women say the "worst aspects" of rape are the possibility of being killed and the possibility, perhaps the likelihood, that if they survive, they nonetheless will be humiliated and stigmatized. In addition, feelings of guilt and self-blame, that they are being punished for past wrongs, and loss of control over their lives are aspects that make the threat of rape terrifying. Women also dread the impact on family and friends; interruption of work, school, and other aspects of daily routine; interruption of normal sexual relations; and the physical pain associated with the rape and other injuries. Unlike death, rape is not a certainty; yet it is dreaded for many of the same reasons.

Most rape victims report having feared for their lives during their attacks, and some women say they would *rather* die than be raped and live. For many women, to be raped is, in essence, to die. Some women have killed themselves after surviving rape attacks, and many other victims consider it.

The threat of death during a rape attack is a very real one to many women, since women believe that on the average at least 25 percent of rape victims are killed during their attacks, and that a majority of victims get seriously injured. (In fact, the figures for death and injury are about 3 and 8 percent, respectively.)

Another aspect of female fear is even more common. Women across the country do not feel safe out alone in their neighborhoods at night,[4] especially if they live in large cities. Just over 61 percent of women—six out of every ten—living in the twenty-six largest U.S. cities say they feel "very unsafe" or "somewhat unsafe" in that situation.[5] Forty-four percent of women living in Philadelphia, Chicago, and San Francisco (cities we will look at in detail later) reported feeling somewhat or very unsafe.[6]

Race, marital status, and age are all related to women's sense of safety. In general, blacks report feeling less safe than persons of other races or ethnicities; those widowed, separated, or divorced feel less safe than the never or currently married; and older people report feeling less safe than younger people. Within each of these demographic categories, however, women are twice as likely as men to feel very unsafe. Blacks, whether male or female, feel the least safe of any ethnic or racial subgroup, but about half as many black females report feeling safe as black males. Gender differences in feelings of safety by age are especially pronounced. Young women feel the safest, with only 26 percent of the twenty- to twenty-four-year-olds saying they feel "very unsafe." Very few young men report feeling very unsafe. Larger percentages of middle-aged women feel very unsafe, and a few middle-aged men do. But close to half (49.7 percent) of the women aged sixty-five or over report feeling very unsafe, while about 26 percent of men in that age category say they feel very unsafe (see Table 2.1).

In addition to city, race, age, and marital status, the neighborhood one lives in bears directly on how safe one feels (see Table 2.2).[7] There are significant differences *within cities* by neighborhood and, not surprisingly, by time of day. Women feel less safe at night (see Figure 2.1).

In order to understand some of the physical realities that might

TABLE 2.1

Percentage Distribution of Feeling of Personal Safety When Out Alone in the Neighborhood at Night by Gender, Race/Ethnicity, Marital Status, and Age

		Very Safe	Reason-ably Safe	Some-what Safe	Very Unsafe	Sample Size
Gender						
	Male	21.8	46.5	19.2	12.5	5230
	Female	7.7	31.2	28.1	33.0	6368
Race/Ethnicity						
Male	White	24.7	47.5	18.2	9.7	3773
	Black	13.8	43.3	22.2	20.8	1337
	Other	21.5	50.5	17.8	10.2	121
Female	White	8.7	33.3	29.1	28.9	4322
	Black	5.3	26.3	25.6	42.8	1924
	Other	8.5	35.6	32.6	23.3	122
Marital Status						
Male	Married	2.0	47.0	19.9	13.1	3252
	Widowed	11.1	35.1	27.0	26.8	182
	Never Married	27.1	48.2	16.7	8.0	1434
	Separated/ Divorced	21.2	41.2	19.6	18.0	344
Female	Married	7.6	32.2	30.1	30.1	3303
	Widowed	6.5	24.9	24.4	44.1	922
	Never Married	8.9	34.6	28.0	28.5	1365
	Separated/ Divorced	6.8	28.9	24.4	39.9	761
Age						
Male	16–19	26.8	49.7	16.2	7.2	553
	20–24	30.1	51.5	13.1	5.3	612
	25–34	27.1	51.2	15.1	6.6	1006
	35–49	21.5	47.3	20.7	10.5	1146
	50–64	17.2	43.1	22.3	17.3	1212
	65 or over	11.4	37.2	25.1	26.4	701
Female	16–19	10.9	35.4	27.5	26.2	607
	20–24	9.3	36.5	28.2	26.0	734
	25–34	7.9	34.5	28.9	28.7	1214
	35–49	8.6	34.6	29.3	27.5	1427
	50–64	6.3	27.2	29.6	36.9	1384
	65 or over	5.0	21.7	23.6	49.7	1003

SOURCE: 1975 National Crime Survey, five-city sample.

TABLE 2.2
Women's Mean Scores on Fear, Worry, and Rape Risk by Neighborhood

	Safety (1 = very safe, 4 = very unsafe)	Worry (0 = no worry at all, 10 = very worried)	Women's Risk of Rape (0 = not likely, 10 = very likely)
Philadelphia			
West Philadelphia (n = 47)*	2.5	5.7	4.6
South Philadelphia (n = 37)	2.1	4.6	2.8
	p = .021†	p = .0255	p = .0034
	eta² = .066‡	eta² = 0542	eta² = .089
Chicago			
Lincoln Park (n = 53)	2.2	5.3	3.5
Wicker Park (n = 32)	2.9	7.3	5.5
	p = .0002	p = .0001	p = .0009
	eta² = .150	eta² = .181	eta² = .114
San Francisco			
Sunset (n = 50)	2.6	5.7	4.2
Visitacion Valley (n = 48)	2.8	7.1	5.3
	N.S.	p = .0082	p = .071
		eta2 = .063	eta2 = .030

* n = sample size (Value varies because of missing cases.)
† p = probability.
‡ eta = variance explained.

FIGURE 2.1
Safety by Neighborhood

During the Day   **Out Alone at Night**

contribute to a sense of safety, women in three selected cities were asked about "dangerous places" in the neighborhood. Over three-quarters of the women (78 percent) felt there was an especially danger-ous place in their neighborhood (see Figure 2.2) and over half reported this dangerous place to be within two blocks of their homes. Figure 2.2 also shows variations in responses by neighborhood.

One woman—Julie, from the Sunset neighborhood in San Fran-cisco—said, "There's a park near here [Golden Gate Park] that's especially dangerous at night because it's dark and empty then." Maria, from South Philadelphia, said a nearby street, part of a busi-ness section, was dangerous at night when all the stores were closed. When asked to describe these dangerous places, women's responses varied as to why they considered the places dangerous, and what kinds of crimes they thought were committed there.

Julie said she wasn't certain that the park was a dangerous place,

FIGURE 2.2
Percent Saying There Is Especially Dangerous Place in Neighborhood,
by Neighborhood

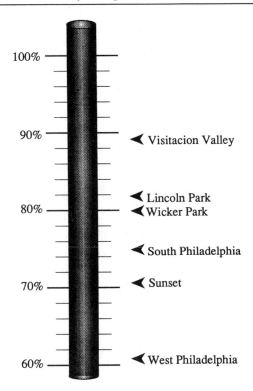

but that it just felt unsafe. If she ever has to go through there, she "surveys the area" and then walks quickly through, usually on the grass so her high heels won't make noise on the pavement. She says "there's no good reason to be there at night," and she thinks "things like assaults, purse snatchings, and rape are likely to occur there."

Patty, from Visitacion Valley in San Francisco, mentioned a "super dangerous" place in her neighborhood—a local park—dangerous because it is unlit and there are "also lots of bushes where people could hide." She thought "every kind of crime" occurred there—especially murder, rape, and robbery. She completely avoids the area, even in the daytime. She knows it is a dangerous area because a daughter of a friend of hers was raped there, and because of the activities of a new neighborhood anti-crime organization. At the first meeting, they talked about what goes on there.

Maria, from South Philadelphia, said an empty business street in her neighborhood was dangerous because most of the people "traveling there are violence-prone, lower-class blacks." She thought mugging was the most likely crime to occur there, and that there was a "good possibility of sexual assault and murder" as well.

In general, women consider certain streets or alleys to be the most dangerous places (39 percent); the next most dangerous is a park (19.5 percent). The most frequent reasons given for considering the place dangerous are "kids hanging out" (30.5 percent), darkness (27.4 percent), a deserted area (23.5 percent), and a location near certain groups of people thought to be responsible for crime (22.6 percent). The crimes most frequently mentioned by women as most likely to occur in these dangerous places were robberies (54.6 percent), street muggings (45.8 percent), and rapes and sexual assaults (41.0 percent).

In addition to feelings of safety or lack of it in certain places, women worry that someone will try to harm them in certain situations. When women were asked how much they worried when alone at night, the degree of concern depended on the situation. Not surprisingly, women were most worried about riding with a male stranger after dark (an average of 9.2 on a 10-point scale) and about giving a stranger a ride after dark (average = 8.8; see Table 2.3). Most reported they never did those things. In contrast, they did not worry very much about being home alone after dark (3.3 on the average), an irony given the fact that more rapes take place in or near the home than any other single place. They worried significantly more about many often unavoidable situations: going to laundromats (5.7), using public transit (6.6), walking by bars (7.2), and walking by parks or empty lots (7.8).

Women worry more than men do in the same situations: going to laundromats, using public transportation, or being downtown alone after dark. And women put themselves in those common situations significantly *less often* than men, with the sole exception of being home alone after dark, which both sexes report doing with equal frequency (see Tables 2.3 and 2.4).[8] In every instance, how often women engage in these activities is related to their worry levels. Women who never pursued an activity in question consistently had the highest level of worry, and the frequency with which women engaged in an activity was consistent with their level of fear (Table 2.4). Thus, women restrict their behavior—even isolate themselves—in order to avoid being harmed.

Women's perceptions of their own personal risk in any given

TABLE 2.3
Percentages of Women and Men in Sample Who Responded "Never" When Asked How Frequently They Engage in Common Activities and Women's Degree of "Worry" in Those Situations

Activities	% Who "Never" Do Activity		Gender Difference (probability)	How Much Women Worry in Situation*	% Variance Women's Worry Explained†
	Women	Men			
Home alone after dark	8.7	9.0	ns‡	3.3	3
Walk in neighborhood alone after dark	25.3	2.9	.01	5.2	18
Go to laundromats alone after dark	68.2	61.8	.01	5.7	20
Go to bars/clubs alone after dark	68.4	5.4	.01	6.5	33
Go to movies alone after dark	74.9	32.4	.01	6.1	30
Walk by groups of boys alone after dark	33.6	11.8	.01	6.9	10
Use public transit alone after dark	46.3	29.4	.01	6.6	16
Walk by bars/hangouts alone after dark	46.5	10.3	.01	7.2	18
Go downtown alone after dark	47.0	7.5	.01	6.4	20
Walk by parks/lots alone after dark	52.8	13.2	.01	7.8	16
Give rides to strangers alone after dark	96.7	82.1	.01	8.8	31
Ride with male strangers alone after dark	98.0	91.2	.01	9.2	25

* Mean on a 0–10 scale: 0 = no worry at all; 10 = very worried.
† By how often respondent does it.
‡ ns = difference is not statistically significant.

TABLE 2.4
Correlation Between Fear and Use of Strategies by Gender

	% Who "Never" Do Activity*		% Who "Always" Do Activity†		Correlation of Fear with How Often Done	
	Male	Female	Male	Female	Male	Female
Strategies which women use more frequently than men:						
How often do you restrict your going out to only during the day time?	72	25	9	26	.3106	.5250
How often do you avoid doing things you have to do because of fear of being harmed?	78	32	6	15	−.0279	.3050
When you go out, how often do you drive rather than walk because of fear of being harmed?	56	18	13	40	.1335	.2925
How often do you not do things you want to do but do not have to do because of fear?	75	30	6	15	.1682	.2813
When you are looking for a parking place at night, how often do you think about safety?	15	5	33	71	.1512	.2350
How often do you ask for identification from salesmen or repairmen?	18	11	33	50	.0282	.2342
How often do you go out with a friend or two as protection?	50	10	4	51	−.0371	.2031
How often do you check the backseat of your car for intruders before getting in?	38	12	31	59	.0048	.1826
How often do you check to see who is at your door before opening it?	10	2	60	87	.2184	.1789

	% Who "Never" Do Activity*		% Who "Always" Do Activity†		Correlation of Fear with How Often Done	
	Male	Female	Male	Female	Male	Female
How often do you try to wear shoes that are easy to run in, in case of danger?	61	19	13	36	.1500	.1779
How often do you lock the outside door when home alone during the day?	12	3	63	79	−.0769	.1567
On the street, how often do you avoid looking people in the eye whom you don't know?	31	18	22	29	.1334	.1531
How often do you try to avoid going downtown when making plans to go out at night?	37	21	19	24	.2715	.1489
When you are out alone, how often do you try not to dress in a provocative manner?	63	18	10	58	−.0017	.1402
How often do you lock the doors when home alone at night?	87	.3	85	95	.0215	.1340
When in a car, how often do you lock the doors?	10	1	64	79	−.0665	.1288
How often do you cross the street when you see someone who seems strange or dangerous?	11	6	25	52	−.0247	.1261
How often do you stay out of parts of town you think are dangerous?	9	9	38	55	.2774	.1109
When walking on the street, how often do you make a point of being alert and watchful?	3	2	66	81	.1972	.1101

Continued on page 18

	% Who "Never" Do Activity*		% Who "Always" Do Activity†		Correlation of Fear with How Often Done	
	Male	Female	Male	Female	Male	Female
How often do you deliberately leave on lights or a radio when no one will be home?	14	5	57	65	.1504	.1037
When out alone, how often do you take something for protection like a dog or whistle?	73	50	6	23	.1961	.0656
How often do you carry keys in your hand when going to your car?	20	4	44	82	.2260	.0596
Did you install or make sure there were special locks or bars on the doors?	43	28	57	72	.1081	.0452
Did you get an unlisted phone number?	60	43	40	57	.1985	.0399
When at a movie or on a bus, how often do you change seats if someone strange is nearby?	26	18	13	28	.0125	.0375
How often do you ask neighbors to watch your house when no one will be home for several days?	16	5	60	75	−.1094	.0323
How often do you get your house keys out before reaching your door?	15	4	50	81	.2216	.0265

* Percent of people who responded "Never" or "No" to questions about precautionary behavior.
† Percent of people who responded "Always" or "Yes" to questions about precautionary behavior.

situation are the result of calculated assessments; that is, women rationally, and automatically, take account of the situation and do a mental calculation of the dangers present before deciding how to behave.[9] Although women can't always articulate precisely what factors went into their calculations, they are able to estimate, on a scale from zero (no possibility at all) to ten (extremely likely), their chances of being raped or sexually assaulted in their neighborhoods and "downtown." They also are able to estimate what they think the chances are that their homes would be broken into, their children (if applicable) harmed, or their money stolen. Figure 2.3 summarizes their responses according to type of crime.

Among these crimes, women consider themselves to be most at risk for rape in the downtown area at night. They also feel quite at risk in their own neighborhoods. Nearly half estimated their

FIGURE 2.3
Assessment of Risk of Becoming a Victim of Different Crimes*

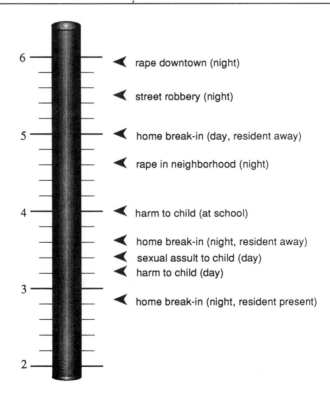

6 — ◄ rape downtown (night)

◄ street robbery (night)

5 — ◄ home break-in (day, resident away)

◄ rape in neighborhood (night)

4 — ◄ harm to child (at school)

◄ home break-in (night, resident away)
◄ sexual assult to child (day)
◄ harm to child (day)

3 — ◄ home break-in (night, resident present)

2 —

* 0 = not likely; 10 = very likely.

chances of being raped in their own neighborhood as five or higher on the ten-point scale. Women feel least risk associated with having their homes broken into at night while someone is home. Of the four crime settings in which women feel most at risk, two involve rape (downtown and in the neighborhood).

Women's fear also is fed by and related to feelings about the extent and seriousness of crime in a particular area.

When asked *how often* they think about their own safety in their own neighborhood, 40 percent of women replied "fairly often" or "all or most of the time." Seventy-six percent of women think the most serious problem facing the neighborhood is crime or crime-related. And when asked what crime should be the highest-priority target for an anti-crime campaign in the neighborhood, women most frequently mention rape, drug abuse, burglary, and juvenile delinquency.

In sum, women view rape as a very serious problem. They are well aware of their own degree of risk, and can readily describe their image of a typical rape. Many know of the damaging physical and emotional effects of rape through firsthand accounts from friends or relatives, and they have changed their own lives because of that knowledge. Forty-nine percent of the women interviewed rate their chances of being raped in their neighborhood as five or higher on a zero-to-ten scale. Fifty-two percent of women personally know at least one rape victim, and 4 percent report knowing more than one. About 15 percent of those victims had been severely injured physically in addition to the rape, and 75 percent were said to have suffered long-term emotional damage. Twenty-eight percent of the women report changing their own behavior because of rapes they know about. Ninety-seven percent of women are able to describe what they believe to be a "typical rape," and women believe the worst aspects of rape are the chance of emotional damage (53 percent); the sexual violation (21 percent); the chance of death (12 percent); and shame (9 percent).

Although women do worry about other things, rape is frequently on their minds. A third of the women interviewed said their most common worry is physical harm, and rape is what they fear most. Joyce, a working-class woman from Chicago, is typical:

> Oh, I fear being physically harmed, raped. I worry about it all the time. I think about it whenever I go out of the house, especially at night. In fact, I almost never go out of the house at night because

of it. I get so scared that something's going to happen that I decide going out is not worth it. Sometimes I get friends to come here, but mostly we talk on the phone.

About two-thirds of women indicate their most frequent worry is about something other than physical harm, but even they say fear of rape enters their minds at least occasionally. Jill, a middle-class professional, responded:

> Oh, I don't know. I guess I worry about keeping my marriage together. I'm doing pretty well at work, and the kids seem to be okay. I think about rape when I'm here at home alone, or when there's a scary rape in the news. Then I'm really afraid, and I think maybe it really could happen to me. It's eerie. . . .

How often is worry about rape on most women's minds? About a third of women say they worry about being raped once a month or more often—many indicated more than once a day—and when they think about it, they feel terrified and somewhat paralyzed. Another third of women indicate they worry about rape more occasionally, but that the fear is "one of those things that's always there," part of the background. "Things will be going along as usual" and "then something will happen" that causes the fear to grip them very intensely until the moment passes and the fear subsides. About a third of the women say they "never" worry about being raped, but even those women say they take precautions, sometimes elaborate ones, to prevent being raped.

These responses suggest that fear of rape is central to the day-to-day concerns of about a third of women, a sporadic concern for another third, and of little concern to another third even though these women take precautions to prevent it. Thus, although rape is not the only thing women worry about, it is of significant concern for most, and all women are forced to live their lives in its shadow.

How are these dimensions of female fear affected if one is actually victimized? Thirty-three women who had been victims of rape talked openly about their sense of safety, concern, worry, and sense of risk. These rape victims were similar in most obvious ways to nonvictims. That is, they were similar in age, had similar amounts of formal education, earned similar incomes, were black, white, Hispanic, and Asian in similar proportions, and were just as frequently living with a spouse or boyfriend.

Most of the victims had moved following their ordeals, and having been raped somewhere else did not seem to affect their concern about rape as a problem in their new neighborhoods. There were also no significant differences between victims and women who had never been raped in their estimates of the likelihood of their being raped in the future. Nonetheless, previously raped women felt significantly more fearful out alone at night.

Victims who moved after their rapes may feel they have taken important steps to both reduce their anxiety and prevent future rapes. Having taken this action, they are similar to other women except that their fear is exacerbated.

3

———◆———

The Realities of Rape

SUSAN is now thirty-three, and a minister. Late in 1983, she and five friends (two other women and three men) had gathered in her apartment for a simple Friday evening meal before a religious meeting. One of the men unlocked and opened the apartment door on his way to get something he'd left in his car. He was stopped in the hallway by a man with a gun.

The man with the gun was angry when the group of six could only come up with $40 from their wallets. He waved the gun and cocked the hammer. Fearful, Susan spoke up and said she had some more money hidden in the other room. The man made her tie up her friends with dish towels, electric cords, or anything else she could find. He also made her remove their watches and give them to him.

After Susan gave the man the $140 she had hidden in her dresser, he pulled her to him and whispered, "Now you're going to make love to me." "No, no," was all she could say before he cocked the hammer of the gun again and said, "Don't fight me." Then she said, "Okay. If I go through with this, will you then just leave, and not hurt any of us?" "Yeh," he said.

He forced her onto her own bed and attempted to rape her from the back; then he told her to turn over and close her eyes, then raped her from the front. When he was through, he wiped her off with her own pink bathrobe and told her to dress. Then he told her to lie on the bathroom floor and count to one hundred. She did, and when she opened her eyes he was still there staring down at her. He told her to count to one hundred again. This time when she opened her eyes he was gone.

By the time she got up and went back, shaking, into the living room, most of her friends had freed themselves and one was calling the police. Only her roommate guessed what had happened to Susan.

After the police had been there a few minutes, Susan's roommate told them there had also been a rape. They said, "Why didn't you tell us in the first place?!" and called a rape victim advocate to meet them at the hospital. There the advocate told Susan she didn't have to answer a prying nurse's questions. The nurse then quietly examined her and gave her massive doses of penicillin to prevent infection and other pills to prevent pregnancy by inducing menstruation.

Susan spent that night and many more at another friend's, a fifty-year-old woman whose own daughter had been raped at gunpoint in a suburban restaurant during a robbery about a year earlier.

The next morning there were stories in the major newspapers headlined, "Rapist Invades Bible Study Group." Many of the facts in the stories were incorrect. Two nights later, someone reentered Susan's apartment and took everything but her clothes and large pieces of furniture. The next day the Tylenol case broke in Chicago, and police and the media shifted their attention to that.[1]

Weeks later, Susan still couldn't bring herself to sleep in a bed. She had nightmares. Far from rich to begin with, Susan was without money and many of her belongings. Friends and her minister contributed to a small fund to help her replace some of what was gone, but there was no way to recover personal mementos and belongings with sentimental value. Susan couldn't seem to concentrate on her work. She felt angry and then depressed. She saw a therapist and talked to friends. She said tearfully, "I don't like the person I've become. I'm afraid, depressed, out of energy. I get angry and it sometimes comes out on people who don't deserve it. I don't know what to do, where to turn, where to live or work. I want so much to believe that people can live in the city."

Susan is a sensible woman who took a lot of the precautions women are advised to take. She wasn't raped on the street or in a dark alley after getting off the subway alone late at night. She wasn't wearing provocative clothes. She asks, "If I'm not safe locked inside my own apartment surrounded by five other people, where can I be safe?"

Susan didn't tell her family about the rape, though she did report the robbery to them in order to explain why she moved to a new apartment. Susan was afraid of their reactions if she told them.

The woman she moved in with temporarily was saddened and depressed by what had happened to Susan. Still too afraid to be alone, Susan moved in with a second middle-aged woman (and her son) from church. That woman, too, had been robbed and raped—two years earlier by a young teenager.

Susan's friends and students, part of a group wanting to commit themselves to an urban ministry, grew more afraid than they had been in the past—taking more precautions, avoiding evening meetings and leisure activities outside their homes, avoiding travel alone on public transportation. They, too, experienced fear, anger, and a sense of helpless dismay.

Susan moved several times during the year, looking for a place and for roommates with whom she could feel comfortable. About ten months after the rape she and two young women—an artist and a teacher—moved into a three-bedroom flat several miles from her old neighborhood, but still in the city. The police never contacted her again, so she assumes the robber-rapist is at large, maybe not too far away.

Susan's story makes clear the complexity and the difficulty in defining both the reality of rape and the pervasive fear it engenders. How indeed can we classify Susan's rape and approximate its terrifying and enduring consequences?

Police, victim surveyors, and other analysts classify rapes according to the relationship of people involved, as "stranger" or "acquaintance" rapes.[2] "Stranger" rapes are what most people think of as "typical"—a stranger, wearing a ski mask; lurking in bushes in a darkened area; grabbing a young, innocent passerby; raping and brutalizing her; leaving her minutes later, clothing ripped, half-naked, shaken and terrified, to be found by a passerby who may or may not give her aid.

Most women think most rapes are "stranger" rapes:

> It occurs most often out on the street. A woman is jumped by someone she doesn't know. . . . A stranger would be the only way it could happen to me.
>
> —Sara

> I remember something told by a friend of a friend who was assaulted under the high-speed [train] line from Jersey, which surprised me. I thought it would be safe there, I don't know why. She was a young white girl, twenties, and was assaulted by a black man. It

was underground and he evidently got hold of her and forced her to go to another area of the subway where he raped her. . . . I know that the family was very upset by it and of course the victim, but the mother was completely distraught. It caused quite a turmoil, a very nice, pretty girl, you know . . . the rapist was a big, black man, very tall and broad. . . . The victim became very depressed and morose and couldn't work for a while. . . . She never took the high-speed line again . . . in fact, I became more cautious, too. I've never taken the high-speed line after that.

—Patty

Well, it's got to be a man sexually assaulting a woman . . . probably a man who is strong . . . and frankly, I know it sounds prejudiced, but I'd pick a black man as a rapist, more so than a white man although there are white men rapists, and I think of it as happening in a dark area where you shouldn't be, a section of the city that is not well lit up, some side street away from the regular flow of pedestrian traffic or maybe under a subway or near a train station . . . a dark area of some big institution like a hospital where there are nurses coming out late at night . . . usually late. I mean it happens during the day too and the area, like I said, is a bad area, an out-of-the-way area. In other areas, even better areas, they might not be bothered. . . . I think in general it's done by strangers, mostly happening in those areas and sometimes they are breaking into a house but more often out on the street.

—Maria

While stranger rapes may constitute people's image of what is typical, acquaintance rapes or nonstranger rapes, are an increasingly large proportion of actual rapes and now account for 55 to 60 percent of rapes reported to police. Such rapes may be even more frequent than the figures imply since many women do not tell the police about rapes by people they know.[3]

But the words "nonstranger" or "acquaintance" cover a wide range of types of relationships. In some jurisdictions a rape is classified as nonstranger or acquaintance if the victim is known to the rapist, even if the rapist is not known to the victim. That is, the rapist may be in, or live in, the geographical vicinity of the rape, and is thought to have been watching or stalking his victim. Some women think this kind of rape is typical.

I feel as though a man will announce a rape. If a woman gets raped the man has been watching her. The way she acts, looks, or the way she's dressed. The company [she keeps]. The rapist knows the victim, but she doesn't know the rapist.

—Mary

This woman, who now lives in a housing project, told of an attack on her by a man whom police would classify as an acquaintance.

> I was on my way to work very early in the morning. This bastard asked me for a cigarette and I gave him one; then he grabbed me and put his fucking hands all in my face. I was scared so I grabbed a pair of scissors that I was carrying in my purse and stabbed his fucking guts out. He pushed me down and tried to hit me, but I got his ass; I stuck those scissors in his filthy belly . . . that white motherfucker was shocked. Then he started screaming for the police. I was OK though. The cops told me that I had to go to the hospital. I told them that he didn't get nothing and that I wasn't going to the hospital. . . . I didn't know the guy, but when we went to court I figured that the SOB had been watching me every morning. I used to leave for work about 5:30 A.M. I was living in South Philly then. He was big, but I was determined that he wasn't gonna rape me and he didn't.
>
> —Mary

Another type of acquaintance rape is referred to as date rape; this occurs when the victim initially is willing to be in the company of a man who then becomes violent toward her. For several reasons, many of these rapes are not reported to police or to those interviewing victims about crime experiences. Although the victim may have resisted and been forced, she herself may not recognize it as rape *because* she was on a date. Even if a victim does define the attack as rape, she may hesitate or not want to charge the perpetrator—frequently for such reasons as they work at the same place or they were fixed up by mutual friends. Most important, date-rape victims often feel they won't be believed or will be perceived as having "asked for it"—by the police, the courts, and everyone else and, therefore, there is no point in reporting it.[4]

> She was on a date and he raped her. She didn't know him before. It happened in Berkeley, in his car. She resisted the attack. She reported it to the police and the guy was arrested, but I don't know if he was convicted. She is still fearful, very fearful of going out, particularly with someone she doesn't know *very* well. It has increased her general anxiety. She was very depressed and self-derogatory. The situation—being out of control—elevated her general sense of low self-esteem and reinforced it. Anxiety, fear, and lowered self-esteem. Now she's a lot more careful in dating. You don't expect it on a date.
>
> —Sara

I was out on a date with a cop. . . . I'd met him when I interviewed him for one of my classes. I'd been out with him once before. After dinner that night we went back to his place so he could get a book I wanted to borrow. He grabbed me and I fought. I'd taken self-defense, but he was so strong. I told him I'd report him and he just laughed and said, "Who'd believe you? I'm a cop!"

—Ellen

A special form of date rape is being increasingly reported on college campuses. In what may have become a typical campus rape, a young woman is assaulted by a young man she has met (often the same evening) at a party on campus. She may have danced with him, gone for a walk with him, gone to his room, or allowed him to walk her to her room. Many campus rapes seem to involve the use of excessive amounts of alcohol by one or both persons involved. One victim of campus rape blamed herself because she was drunk. When a faculty member reminded her that it is a crime to rape, but not a crime to get drunk, the coed decided to file charges. Experts in this field say, "Clearly, among college students, sexual aggression is rare among strangers and common among acquaintances."[5] Another researcher surveyed a midwestern college and estimated that more than 20 percent of college women are victims of rape or attempted rape, and that student victims almost always know their rapists.[6]

These and other researchers argue that campus rape may be so prevalent because of norms in our society that condone sexual violence. People are conditioned to accept sexual roles in which male aggression is an acceptable part of our modern courtship culture. According to this line of reasoning, campus rapists are ordinary males operating in an ordinary social context, not even knowing they are doing something wrong, let alone against the law. Obviously, the climate on college campuses must be changed so that this kind of behavior is no longer regarded as acceptable.

College campuses are also common settings for gang rapes. Most reported rapes involve only two people, usually a male and a female. Rapes involving one or more rapists are known as gang rapes. The perpetrators may or may not be known to the victim or victims. Until recently, gang rapes seemed to occur rather infrequently, usually involving a single victim attacked serially by several strangers who knew one another but were not known to the victim.

However, there have been increasing numbers of gang rapes on college campuses, where the victim(s) and perpetrators are likely to know one another. Gang rapes among acquaintances in 1983 at Duke University and at the universities of Florida and Pennsylvania received extensive news coverage.

Such gang rapes on campuses are much more frequent than indicated by police records since knowledge of them is often hushed up by victims, perpetrators who fear embarrassment, dismissal and/or public censure, and by college administrators who fear legal repercussions.[7]

One victim reported:

> It was at this fraternity party. Everyone, including me, had had pretty much to drink. I wasn't really with anyone—it was our sorority and their fraternity. This guy there—I'd been out with him a couple of times—got me to go up to his room. When we got there there were five or six other guys there, I don't really know how many. They started touching me, laughing, pushing at me. The next thing I knew they'd locked the door and were ripping my clothes. They all did it. I don't even know who some of them were. Later that night I told my resident assistant in the dorm and she told the dorm master. By that time I was sick. The next day they said I was contradicting myself, that the whole fraternity would be censured, and they kept asking if I was sure I was telling the whole truth. I was scared and hurting. I went to the student health center and they gave me something to be sure I wouldn't get pregnant. I really thought it was all my fault since I'd been drinking and I went upstairs. Anyway, I decided not to report it, because my parents would have found out. But I couldn't concentrate and a couple of weeks later I decided to drop out of school.
>
> —Joan

College campuses are not the only site of rape among acquaintances. Sexual violence also occurs in marriage and in parent-child relationships. Marital rape, sexual child abuse, and incest have always been treated separately and differently from other forms of sexual assault, by the law, by agencies dealing with victims and perpetrators, and by the public at large. Perhaps for that reason, victims of such assaults often do not think of them as rapes.

Some women who have been raped by their husbands define it as rape while others do not. When asked if anything had ever happened to her that might be considered sexual assault, an Italian woman from Philadelphia said:

> As far as being touched in a way that made you feel uncomfortable, does that include the husband? I had more problems with that than with strangers. My husband was actually very intoxicated,

he tried to press his attentions on me. I think this was getting close to a physical assault, actually. I felt revolted and disgusted. I started sleeping in my daughter's bedroom and locking the door. Once he broke down the door, dragged me into the other room, and forced me to have sex.

—Maria

Yet when asked if she or anyone she knew had been raped or sexually assaulted, Maria replied, "No." She also said no to a question about whether unwanted or forced sexual intercourse between a husband and wife ought to be covered in laws about rape.

Nancy, a middle-class professional woman, said she had been physically abused by her ex-husband and often felt forced to have sex with him, but it wasn't until after she was divorced that she realized she had been the victim of marital rape.

Sexual violence between acquaintances can also take the form of attempted rape. Attempted rapes often go unreported to the police, and if they are reported, they usually are treated with less seriousness than completed rapes. Sometimes attempted rapes happen between people who once knew one another and then became estranged. One young woman told of an attempted rape by a former boyfriend.

Well, it was an old love of mine who came over very drunk and wanted to go to bed and I said no. And he basically dragged me into the bedroom . . . took me by the wrist, and his, well the main reason he didn't succeed was that he couldn't get an erection because he was so drunk. I kept trying to get out, and I finally did after about half an hour. I got out of the room, and that's when he said he would leave. Basically I thought at first I could talk him out of it. And then I started fighting. He's big, about six-foot something, about 265 pounds and just would, you know when I would try and run out, he would just pull me back, push me down. He didn't hit me, but he was a lot stronger than I was. He would tell me to lay down, that sort of thing. He didn't make any other threats. It doesn't surprise me entirely. He was abused very badly as a child by his family—neglected. He didn't have a very high opinion of women. He's sort of a street person. And he was very upset at the fact our relationship wasn't continuing.

—Rebecca

Attempted rapes also may involve strangers and can often be devastating and have long-lasting consequences for victims. Martha, a resident of a high-income lakefront neighborhood in Chicago, is a young, well-educated, sophisticated, and self-confident young woman. Nonetheless, she feels considerably less safe and more fearful now than she used to, and, she thinks her risk of being raped is high. She attributes her fear to an incident in a park.

It was about—actually it was about ten years ago. I was at Foster Avenue Beach [in Chicago]—three o'clock on a sunny Sunday afternoon—in May. There were a lot of people around—there were people pushing their baby carriages and whatever—it was just such a beautiful day—early in the spring—that it brought everyone out. And I had to use a public washroom, and I was with two friends and they were just sitting down and they didn't want to get up so I went alone. And I remember I was in the compartment and I heard someone come in after me, and I was really aware of how big they sounded, and I just pictured that it was one of these big women that were outside taking care of people's kids. I thought it was just one of them because the footsteps sounded so heavy. And it was really crazy—I never looked down—they were in the one right next to me—I would have known there was a man there but I just—it wasn't until I pulled the lock on my door, I heard the lock click on the next one, and I opened the door, and there he was standing. He was probably thirty, he was dressed in a suit. Initially—it seemed like a long time, but I'm sure time was all mixed up—but we just kind of both stood there. And I didn't say anything—I didn't do anything—I just stood. And it wasn't until he actually touched me—put a hand on my shoulder—that I realized it was real. Something was going to happen, and I started to struggle a little bit. And I was really cornered because he was the fourth wall. And he was so strong and I thought, this is how it happens. You always think it's other people, and now it's you and there's no way you can get away and he's so strong—you know, it's like trying to plow your way through a brick wall—it's just not—you're not getting anywhere. And I could feel—I just really felt weak, and then all of a sudden I just got really angry. I got angry at myself first—you're just going to let this happen to you—and then I got angry at him—who does he think he is—and all at once I kicked, kneed him. Well, one of my fears was if I kneed him—it's amazing how I was thinking all these things—if I kneed him, he'd fall forward and I wouldn't get away. All the time, I was thinking all these things, I was screaming. I never stopped screaming. I almost forgot that—that was important because initially when I first started struggling and I wasn't successful, I thought, well, I'm screaming and people will come—I know all those people out there. And so I screamed. Lucky for me, his intention seemed to be to get me to stop screaming and so I was screaming and he was really trying to stop me from screaming. He had his hand in my mouth and he did a lot of damage to the inside of my mouth but I think I also did a lot of damage to his hand. You know, I bit. The noise reverberated around the room, but apparently the noise just really didn't carry outside because people that helped later on said they didn't hear anything. So anyways after I went through the stage of feeling helpless and then getting angry, what I—I kind of quickly made a plan of action and I kind of executed it all at once. I kneed him as hard as I could. I hit him in the stomach with my purse and I grabbed his glasses with my hand and dug my nails down his face and then I threw the whole weight of my body against him—just like I tried to throw my whole self against him. And he fell backwards on the ground and his glasses flew in the corner and I kind of landed on the ground, too, on all fours and I was shaking so much from it—from the fear and the activity and the power that I had for that one moment—I couldn't even walk. I literally crawled out on all fours and he apparently went to get his glasses. And I got outside the door and I stood up and I just couldn't do any more.

—Martha

All of these forms of sexual assault—attempted or completed— provoke fear and generate important emotional consequences for the victims and for people who know them. Some people believe the stranger rape to be the most difficult for victims to deal with since it is often perceived as unprovoked or "out of the blue." It leaves the victims and others who learn of the crime with the feeling there is no way to prevent such attacks. Others believe acquaintance rapes—especially date or family rapes—to be the most troublesome because they are perpetrated by people the victims know and often have loved and trusted. These rapes often leave the victim feeling that *no* one can be trusted. Since these rapes are often never reported to anyone, the victim may also bear burdens of secrecy, shame, and other feelings which she believes cannot be shared.

The emotional devastation accompanying rape is of particular concern to our society because rape occurs so frequently. At the moment, it is impossible to specify exactly how much rape there is in the United States. The best anyone can offer is a series of estimates, each based on assumptions and often on differing reporting procedures and definitions of the crime. Official rates differ from year to year, time of year, region of the country, urban versus rural locations, race and age of the victim, type of rape, and several other factors. Many observers and experts believe the true rate of rape in the

United States is at least twice the official rate and may be as much as twenty times as high.

Rape statistics generally are based on police reports. Citizens' reports of crime to police are in turn reported by local police to the Federal Bureau of Investigation (FBI), which uses them to compile national statistics referred to as the Uniform Crime Reports (UCR). As Table 3.1 shows, in 1986 there were 90,434 forcible rapes reported by police across the country to the FBI, representing an increase of 3.2 percent over 1985 and a rate of 73 per 100,000 women. This is one rape every six minutes. Rapes accounted for 6 percent of all violent crimes.[8] Rape rates increased 4 percent in 1985 and 7 percent in 1984 from the previous years. While the increases in this crime from year to year may appear modest, the increase between 1982 and 1986 was 15 percent, and between 1976 and 1986 an astonishing 58 percent.[9]

The numbers and rates of rape vary considerably by city size, season of the year, and region of the country. For several years, the absolute *number* of rape offenses has been highest in the South, the region with the largest population, but the *rate* (number per thousand people) has been highest in the West. More rapes take place during the summer months, especially August, than during other seasons.[10] And both the absolute number of offenses and the rates are higher in large metropolitan areas than in either smaller

TABLE 3.1

Trends in Forcible Rapes Reported by Police to the FBI, 1979–1986*

Year	Number of Offenses	Rate per 100,000 Inhabitants	Rate per 100,000 Women
1979	75,989	34.5	69
1980	82,088	36.4	73
1981	81,536	35.6	71
1982	77,763	33.6	67
1983	78,918	33.7	67
1984	84,233	34.3	69
1985	87,671	36.7	72
1986	90,434	37.5	73

* Forcible rape for these data is defined as the carnal knowledge of a female forcibly and against her will. Assaults or attempts to commit rape by force or threat of force are also included; however, statutory rape (without force) and other sex offenses are excluded.

SOURCE: Uniform Crime Reports, *Crime in the United States*, FBI, U.S. Department of Justice, Washington, DC 20535.

cities or rural areas. The most recent data, for 1986, indicate that these same patterns persist, but that the rates in midsize cities are increasing faster than the rates in the largest cities.

Black women are more likely than white or Hispanic women to be victims, and younger women are more likely to be victims than older women. Of the men arrested for rape in 1986, 52 percent were white and 47 percent were black. Forty-five percent were under twenty-five years of age and a third were between eighteen and twenty-four years of age. These patterns also are similar to those in previous years.[11]

Analyses of how UCR data are gathered and compiled have indicated errors of omission and commission, most of which lead to the underrepresentation of the actual rate of rape.[12] For example, in the UCR each reported or attempted crime is tabulated in a single crime classification, according to the most severe offense.[13] Thus, a rape-murder would be classified solely as a murder.

In addition, police may "unfound" a rape (declare there is not enough evidence to warrant a charge of rape) reported to them, thus lowering the statistics still further. Some police departments regularly conclude that as many as 50 percent of the charges of forcible rape received are not classifiable as offenses.[14] A 1982 investigative report of unfounding practices in the Chicago Police Department discovered an unfounding rate for rape in that city of 54 percent.[15] Correcting the reporting procedures led to much higher reported crime rates the following year, with apparent increases as high as 74 percent for rape. Unfounded rates for other crimes are generally much lower than those for rape.

Because of the problems with the Uniform Crime Reports, in order to obtain more accurate estimates of the rates of rape and other crimes and to assess the magnitude and significance of unreported crime in the United States, several organizations began in the 1960s to interview people about crime victimizations in their households. The National Opinion Research Center (NORC) interviewed 10,000 households in 1965 and determined that the rate of rape per 100,000 persons for that year was nearly four times (42.5 per 100,000) what the UCR showed for the same year (11.6 per 100,000). Studies in subsequent years by the Bureau of Social Science Research (BSSR) in high-crime neighborhoods in Washington and by the Survey Research Center at the University of Michigan in several other cities showed even higher rates.[16]

These findings and others gave rise to the National Crime Surveys (also often referred to as the victimization surveys) now regularly conducted in conjunction with the U.S. Census. Although not without flaws, the National Crime Survey constitutes the most complete body of information about victims and their experiences with crime. These surveys identify many victimizations even when they have not been reported to the police.

In 1979 there were 192,000 rapes reported to victimization surveyors (Census Bureau interviewers, overwhelmingly women) for a rate of 110 per 100,000 people, or approximately 220 per 100,000 women, more than three times the police-based UCR data of the same year. About half the victims said the rapes had been reported to the police.

Since 1980, however, the number of rapes reported to Census takers has declined[17]—rapes reported to surveyors in 1986 yield a rate of about 140 per 100,000 women, with 48 percent having been reported to the police. Thus, the most current victimization surveys indicate a rate of only double that indicated by the UCR data.

Although the numbers and trends differ, both UCR and survey figures show that the greatest number of rapes in the United States take place in the largest cities. UCR data from 1986 show San Francisco with approximately 140 rapes per 100,000 women, the Chicago area with an estimated rate of about 240 per 100,000 women,[18] and Philadelphia with a rate of about 134 per 100,000 women— all double or triple the national rate of about 73 per 100,000 women.[19] Victimization survey data for these same three cities (available only for 1973 and 1975)[20] indicate even higher rates: over 500 per 100,000 women in San Francisco, 440 per 100,000 women in Chicago, and 230 per 100,000 for Philadelphia, as compared with national rates of 170 (in 1975) and 140 (in 1986) per 100,000 women.[21] Thus women who shared their stories and fears in this book are not only living in the *nation* with the highest rate of rape in the world, but also in *cities* within that nation with higher than average rates of rape.

Perhaps the greatest source of error in the reported rate of rape is the nonreported incidents. This "doubly dark" figure of crime,[22] which is reported *neither* to the police *nor* to a victimization survey interviewer, remains elusive. Research indicates that rapes by known assailants are particularly likely to go unreported, resulting in a serious underestimation of the extent of violence against women. In addition, the National Crime Survey does not ask victims directly if they have been raped, but rather asks those who indicated they had been attacked if the assaults they reported were rapes. Thus, it is very possible that many rapes are not mentioned or are misclassified as assaults.[23]

When women living in the three selected cities were asked in telephone interviews if they had ever been raped *or* sexually assaulted *at some time during their lives,* 2 percent said yes. That is a rate of 2,000 per 100,000, much higher than either yearly UCR or survey rates for these cities. But when women were asked the same question in person, the figures were even more startling. Eleven percent (or 11,000 in 100,000) said they had been raped or sexually assaulted.[24] These rates are surprisingly high and help to underscore the problems with any of the figures now available.

One source of variation in rape rates may be the time frame used in compiling these statistics. The rates from women in the three selected cities are based on a much longer time frame than the UCR and victimization survey rates, which are based on the preceding twelve months. For example, the 192,000 rapes in the United States reported in victimization surveys in 1979 translates into one-fifth of one chance in one hundred of being raped in that single year, but a one-in-twelve chance of being raped over a twenty-five-year period.[25] Many women live in large cities more than twenty-five years. Therefore, an urban woman's chances of being raped *during her lifetime* may be much closer to one in eight or one in five. Another researcher reported the one-in-five figure was much closer to the reality for San Francisco women. In that city, 22 percent of a random sample of women answered yes to the question, "Have you *ever* been the victim of rape or attempted rape?" That figure doubled when respondents were then asked about "other incidents," such as incest, marital rape, and forced intercourse while on dates.[26] Data reported for the Chicago area indicate the "during your lifetime" rate in that city may be as high as one in three.[27]

During-your-lifetime figures also would seem to be more relevant in terms of the *consequences* of rape than the annual rates. That is, the consequences of victimization, especially female fear, often last a great deal longer than twelve months. Indeed, for most victims, they last a lifetime.

Until relatively recently, rape victims who reported the crimes to police were often subject to treatment by them and by medical personnel which many described as double victimization. Women often were subjected to humiliating and sometimes brutal examination, and questioned by disbelieving officers who teased and taunted them while often failing to get the information needed for subsequent apprehension and successful prosecution of the suspect.

Due largely to the sustained efforts of feminists, the situation, especially in the nation's large cities, is often quite different today. Many police departments and hospitals have cooperative arrangements with rape crisis centers, or have their own victim witness units staffed by on-call volunteers and advocates. They are trained to help victims sensitively through each stage of the legal and medical procedures.

One result has been increased sensitivity on the part of police and medical personnel. Another has been increased willingness of victims not only to report the crime but, if the suspect is apprehended, to prosecute. This increased willingness to report the crime increases the statistics.

There is no easy answer to the question, How much rape is there? There is general agreement that all official or publicly ascertained rates are underestimates, but no one yet knows how much higher the true rate is. Further, it is not known whether recent increases in the reported rates reflect true increases in the crime or increases in reporting the crime, or both.

Whatever the true figures are, it is clear that women living in the United States, especially those living in large U.S. cities, are more at risk than anywhere else in the world.

Although comparative data from foreign countries are difficult to come by, comparisons reported in several sources indicate that the rate of rape as recorded by the police is substantially higher in the United States than in other industrialized, record-keeping countries, and that it has been for at least twenty years. In 1967 there were striking differences among rates in Belgium (.08 per 100,000 persons, [male and female]), France (1.9 per 100,000), Luxembourg (2.7 per 100,000), the Netherlands (1.2 per 100,000), and the United States (18.2 per 100,000).[28] There were fifty-two cases of rape reported for the entire country of Sweden in 1969. Other data indicated rates per 100,000 persons of 1.2 for Spain, 1.4 for Switzerland, 1.6 for Great Britain, .26 for Greece, but nearly 20 for the United States. Only Yugoslavia, with a rate of 15.1 per 100,000 in 1976, seemed to come close to the United States in rates of rape.[29]

International data collected by the Gallup Poll Organization and reported in late 1984 indicated a pattern similar to that of previous years.[30] Yugoslavia seems to be the only nation with personal violence rates approaching those of the United States.

How do the international, national, and city figures about the incidence of rape relate to women's fears? In other words, how realistic are those fears? In order to try to understand female fear in terms of *actual* risks in their neighborhoods, we plotted the actual (according to police data) rate of rape per thousand female residents in each of six neighborhoods against what women living in those same neighborhoods estimated their risks to be (see Figure 3.1).[31] The actual rape rates, according to police statistics, are lowest for

FIGURE 3.1
Actual Rape Rates (Police Data) by Perceived Risk of Rape

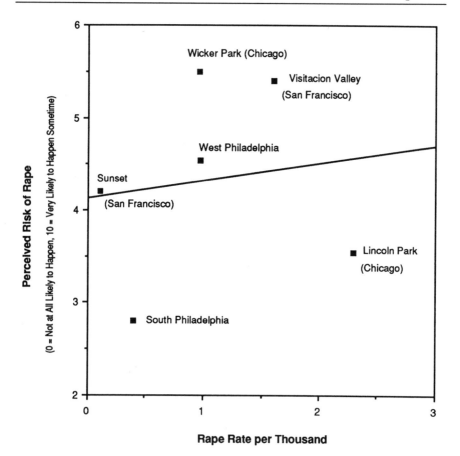

Rape Rate per Thousand

South Philadelphians and the Sunset area (of San Francisco) and highest for Lincoln Park (in Chicago) and Visitacion Valley (in San Francisco). The line on Figure 3.1 indicates the average risk for rape of women in those neighborhoods. For each neighborhood, the squares show women's perceptions of their risk of rape, taking into account the actual (police data) rate of rape in those areas. The figure shows that Sunset women as a group quite accurately estimate their risks, but women in both South Philadelphia and Lincoln Park vastly underestimate theirs, whereas Wicker Park and Visitacion Valley women markedly overestimate them. Thus, at least the official rates of rape (based on police data) are quite imperfectly related to women's perceptions of their risks in the neighborhoods they live in.

Such discrepancies between actual and perceived risks may contribute to women's ambivalence about appropriate responses to the threat of rape. Men's estimates of women's risks in those neighborhoods were consistently *higher* than the women's own estimates. This, taken together with the lack of certainty about actual rates, may be used to justify men's insistence that their wives, mothers, daughters, and sisters are unsafe out alone and should therefore go out only in the company of men, thereby giving further support to a culture of male dominance.

4

The Aftermath of Rape

IN a Chicago suburb, a young woman and her roommate were bound and gagged by a burglar who ransacked their apartment. Before he left, he decided to rape one of the women. Both women were in the room, but he forced one of them to face the wall while he raped the other. The victim was a virgin. The assault involved both oral sex and vaginal penetration. Two or three days later police arrested the suspect, who was positively identified by both women and by a third person who had seen the man entering the building. He had an arrest and conviction record and had served time in jail for two previous felonies. A third conviction could mean his being jailed for life.

After months of inaction, and having heard little or nothing from her attorneys, the young victim, who by then had moved to Boston, decided not to testify on the rape charge. She couldn't bear to have lawyers grill her about the incident in front of a roomful of strangers. She felt guilty that she hadn't resisted, although he had a knife and she had been afraid he would hurt or even kill her. She felt she needed to get on with her life and that she couldn't do that until the court case was over. And she worried that, even if convicted for breaking and entering and burglary, the assailant might get no additional penalty for the rape. The prosecuting attorney and the girl's roommate wanted her to testify because of the chance of getting this man "put away for good," but the roommate also felt the victim's mental health was the most important issue to consider. She and the lawyer ultimately decided to honor the victim's wishes in this matter.

A couple of years after this incident, the roommate who had

not been raped found that her own life had been completely altered by the event. She feared the rapist would find her and rape her in a new attack, and she found she distrusted nearly all men.

Most women fear going through what this victim and her roommate experienced. They fear rape because they know some victims get killed during an attack and because the consequences of rape can be devastating for months or years after. The pioneering research on rape victimization was done in 1974 when Ann Burgess and Lynda Holmstrom interviewed about one hundred victims who were admitted to emergency wards of the Boston City Hospital. They found that these victims experienced the "rape trauma syndrome," a combination of emotional and physical reactions to rape. As the researchers put it, "This syndrome of behavioral, somatic and psychological reactions is an acute stress reaction to a life-threatening situation."[1]

During the first phase, which often lasts two to three weeks, victims experience a wide range of emotions which they may express through crying, sobbing, smiling, restlessness, or through a more controlled calmness. The feelings often include fear, humiliation, embarrassment, anger, revenge, and self-blame. "Fear of physical violence and death was the primary feeling described. Victims stated that it was not the rape that was so upsetting as much as the feeling that they would be killed as a result of the assault."[2]

The researchers reported that during the second phase, victims did not all experience the same symptoms, or in the same sequence, and that their coping behavior was affected by such factors as their own ego strength, the network of support available to them, and the way people treated them as victims.

Most victims reported increased fears of many situations, often involving idiosyncratic factors associated with their own rapes. For example, one woman had been raped in her bedroom by a man who broke her window with a baseball bat which he was holding over her when she first awakened. Months later she could not attend baseball games, or even watch them on television. Some women who had been attacked indoors were afraid of being indoors; others who were attacked outdoors were afraid whenever they were outdoors. Some were afraid of being alone whereas others were afraid of crowds, or of people who walked behind them. Many victims also experienced nightmares. Nearly half changed residences and had their telephone numbers changed, and most visited with family members and friends more frequently.

After several months, the majority of the victims studied eventually were able to recover sufficiently to return to work (if they had been working before the attack) and in other ways to lead more-or-less normal lives. A major post-rape focus of all the victims was on protecting themselves from future attacks.[3]

Still other researchers studied clinical data from victims taken to hospitals in the Southeast.[4] Their work describes more fully how victims feel. The researchers gathered information two to three hours after the attack and again at one-month, six-month, and yearly intervals. Shortly after the attacks, "victims reported feeling scared (96 percent), worried (96 percent), terrified (92 percent), confused (92 percent) and having racing thoughts (80 percent)." They also evidenced physiological symptoms including shaking or trembling (96 percent), racing heart (80 percent), pain (72 percent), tight muscles (68 percent), rapid breathing (64 percent), and numbness (60 percent). Two to three hours post-rape, more than 80 percent of the victims still were experiencing strong fear reaction, although withdrawal, depression, and exhaustion were also preeminent.

One month after their victimizations, women were significantly more disturbed than a matched sample of nonvictims on twenty-five of twenty-eight measures of anxiety, fear, depression, mood, and self-esteem. Victims improved considerably between one and three months, but after a year the researchers found that the majority of victims (75 to 80 percent) still continued to suffer from rape-related fear and anxiety.

Being raped also appears to affect the sex lives of most victims.[5] Women who were virgins when they were attacked and women who had not been sexually active had the greatest difficulty engaging in normal sexual relations after the rape, even many months after. Most victims who had been sexually active before their attacks experienced marked disruption in their sex lives, and although sexual satisfaction gradually improves in the months and years after rape, it rarely reaches pre-rape levels. Further, some partners of victims, while trying to understand what their loved ones are going through, may secretly believe they could have prevented their rapes. Just as victims sometimes are overwhelmed with a desire to cleanse themselves, so sometimes partners—even sympathetic, concerned ones—are overwhelmed with a desire to "repossess" their loved ones. These feelings can emerge at unpredictable times and places. Rape counsellors estimate that 75 to 85 percent of married victims are divorced within two years of their attacks.[6]

In 1978, four years after Burgess and Holmstrom originally interviewed the hundred or so victims of rape, they reported on the subsequent experiences of these women. None of the victims believed their lives were "back to normal," or back to a pre-rape state. By 1979, some of the original victims still had not recovered from their rapes.[7] Some women never recover, and many repress their feelings about their attacks only to have them emerge many years later, sometimes in confusing ways.

Twenty years after the fact, a Chicago woman, Ellen, had nightmares about a rape which had taken place long ago when she was baby-sitting for family friends. She didn't tell her parents or the parents of the baby; the assailant was a houseguest in their home. Ellen did tell other friends when she was an adult. She didn't think the rape had affected her sexually, or in her relationships with other men or women, but she did think the incident had another psychological impact. Ellen thinks the lesson she learned from that rape was that she could not be open, friendly, outgoing, assertive, or competitive without getting taught still another lesson—that all of her initiatives would end in disaster. This feeling controlled and limited her behavior for years. She related her current nightmares about the incident to current initiatives she was making with respect to her career, and she feared she would get taught another damaging lesson.

Victims who tell no one are frequently haunted years later by nightmares and guilt over having "hidden" the event from friends and loved ones. One victim eventually told her minister. She had never told her husband, or anyone else, about her victimization. It had happened when she was nineteen, before her marriage, and she had been afraid to tell her fiancé for fear he would refuse to marry her. Then, thirty years after the fact, she had nightmares which seemed to be rooted in her guilt for concealing it.

Another victim, also a middle-aged woman in Chicago, Hilda, said:

> Well, I was raped twenty-five years ago. I never told *anyone* until now. It was in Germany. He was an American soldier. He forced me. I got pregnant as a result. I was humiliated, but had nowhere to turn. My father would have killed me. I moved to the United States and had the baby here. I'm Catholic and just couldn't get an abortion . . . and it was much harder in those days. [A few minutes after she finished describing her rape, Hilda's twenty-five-year-old son walked through the living room. Hilda nodded, indicating he was the product of the rape. Then Hilda added,] The trouble with rape is that it ruins your life, the whole rest of your life.
>
> —Hilda

Whether or not victims conceal their rapes, many feel guilty and search their minds and hearts trying to think of what they could have done to prevent it. Often the circumstances indicate no basis for the guilt, but it burdens victims anyway.

Researchers, noting that self-blame is a common reaction to rape, have studied the situational conditions surrounding the rapes of a sample of victims and the nature of their self-blame.[8] Janoff-Bulman distinguished between what she labeled behavioral self-blame and characterological self-blame. Behavioral self-blame (experienced by 69 percent of those who blamed themselves) is limited to the victim's behavior in the specific situation, whereas characterological self-blame (experienced by 19 percent of those who blamed themselves) involves a general negative evaluation of oneself as a person. She speculated that women who believed they could have behaved differently (for example, by not going to the site, or by dressing differently) would be better able to cope than women who blamed themselves characterologically, that is, thought they were bad people deserving of victimization. She reasoned that women who blamed their behavior would think they could do something—that is, change their behavior—to prevent future rapes, while those who blamed themselves characterologically would feel it was hopeless or futile to try. Other researchers, however, find that self-blame in either form is a symptom of psychological distress. They regard regaining a sense of control over one's life as important to recovery for victims, but identify several routes other than self-blame for doing so. The fact that so many victims do cope and survive is impressive.

Whether they blame themselves or not, victims' stories indicate that the realities of rape are devastating, that no two rapes are alike, and that since victims all have different backgrounds and experiences, no two victims experience it the same way. In short, there is no typical rape, no typical victim, and no typical rapist. Yet the sexualization of the violence in this crime has engendered a similarly experienced, widespread fear among victims and potential victims and those who hear about the crime. Many women, especially those in their twenties and thirties, know someone who has been a victim of sexual assault, and what they have learned about the victim's experiences becomes an important component of their own fear.

The aftermath of rape for victims and those who hear about their attacks can be devastating not only for them, but ultimately for the quality of urban life in America. Widespread fear, especially fear of attack, is primarily a concern of women in our nation, and that female fear is the legacy of rape in America. It limits women's lives because it prompts them to take precautions which may not protect them but do constrain them. Many feminists argue that rape is not a crime of sex or sexual passion, but rather a crime of political dominance, perpetrated by men who want or feel the need to control and humiliate women. This perspective has led feminists to argue that the function of rape in our society is to keep women afraid, "in their place," and dependent on men.[9]

If rape is most often and primarily an act of dominance or aggression, why don't rapists simply beat up or mug the women? Why do they rape them? Many arguments revolve around this question of whether rape is purely an act of political dominance or whether it is an act of lust and sex, or some combination of the two. To show power and anger through rape—as opposed to mugging or assault—men are calling on lessons women learn from society, from history and religion, to defile, degrade, and shame in addition to inflicting physical pain. Rapists have learned, *as have their victims,* that to rape is to do something worse than to assault; this sexualization of violence adds a range of long-term emotional consequences to the physical injury.

Sorting out sexual from dominance motives with research on rapists is problematic,[10] since in fewer than half of reported rape cases is anyone arrested, and only 5 percent of those arrested are convicted. Studies of rapists have always concentrated on convicted men in prison; they may tell very little about the much larger number of rapists who are never caught or convicted.

Research on rapists in prison indicates that about a third are married and were sexually active with their wives at the time of the assault. Of those not married, the majority were involved in consenting relationships. The profile of convicted rapists is remarkably similar to that of any other felon. Most have committed other crimes and learned at an early age to deal with stress through violence. They committed rape in order to dominate or possess the victim or to lash out and attack another person. Often the anger or aggression is not even intended for the woman attacked and often the rapists cannot even remember what their victims looked like.[11] More than 70 to 80 percent of convicted rapists have been sexually abused as children (as opposed to 30 to 40 percent of the general prison population). Therapists treating these rapists believe sexual child abuse is so traumatic for young boys, and halts their emotional growth to such an extent, that the emotional age of the victim-turned-aggressor remains at the chronological age when first attacked. Treatment involves regressing these men back to the age of attack, dealing with the emotions felt at that time, and then bringing them back emotionally to their current age.[12]

Convicted rapists (and child molesters) express anger and frustration through aggression and transgression, and are often unskilled in expressing emotions verbally. The majority of men convicted of rape have raped more than once, are likely to rape again, and are likely to exhibit more violence against the next victim.[13]

Violent men who choose rape over another form of physical attack may be especially immature emotionally, and want to do something more demeaning than simply assaulting another person. They want to add long-term emotional injury—shame, humiliation, and degradation—to physical injury. They may also know that women fear rape second only to murder, and it may increase their aggressiveness to know that their victims have learned to fear this particular violation more than other things they might do.

Of the 348 convicted rapists in one of the studies,[14] about half had raped adult women; the remainder had been convicted of raping children, other men, or elderly women. Of those who had raped adult (but not elderly) women, 55 percent were classified as having committed "power" rapes; that is, the rapists wanted to exert control or to possess the victim. Another 40 percent of the rapes were classified as "anger" rapes, cases in which the rapist lashed out, wanted to attack the victim. The final 5 percent of rapes were classified as "sadistic" rapes in which anger and power motives were combined.[15]

Thus, the feminists are right that—from the point of view of the rapist—rape is rarely only an act of passion or lust. But from the point of view of the victim, rape is rarely experienced only as an act of political dominance because it involves sexual organs as well as physical violence. It exploits the physical differences between men and women in size and strength. It exploits the power and status differences between men and women in our society.

Such exploitation is possible because rape continues to be viewed by most as a private experience which people believe can be prevented if victims and rapists learn to behave differently. Rape is rarely also viewed as a collective problem, a problem of society that results from years of inequity and reinforcement of myths and social lessons taught to both women and men by the way rape has been handled in the criminal justice system, medical facilities, media, schools, churches, and other important institutions in our society.

5

Society's Response

ALTHOUGH each woman develops her own attitude toward rape based on her knowledge and experiences, female fear is one of the most commonly experienced aspects of women's everyday lives. It is not an idiosyncratic, private emotion, but a social fact with considerable impact on our society and on the quality of life in our cities.[1] It is a rational phenomenon resulting not only from women's personal backgrounds but also from what women as a group have imbibed from history, religion, culture, social institutions, and everyday social interactions. Learned early in life, female fear is continually reinforced by such social institutions as the school, the church, the law, and the press. Much is also learned from parents, siblings, teachers, and friends. While the impact of the lessons varies, the message is uniform: (1) men are in charge of institutions and define how the institutions will view issues; (2) women and women's issues are not important; (3) rape is a women's issue and therefore not important; and (4) institutions do not devote resources to combatting rape. Since women know the devastating emotional consequences of rape and know they are held responsible for preventing it, their heightened fear is a rational response.

Throughout much of history, the organization of society placed women mainly in the private, domestic sphere while men occupied the public arena. Presumably, the initial reason for this was centered in the biological differences between men and women and the fact that only women can give birth. Yet the birthing process itself incapacitates women for very little time; many women are able to perform everyday work until a few days or even hours before delivery and to resume many tasks only a few days or weeks later. However, in most cultures women have also been assigned the social role of caring for the children, usually in isolated or semi-isolated settings such as individual households or extended family compounds. Men, meanwhile, have been expected to carry on other activities outside of the household. In much of the world, the private, more secluded world of women became over time more and more separated from the more public life of men, and the day-to-day activities of women and men overlapped very little if at all.[2]

The social separation of men and women, and the social definitions of men's and women's roles, have been reinforced by religious teachings. An extreme example occurs in Islam where the practice of purdah—total seclusion and segregation of women—includes the covering of women from head to toe with a thick burka that is regarded as "the bulwark against sexual anarchy."[3] The Ten Commandments of the Jewish and Christian faiths warn against committing adultery or lusting after a neighbor's wife, and the Scriptures warn in many ways against the "ways of the flesh." These beliefs and practices gave rise to the notion that women are to be honored, but that they can be dishonored, defiled, and shamed through a range of actions involving sexual organs. It was believed that women could be better protected from shame-producing events if they were secluded in homes. This belief further accentuated the division between the public and private lives of men and women and, coupled with the need to care for the children, gave rise to the long-held belief that "a woman's proper place is in the home."

This belief was most strongly held by those segments of ancient and medieval, Christian and Moslem cultures that could afford it.[4] That is, men who were economically successful could afford to "keep" their wives at home; those who couldn't afford it had wives who worked outside the home. One result of this state of affairs was that men whose wives did not work outside the home had higher status in their local societies than men whose wives "had to work" outside the home. Another result was that women who stayed at home acquired the higher status of their husbands, which benefited them in any social interactions outside the home, while within the household they had very little status as they were completely dependent economically on their husbands. In contrast, "working wives" had lower status in the larger society, but more equal status within their own households.[5]

Religion also buttressed the seclusion of women by treating sex and bodily changes associated with childbearing as dirty or somehow bad. Women in purdah in India are prohibited while they are menstruating from praying and from preparing food to be eaten by visitors to the shrine their husbands serve. Some Jewish men and women believe women can reenter "normal" life after menstruation only by participating in a cleansing mikvah, a ritual bath. A remnant of this belief is evident in the fact that many modern women still refer to menstruation as "the curse."

These traditional and religious ideas also led to a belief that it was up to women to dress modestly, lest they be thought provocative or licentious. By the time of Victorian England, "woman . . . was to be chaste, delicate and loving."[6] Much of the Puritanism of Victorian England with regard to sexual relations seems to have been rooted in some fear related to the "uncontrollability" of women's sexuality: "Women's reproductive organs were thought to control not only her physiology but also her emotional life, in contrast to male sexual impulses, which were subject to man's will."[7]

The social isolation of Victorian women and their relative lack of knowledge about the public arenas of life meant that the world outside the home was experienced by them as strange and unpredictable. In that unknown world they were vulnerable and dependent on intuition for ascertaining how to respond, especially to perceived danger. At home they were surrounded by the familiar, protected (supposedly) from danger, and secure.

Thus, by the end of the Victorian era and the beginning of modern industrialization and urbanization, several traditions, mores, and myths about the place and role of women, their sexuality, and how it was to be controlled were well established. First, a woman's proper place was believed to be in the home, caring for the home and children, providing an emotional haven for her husband. Furthermore, proper women were expected to be modest, taking care not to dress or act in a manner that could be thought provocative. This included speaking in a quiet voice, avoiding strong food and liquor, and avoiding conversation with men, especially about serious topics. Discussion about sex was rare and proper women did not engage in sexual relations before marriage or, once married, with anyone other than their husbands. Couples were expected to remain married. Finally, women were considered emotional and rarely capable of rational thinking, not as amenable as men to education, and more dependent on intuition for their sense of reality than on reading or rational thinking.

As modern urban life evolved, many of the traditions and mores concerning women that had developed in the Victorian era were heightened and exacerbated by general changes in society. The industrialization of the late 1800s and early 1900s was accompanied by the growth of rational bureaucratic organizations built around a hierarchy of positions which represented power and authority. Persons who occupied those positions were accorded prestige and esteem commensurate with how well they exercised that power and authority. The public world of power and authority was largely a world of men.

As cities increased in size, people did not lose the capacity for deep personal relationships, but they did develop the ability to engage in superficial, fleeting relationships; and with that ability came fear and distrust of foreign groups or strangers in the public sphere.[8] People increasingly felt themselves surrounded by a "world of strangers,"[9] who were perceived as "odd, different, unconventional and potentially threatening."[10] Thus, the increase in urbanization meant that urban dwellers experienced increased stress, alienation, personal estrangement, and a weakening of social bonds.

Before the growth of large cities, people tended to live in small communities where they knew everyone, and each person's rank or place in society. People behaved as befitted their social rank and it was very difficult for anyone to "rise above" his or her station in life. In today's large cities filled with strangers, social rank generally is much more difficult to assess; it is much more difficult to know whom to trust. This makes social control through mores, custom, and tradition much more difficult. Some urban neighborhoods, those filled with families that know and interact regularly with one another, call up memories of how it used to be.[11] But even in these neighborhoods, strangers are common today and the traditional social bonds are weakened.

While it may be difficult to ascertain status, in most instances it is not difficult to ascertain race. And since race and social status have for many years been linked in the United States, there is an unfortunate, almost automatic distrust by persons of one race for those of another. In terms of crime and fear of crime, urbanites (especially whites) tend to believe that strangers, (especially blacks) are the persons responsible for crime.[12] While whites may fear blacks, in fact most victims of crime, including rape, are of the same race as the perpetrator.

The lack of relatedness and consequent feeling of isolation in modern cities strains both individual psyches and social relations.

It is not surprising, then, that various types of group and interpersonal conflict, including crime, are disproportionately likely to occur in large cities.[13] City dwellers often feel more vulnerable than people living among acquaintances to whom they can turn for help in a time of need. Many people, especially women, believe that if they called for help no one would respond, as in the case of Kitty Genovese who was raped and killed in New York, her screams unheeded by the dozens who later admitted hearing her.

For many of these reasons, then, crime has been viewed as primarily an urban problem,[14] and analyses of crime statistics attest to the fact that violent crime has increased very dramatically in the past fifty years and that the rate of victimization is much greater in the nation's large urban areas than in small towns and rural areas. Further, the rate of violent crime in the United States is estimated to have increased 336 percent between the years 1964 and 1975.[15] Crime has become a "nationalized" problem, and it is affecting all of our major cities in a similar manner.[16]

Other forces of industrialization and urbanization which have changed the face of America also have resulted in many changes in women's lives—from machinery to help with housework to a near revolution in the attitudes of many toward women's roles.

But in some quarters, attitudes and behavior are quite unchanged. In many U.S. social settings, women's "place" is still regarded to be the home. Many believe women should work only if they must because of economic need. In such situations, modern women—like their sisters of years past—may resent having to work; husbands may feel inadequate because they don't earn enough so that their wives won't have to work. Men who are successful enough that their wives can choose to stay home are accorded higher status, especially if their wives then devote considerable time and energy to volunteer activities.[17] And like women from earlier eras, those women have relatively high status (their husband's) in interactions outside the home, but are likely to have little power within the household.

Work in the home and in volunteer situations of such women is relatively "invisible," but necessary if those on the "overside"[18] of history are to function effectively.[19] For example, the *pirzada* men who maintain the modern shrine outside Old Delhi would be unable to do so without the women kept isolated and invisible in purdah to make food and other preparations (which men are prohibited from preparing) for visitors to the shrine.[20] And many modern corporation men would be unable to do their jobs were it not for the invisible work done by their wives, who learn to entertain elaborately and take full responsibility for children and home management. Similarly, politicians depend on women volunteers to set up rallies and fundraisers.[21]

Industrialization and urbanization, rather than liberating women, may have resulted in even greater sexism and an even greater loss of power for the vast majority of women. One philosopher-historian argues that until the modern era, in all cultures, men and women did gender-linked work, and that very linkage involved a mutual interdependence and thus resulted in shared power. Industrialization moved many functionally important jobs from the home and control by women to the factory and control by men, and in the process created many unisex jobs, destroying the complementary, mutually dependent forms of work. Although many women now do jobs formerly done only by men, the systems, institutions, and bureaucracies controlling the conditions of work are still controlled by men. Thus, despite appearances of progress, women may actually be worse off.[22] Ironically, while not gaining equality in the public sphere, women may be losing their traditional arena of power if they encourage men to extend their range of functions to the home by sharing in housekeeping, cooking, and child rearing.[23] (Needless to say, such ideas on this topic are debated by many feminists!)

If women work outside the home at unisex jobs, they are still frequently subject to many of the traditions and mores that affected women in the past. There are few working mothers who have not experienced at least some emotional strains associated with the conflicting roles they are expected to perform at work and at home.[24] Those who have a choice and choose *not* to work outside the home may also feel strain associated with pressures they attribute to the women's liberation movement, resulting in a feeling that they are "only housewives."

Industrialization and modernization, and the accompanying weakening of social bonds, have brought additional pressures on women that conflict with sexual norms and mores in the past. Now women are expected to be physically attractive to all men, and the fashion, cosmetic, beauty, diet, and advertising industries are dedicated to this end. Yet such attractiveness may not only send men a mixed message, it may also make women even less powerful. Wearing high heels makes women's legs more attractive, but also makes it more difficult for them to run away and protect themselves in dangerous situations.

In magazines, men are portrayed as lavishing money and gifts—if not sustained attention—on the beautiful women in the ads. In return for such gifts and attention, there seems to be some suggestion that women will bestow "sexual favors." Nonetheless, a woman may lose respect if she bestows too much, too easily, or too soon. If she doesn't bestow enough, she may be forced. And if she is forced, others may think that although she resisted she "really wanted it," that she "asked for it," or that somehow it was "her own fault." While a woman in this situation may believe she's been raped, a man may think of it as sexual seduction gone awry:

> It is hardly surprising that there should be such widespread confusion over the distinction between rape and seduction, given the legitimacy of sexual coercion in our society. The socialization of both men and women takes coercive sexuality as the normal standard of behavior. Men are expected to apply a certain amount of pressure to have women submit ("agree") to sexual intercourse, and women are expected to resist such pressure, whatever their own desires might happen to be.[25]

The principal lesson women learn from these interactions results in a double bind: be sexy, but modest; attractive, but not provocative.

Now, in the 1980s, the traditions, mores, and myths about the place and role of women, their sexuality, and how it is controlled are in great flux; and the modern urban woman is confronted by what appear to be multiple paradoxes concerning her sexuality, her economic security, and her physical safety. For example, while a woman's proper place may be in the home, it may also be in the world outside the home. Women often are expected to be both modest and sexually attractive. The messages for women are very mixed with respect to assertiveness, courage, intelligence, and decision making. Messages are also mixed about the advisability of sexual activity before marriage, with other partners during marriage, or between marriages. Divorce and extramarital sex are common.

Over time, these lessons from history, religion, and modern urban life have influenced the manner in which families raise their children. Young girls are warned at an early age to stay away from strangers lest one of them turn out to be a child molester. All women recall being warned as children, and they warn their own children. As one woman said about her daughters,

> I mostly try to keep them in as much as possible. I tell them to walk toward the middle of the street . . . don't go out alone but walk with a friend. They both take karate. None of these things

really relieve my mind though. They are both well-instructed, probably overinstructed, but it still doesn't relieve my mind. I don't
think my fifteen-year-old is a bit afraid, and that worries me. She's
too friendly.

Another woman warns her daughter to "be careful how she acts
and carries herself," and "don't trust strangers." But she tells her
fifteen- and sixteen-year-old sons to "fight back . . . if they're too
small to beat the person, they should get me. Don't be a punk.
Don't take no crap from no bums."

Perhaps because of childhood and adolescent experiences, girls
are more willing to admit fear than boys, and girls report higher
levels of fear.[26] Boys feel it is not acceptable to admit fear for themselves. However, although girls report more fear, they do not exhibit
any more fear-related behavior than the boys. As the girls mature
into women, however, they increase their fear-related behavior by
taking more precautions against crime. As boys mature into men,
on the other hand, they report fear for their mothers, wives, and
daughters, but take few precautions themselves, despite the fact that
statistics indicate men are more likely than women to be victims of
all crimes except rape.

Women's awareness of danger may be reinforced by the fact
that most women grow up without much knowledge or experience
in defending themselves. Rarely are they taught to fight or run fast;
instead the emphasis is usually on being feminine, and at least appearing relatively weak and delicate. This behavior magnifies the differences between the sexes.[27] Some researchers suggest that such attitudes, learned while young, account for the greater fear of crime
experienced by adult women than men.[28] Other research suggests
that women's perceptions of their own physiques are also important
in accounting for their level of fear.[29] When asked how strong they
thought they were and how fast they thought they could run compared
to the average woman and man, 63 percent of women[30] thought
they were less physically competent than both the average man *and
the average woman;* only 28 percent perceived themselves to be
better or even similar in speed and strength when compared to the
average woman. These perceptions of physical competence are significant predictors of women's fear levels; women who perceive themselves as less physically able are more likely to say they are afraid.
However, after taking self-defense training courses, women reported
feeling stronger, braver, more active, more in control, bigger, more
efficacious in a variety of arenas—and less afraid.[31]

Women's early training to be alert to danger, coupled with lack of a sense of physical efficacy, may leave them particularly vulnerable. This vulnerability is compounded by women's hesitation to reproach others for their behavior, especially if they are not certain about these others' intentions. The "failure to condemn allows those who ignore moral requirements to do so more easily."[32] Those of lower status, whether determined by age, sex, race, education, or income, are less likely to make a moral reproach.

The inhibitions women learn while growing up about reproaching others—especially if they have greater power or status—may be important in understanding why women who are about to be attacked may appear to wait too long before they act to protect themselves.

If a woman is aware and *certain* that a man intends to rape her, she is likely to take action—however effective or ineffective— and much more quickly than if she is unaware or uncertain. But at what point can she be certain? The ramifications of accusing a man of *thinking about* or *intending* to rape her could be severe enough to prohibit even the most assertive woman from making such accusations. Yet many rapes begin in situations in which the woman is initially uncertain about the rapist's intentions. By the time she is sure, she may have lost the opportunity to escape. Women who successfully resist a rape attack are often those who attend to feelings early in the interaction signaling that something is wrong.[33] Thus women are forced to become extremely sensitive to nuances of language and style, and to trust most in the accuracy of the resulting, often inexplicable, intuitive feelings. Women's fear is a survival mechanism.

Analyses of crime data from Chicago neighborhoods suggest that women are particularly sensitive to the presence of signs associated with danger and social disorder, such as graffiti, abandoned buildings, and teenagers hanging out on street corners.[34] Such disturbing (although not necessarily criminal) "incivilities" are related to increased use of precautionary tactics. Incivilities suggest that local social-control mechanisms are not operating effectively. Residents then perceive that, in the aggregate, a community is unable to regulate behavior within its boundaries.

Women's comfort and familiarity with their communities are related to their fear levels.[35] Those who find it easy to distinguish local residents from strangers, who know neighborhood children by name, and who feel a part of their area rather than "it's just a place to live," tend to report less fear. Those who feel detached may read the environment incorrectly whereas neighborhood bonds may enable a woman to have an impact on her environment.

Discussion or gossip about crime in the neighborhood may also affect women's fear levels. Talk about crime seems to be stimulated by the perception that the local crime problem is serious, and those with strong local ties tend to speak more frequently with neighbors about such problems.[36] Such gossip tends to center on women and the elderly. Researchers speculate that such stories become the focus of discussion because they concern violations of the unwritten rules about how the elderly should be treated.[37] They induce greater fear because they seem to indicate lack of social control in the community. Women may also respond to these stories because they identify with the victims.[38]

Whereas signs of incivility, neighborhood ties, perceptions of risk, and other factors all affect fear levels, they do not necessarily determine who gets victimized. An extensive analysis of data from the National Crime Survey suggests that victimization is related to lifestyles, since "lifestyles are related to the probability of being in places (streets, parks, and other public places) at times (especially nighttime) when victimizations are known to occur."[39] Yet the demands set by occupational schedules may necessitate exposure to risk, and indeed employed women do report less avoidance of danger than those who do not work outside the home.[40]

Women may not go out alone at night because of sex-role expectations or child-care obligations, or because of fear. Whatever the reason, the result of circumscribing their activities is that women are less exposed to the possibility of being victimized. Perceptions of the rate of rape generate fear in women and fear leads them to reduce their exposure to risk, which in turn lowers the frequency of victimization. In many ways, then, female fear is adaptive. It is also the best predictor of the lengths to which women will go to protect themselves.[41] However, although fear leads to self-protection, this may in itself lead to more fear by making women aware of their feelings.[42] This relationship between fear and precaution, whatever its causal direction, means that fewer women are exposed to risk and hence are less available as victims of crime. But the relatively high frequency with which women are victimized within the home by known assailants raises the question of whether restricting their movement through public places really keeps women safe. While it does keep women safe from some attacks by strangers, it certainly does not prevent attacks by all strangers. Nor does it prevent women's victimization from other forms of domestic violence.

6

Views from the Law

THE treatment of rape by the powerful legal and justice systems is linked to the political system (since elected legislators make the laws) and to the medical institutions which collect (or don't collect) evidence needed in the prosecution of rape cases. The outcome of rape cases contributes to female fear.

U.S. common law and the FBI Criminal Code define rape as the "carnal knowledge of a female forcibly and against her will." Yet since rape is a personal crime, it is governed by state rather than federal laws.[1] The states' statutes and penalties for the commission of the crime vary, reflecting the attitudes of local citizens and legislatures. Some state laws—fewer and fewer—still reflect outdated myths and stereotypes; the laws "mirror values regarding the social position of women and the nature of the crime."[2]

Although state definitions of rape vary, three elements are crucial to the successful prosecution of any rape case in all states: *identification* of the rapist, the use or threat of *force,* and penetration *against the victim's will* and without her consent. Since the victim is usually the only witness and her veracity is often doubted, rape traditionally has been difficult to prove. It is often difficult for a woman to present evidence of all three aspects, especially that it was against her will. In many jurisdictions, a victim must take a polygraph test to substantiate her accusation of sexual assault. Thus, unlike burglary or mugging victims, the rape victim may be called upon to "prove" that a crime has been committed before the prosecutor will even begin to establish a case.

A review of rape laws shows that persons accused of crimes in the United States are considered innocent until proven guilty and that the laws in our nation are written, implemented, and prosecuted primarily by men.[3] Thus, rape laws indicate what (usually) male legislators regard as necessary to prove a (usually) man guilty of the crime, in order to protect men falsely accused.

According to legal theory, the commission of a crime requires the concurrence of an *actus reus* (unacceptable act) and *mens rea* (criminal intent with respect to that act). Under the traditional definition of the crime of forcible rape, the *actus reus* is the unconsented act of sexual intercourse and *mens rea* is the intention of having intercourse without the victim's consent.

This definition requires both the victim's perception that the intercourse was nonconsensual and the defendant's perception of the victim's nonconsent. Thus, nonconsent distinguishes forcible rape from mutually desired intercourse. Furthermore, women were traditionally presumed to consent to sexual intercourse unless criminal circumstances could be proved beyond doubt, often requiring active victim resistance or independent corroboration of the victim's report of the crime. (Islamic law requires several male witnesses before the crime of rape can be established.)

U.S. rape laws and law-enforcement officials thus have traditionally regarded force and consent as independent elements. The rape victim is required to prove her nonconsent beyond a reasonable doubt, placing the victim in the status of codefendant charged with the "crime of consent." The victim must show not only that she was forcibly violated, but that she consciously and subconsciously did not desire intercourse. The theory behind this is reflected in a British barrister's well-known statement published in 1847 and still quoted in law school textbooks and by many judges as they instruct juries:

> It's true that rape is a most detestable crime, and it ought severely and impartially be punished with death, but it must be remembered that it is an accusation easily to be made and hard to be proved, and harder to be defended against by the party accused, tho' never so innocent.[4]

This "essentially creates two crimes—consent and force—and two criminals—the woman and her assailant. Because nonconsent is an element of the offense and because a criminal defendant is innocent until each element is established beyond a reasonable doubt, the burden is, therefore, on the prosecutor to establish beyond a reasonable doubt that she did not consent."[5]

The requirement of proof of the victim's nonconsent is unique to the crime of forcible rape. A robbery victim, for example, is usually not considered as having "consented" to the crime if he or she hands money over to an assailant (especially if there was use of force or threat of force). As a result of this requirement, evidence of the victim's reputation for unchastity and acts of prior sexual conduct has been generally admissible in crimes of forcible rape; lawyers infer that an unchaste woman would be more likely than a virtuous woman to agree to intercourse with an assailant.

Common law and the courts have generally accepted resistance by the victim as the outward manifestation of nonconsent in order to distinguish forcible from consensual carnal knowledge. The purpose of the resistance standard is twofold. First, resistance is the behavioral manifestation by which the victim communicates her nonconsent. Second, resistance provides an apparently objective standard for nonwitnesses (jurors, for example) to assess whether there was nonconsent. The theory underlying the resistance standard is that persons worthy of the protection of the law would defend their virtue by undergoing a significant degree of other physical harm before submitting to sexual attack. By requiring resistance, however, the law continues to focus on the victim's reaction to the crime, rather than the offender's criminal conduct.

The basic question for the courts to resolve is the *amount* of resistance sufficient to negate consent and thus show the act was against the victim's will. Resistance by words alone is insufficient and must be accompanied by acts. The most stringent standards require the "utmost resistance": that the victim did everything possible, exercised every physical means within her power, to prevent the assailant from completing the assault. Most courts, however, have accepted a "reasonableness" standard requiring sufficient resistance to make nonconsent reasonably manifest. Courts have thus generally required that resistance be relative, and judged with regard to all the circumstances including the victim's age, the relative strength of the parties, and the amount of force exerted by the assailant. Furthermore, the trend in most jurisdictions is toward a liberalization of the resistance standard. Courts have generally accepted that the victim's submission based upon reasonable fear does not constitute consent. Nonetheless, many rape victims who escaped physical harm in addition to the rape are made to feel by police, court personnel, and others who learn of the crime that they must not have resisted enough.

The traditional requirements of nonconsent and resistance suggest that rape laws were designed not to protect women from assault but to protect the male's exclusive possession of his woman's body. Radical feminists put it more strongly, saying that rape is "an offense one male commits upon another" and that rape laws are designed to safeguard male property rights in women.[6]

Women are traditionally conditioned to be passive, submissive, and weak. "The real reason for the law's everlasting confusion as to what constitutes an act of rape and what constitutes an act of mutual intercourse is the underlying cultural assumption that it is the natural masculine role to proceed aggressively toward the stated goal, while the natural feminine role is to 'resist' or 'submit.' And so to protect male interests, the law seeks to gauge the victim's behavior during the offending act in the belief that force is not conclusive *in and of itself.*"[7] By requiring the victim's nonconsent and resistance, the laws are premised upon the belief that a healthy or virtuous woman cannot be raped; that rape victims either "want" or "deserve" it. Nonetheless, both verbal and physical resistance to violent crime are often discouraged by law-enforcement officials, on the grounds they may provoke greater violence or other unpredictable reactions and increase the victim's chances of injury.

Public perceptions of the crime of forcible rape closely parallel traditional legal definitions. Research shows that physically forced, unwanted sexual intercourse (similar to the traditional definition of carnal knowledge of a woman not one's wife, forcibly and against her will) is most clearly perceived by the public as rape and warranting legal protection (see Table 6.1). In addition, intercourse without consent, irrespective of physical force, is also viewed as constituting rape; the victim's nonconsent is thus considered paramount in distinguishing rape from mutually desired intercourse. Unwanted sexual intercourse on a date, however, is less often perceived as rape and thus warranting the protection of rape laws.

These public perceptions reflect the underlying societal belief that the social circumstances surrounding dating *imply consent* to all resulting sexual contact. The American dating system, which constitutes a primary source of heterosexual contacts, legitimizes the consensual "purchase" of women as sexual objects and obliterates the crucial distinction between consent and nonconsent. The messages are conflicting: women are expected to be alluring enough to attract men and allow them to spend money on their food, entertainment, and perhaps gifts—and yet remain chaste. Furthermore, nonstranger

TABLE 6.1
Percent of Males and Females in Chicago, Philadelphia, and San
Francisco Who Define Various Acts as Rape

	% Yes Males	% Yes Females
1. What about unwanted sexual intercourse with someone when physically forced or overpowered?*	98.5	99.0
2. What about sexual intercourse with someone without their consent? Is that rape?†	94.1	95.6
3. What about unwanted sexual intercourse on a date? Would you call that rape?	82.5	83.4
4. What about a relative having sexual intercourse with a *child?*	83.3	90.6
5. A relative having sexual intercourse with a *teenager* under age 18?	63.5	79.5
6. What about unwanted sexual intercourse between a husband and wife? Is that rape?	43.9	63.0
7. What about a stranger pinching or grabbing in a sexually suggestive way? Is that rape?	10.4	22.9
8. What about a stranger exposing his genitals?	14.9	21.2
9. What about someone whistling or making rude remarks? Would you call that rape?	0.0	3.7
10. Is there anything else you would call rape?	30.3	17.8

* The order of the questions on the survey was 3, 9, 7, 8, 2, 1, 6, 4, 5, 10.
† Responses included forced anal or oral intercourse and the use of objects.

rapes are often not reported because women are afraid of reprisals or believe the police won't take them seriously. Women themselves are imbued with societal myths, and may believe they were somehow culpable. Thus, public attitudes limit the crime of forcible rape to unwanted sexual intercourse accompanied by force and committed by a stranger. But stranger or not, it is *not* a crime for a woman to say no, or to change her mind; it *is* a crime to rape.

The requirement of the victim's nonconsent provides the major legal and conceptual barrier to making forcible sexual intercourse within marriage a crime. "This doctrine is based on the premise that consent is a total defense to a charge of rape. Since a woman is theoretically consenting to all sexual intercourse with her husband as long as she remains married, rape is not possible between marital partners."[8] Thus, some argue, the marriage contract implies consent to all sexual intercourse. Since marriage traditionally also constituted ownership of the wife by her husband, he could not violate or steal his own property. Before recent reforms, the law in the state of Washington was typical of legislation on this issue. It defined rape as "an act of intercourse with a person not the wife or husband of the perpetrator committed against the person's will and without the person's consent."[9]

The movement to make it possible for women to charge their husbands with rape is hampered by concerns for malicious prosecutions. The rationale was expressed by Lord Hale: "There are women who are so unscrupulous that if they were given . . . statutory protection of rape in marriage they might be prepared to commit perjury and bring their husbands into a criminal court for the sole purpose of breaking up the marriage."[10] Furthermore, difficult evidentiary problems threaten the married victim's ability to meet the necessary burden of proof of rape by her husband beyond a reasonable doubt.

Despite legislative proposals in several states to protect married women from forcible rape by their husbands, most continue to permit marriage as a total defense to the charge of rape. Some states permit a charge of forcible rape if the spouses are living apart at the time of the rape; examples are Michigan, Oregon (later repealed), Delaware, and South Dakota. Most of these states, however, require that one spouse has filed for separate maintenance or divorce. By late 1984, seventeen states had abolished the marital rape exemption in some or all cases.[11] The rationale for limiting protection to married women has been summarized as follows:

> There are several considerations that led to the limitation of coverage to couples living apart. Acts between a married couple may provide difficult evidentiary problems. It may be argued, however, that difficult evidentiary problems do not justify withholding the protection of the law from married persons. There is a belief that the situation of spouses living together is susceptible to misrepresentation and likely to allow either spouse to use the law to obtain a better property settlement or child custody. It also might act as an obstacle to reconciliation. . . .[12]

The reluctance to extend protection to married women is attributable partly to the feelings of self-preservation on the part of married American male legislators.

In the struggles in Illinois and elsewhere to reform the law there, legislators, in the course of debating the language, repeatedly insisted that such a law would hurt men by allowing angry wives, or wives who wanted a divorce, to "get back at them" by charging rape. A veteran Miami trial attorney articulated the same sentiment:

> Let's say a wife found out her husband was cheating on her . . . what would be easier for the unhappy, frustrated wife than to claim he had raped her? If she were convincing, and some young assistant prosecutor believed the story, the guy could be indicted. When love turns to hate in marriage . . . there's nothing to match that kind of hate. Anything is possible.[13]

In contrast to both traditional and modern legal definitions, a surprisingly high proportion of women (63 percent) regard unwanted sexual intercourse within marriage as rape. These public attitudes reflect the tension between divergent proponents: those who desire the protection of all women from sexual assault, and those who worry about the stability of the marital relationship.

In response to criticism of traditional rape laws, most states in the last fifteen years have attempted to redefine the crime of forcible rape.[14] Beginning in 1962, the Model Penal Code produced by the American Bar Association (which was intended to be a model and not representative of typical state law) sought to reduce the degree of resistance required of the rape victim by eliminating the independent element of "against her will." The Code, shifting the focus to the conduct of the perpetrator, substituted the requirement that the assailant "compels her to submit by force or by threat of imminent death, serious bodily injury, extreme pain or kidnapping. . . ." Nonetheless, the resistance standard remained an important factor: the drafters noted that "compels . . . to submit" requires that the woman offer more than "token initial resistance."

Legislative reforms, spearheaded by Michigan activists, more successfully define rape in terms of the rapist's conduct (force). Such reform statutes define rape as sexual intercourse under circumstances which *presume* both criminal intent and nonconsent. Thus,

> If sexual intercourse occurred under a dangerous criminal circumstance, then an objective standard has been met and it does not matter whether or not the victim consented. In fact, the law does not allow her to consent under such a circumstance. A determination has been made by the legislature that consent in such a situation is too dangerous to be sanctioned.[15]

Under the Michigan statute, the burden of proof of nonconsent shifts from the prosecution to the defense, once the use of force has been demonstrated. Furthermore, resistance is not explicitly required. Rather, the statute explicitly focuses on the rapist, not the victim, and defines force and coercion, including criminal circumstances in which force or coercion are *presumed* to exist. They are presumed to exist when:

1. Circumstances involve the commission of any other felony.
2. The perpetrator knows that the victim is mentally defective or incapacitated or physically helpless, or the perpetrator uses force or coercion.
3. The perpetrator is armed with a weapon or an object which the victim reasonably believes is a weapon.
4. The perpetrator accomplishes penetration through force or coercion and causes injury to the victim.
5. The perpetrator causes injury to the victim and knows the victim is mentally defective or incapacitated or physically helpless.

Thus, the victim may assess her danger in light of the surrounding circumstances and act accordingly, required only that she believe the assailant has the ability to carry out his threats. Furthermore, no show of force is required when the victim is mentally or physically incapable of resistance.

Traditionally, forcible rape was regarded as a single crime of penetration, frequently accompanied by severe penalties, such as death or life imprisonment. The severe punishment was consistent with both the narrow definition of the crime of rape and the substantial evidentiary burdens placed upon the victim; both made it more difficult to win rape cases.

This situation resulted in the apparently anomalous position of activist women who argued for *reduced* penalties for rape. In states with reform laws, the crime of forcible rape has been divided into degrees with accompanying gradations in penalties. For example, the Michigan law provides for degrees of sexual assault which are determined by both penetration and the actual and presumed injury to the victim, thus more closely linking the severity of criminal conduct to the severity of the punishment. Thus, *penetration with aggravation* (that is, accompanied by threats of injury with a dangerous weapon or serious injury to the victim) constitutes first-degree assault; *contact with aggravation* constitutes second-degree assault; *penetration without aggravation*, third-degree assault; and *contact without aggravation*, fourth-degree. The punishments in Michigan range from a maximum of twenty years' imprisonment for first-degree sexual assault to imprisonment of not more than one year or a fine of not more than $500 for fourth-degree sexual assault. Thus, under this and similar approaches, Michigan and other states have changed their definition and treatment of rape from a sexual crime to a crime of violence, treated similarly to other violent crimes.

The Michigan statute is also innovative in that it protects three classes of people traditionally unprotected by rape laws. First, the new law is sex neutral, thus protecting males from sexual assaults not otherwise criminally prohibited. Second, the law affords limited marital protection by protecting a person from assault by a spouse when they are living apart and one partner has filed for divorce. Third, it eliminates the admission of evidence of prior sexual conduct with persons other than the defendant. This is premised upon the belief that every person has the right to be protected from unwanted forcible sexual penetration, regardless of the victim's past.

Nonetheless, the reforms exemplified in Michigan may prove inadequate. The Michigan statute fails to expressly eliminate lack of consent as an element of the crime, leaving open availability of consent as a defense. And despite the reforms, many jurors and judges (including women) cling to the belief that women cannot be raped.[16]

Several states, including Wisconsin, have eliminated rape as a specific crime and redefined it in terms of existing assault-and-battery concepts. Assault is defined as an intentional showing of force that creates reasonable fear of danger and physical harm; battery is the actual, intentional physical contact. Both assault and battery emphasize the physical harm resulting from the assailant's conduct. This approach, however, minimizes the rape itself. "The seriousness of rape does not necessarily depend upon the degree of force used or on the potential physical harm which results from forced intercourse. . . . The harm of rape rests in the fear of death as well as the degradation and humiliation the victim must experience. The injury is always to the psyche, sometimes to the body."[17]

Although the legal definitions of rape have been altered substantially in some states, basic societal attitudes have been much slower to change. If there is no physical injury or outward sign of violence and if the attacker is not a stranger, the incident is often not seen as a "true rape" by society, by the rapist, by police, by prosecutors, by judges, or even by some victims. Some argue that "the main impact of the statutory reform has been a symbolic and educative one for society at large, rather than an instrumental one for law enforcement."[18]

Thus, the lessons women learn from a study of laws pertaining to rape do not comfort them; on the contrary, they further justify women's fear.

7

———◆———

Exploitation of
Women's Fear

THE mass media are another institution important in teaching women
to worry about rape. Ever since the mid-1800s, when the penny
presses learned to exploit the human interest angle of violent crime,
editors have relied on stories about rape to provide a major ingredient
in their success formulas.[1]

Social critics, feminists, and academics all assert that the mass
media contribute to the prevalence of fear of crime, and more specifically to female fear. They reason that the attention the media give
crime and violence teaches women to fear, and continually reinforces
those lessons through frequent portrayals of violence against women.
The issue is complicated by the fact that the media portray crimes
as they do because it serves their best commercial interests.

Even though an urban woman's chances of being raped *may*
be as high as one in five, or even one in three, most women have
not been raped. Most people do not know—or do not know they
know—a rape victim. Most people do not even know someone who
has been the victim of any serious personal assault. Therefore, given
the dearth of firsthand information most people have about violent
crime, the media play a vital role in creating for the public the
vicarious reality about criminal victimization, and about the capacity
(or incapacity) of American society's institutions to deal with it.
After examining the issue in detail, the Crime Commission Task
Force Report concluded years ago that the media exaggerate both
the prevalence and the seriousness of crime in general, and that

their emphasis on violent crime prompts unrealistic fear.[2] If this is true about crime in general, it is likely to be even truer of the crime of rape.

What is the picture of rape that emerges from the pages of the newspaper? What can women conclude from newspaper portrayals about the facts of rape—frequency, time of day, age of victims, relationship of victims to assailants, location, and so on?

In order to answer these questions, researchers examined data from the Uniform Crime Reports (UCR), the victimization surveys (National Crime Surveys), and the eight major newspapers published in three selected cities during a six-month period: the *Chronicle* and the *Examiner* in San Francisco; the *Sun-Times,* the *Daily News,* and the *Tribune* in Chicago; and the *Inquirer, Bulletin,* and *Daily News* in Philadelphia.[3]

In each of the eight papers there was an average of 4.4 to 6.8 violent crime stories every day. Although murder is the least frequently occurring crime, about half of the violent crime stories printed were about murder, followed by stories about robbery, assault, and child abuse. Stories about rape, sexual assault, or sexual child abuse appeared two to four times per week, depending on the paper.

These newspaper stories can play an important role in shaping the public's beliefs about rape, beliefs that are not always accurate. For example, people often consider the typical rape situation to be one in which a stranger accosts a young, attractive woman on the street late at night. By extension, this implies that rapes happen only to women who are not being careful enough, who are "asking for it," and who entice men through their appearance or behavior. In reality, the rapist is often someone known at least casually by the victim, rapes occur at all hours and to women of all ages, and a large percentage of rapes occur in the victim's home rather than on the street.[4]

Since beliefs about rape can affect people's assessments of their own risks, ideas shaped by newspaper portrayals of rapes can intensify fears.

One aspect that influences women is the degree to which the newspaper stories allow them to engage in social distancing, that is, the degree to which they can make comparisons between a victim and themselves. Less fear will be evoked if a woman can differentiate herself from the victim in some salient way that will allow her to convince herself she is unlike that victim.

Theoretically, the more a reader can use social-distancing defense mechanisms, the less salient a particular news story should be, and the less the event portrayed should be incorporated into calculations of risk. Two aspects of social distancing are affected by newspaper portrayals: the extent to which newspapers give facts about the victim (and situation) that would allow comparisons; and the extent to which newspapers give "safety" or "risk" cues, indicating that crimes of a particular sort are either quite common or quite rare.

Everything else being equal, if a crime occurs frequently, one is likely to calculate that chances of victimization are greater than if the crime were rare. Yet we have already seen how difficult it is to get an accurate picture of rape statistics, even from law-enforcement agencies themselves. Added to this initial distortion is the fact that although three rapes are reported to the police for every murder, the papers report only one rape for every eleven murders. Editors have decided that almost every murder is news and most rapes are not. In deciding which rapes are newsworthy, newspapers distort their presentation, avoiding the representative rape in favor of the most lurid, in order to capture their readers' attention.

This contention is supported by the ratio of attempted to completed rapes reported by the newspapers in San Francisco, Philadelphia, and Chicago (see Table 7.1). The police data from those cities indicate that in every four attacks, one victim gets away and three rapes are completed; but the victimization survey data indicate the opposite—that in every four attacks, three get away and one rape is completed. The likelihood is that the victimization survey data are more accurate. For example, many women who have been attacked but have gotten away don't bother to report it to the police, but may recount the incident later to a Census surveyor. In any case, the newspaper portrayals show a very different picture. For every fourteen news reports about rape, thirteen are about completed rapes and one is about an attempted rape, often one with a bizarre

TABLE 7.1
Rape Statistics by Source

Rate	UCR 52/100,000 Women	Media	LEAA/Census 315/100,000 Women over 12
Ratio Rapes Completed: Attempted	3:1	13:1	1:3
Ratio Rapes: Murder	3:1	1:11	

angle. This may be why women believe most rapes are completed, and that women have very little chance of getting away. The consequences of presenting such an inexorable view need to be considered.

Other aspects of rape are also distorted (see Table 7.2). For example, the age distribution represented in the media reports compared with the police data is skewed toward the mature. Since teenage women have a three times higher rate of rape than the average woman, the rape of an older woman is less frequent and therefore more newsworthy. One news feature editor, questioned about why his paper seemed to have so few rapes compared with his competitor's said, "They [rape stories] all look the same . . . the typical rape isn't news . . . if a seventy-five-year-old woman is raped, it's more heinous. That will be in the paper."[5]

Some distortion occurs simply because of the media's reliance on police blotters for their information. Comparisons of the UCR and victimization survey data indicate that many rapes of fifteen- to nineteen-year-olds are either hidden by their families or declared unfounded by the police. Similarly, newspapers underrepresent the number of rapes by acquaintances or relatives because family pressures and police unfounding practices often keep these rapes from police records. Further, whereas 50 percent of the rapes reported in the victimization survey were reported to have occurred between six in the evening and midnight, only 5 percent of the rapes reported in the newspapers were assigned to this time slot. Date rapes, acquaintance rapes, and rapes occurring in quasi-social settings are most likely to fall in this time frame, and are also quite likely to be underreported or declared unfounded. Since these crimes don't appear on the police blotters as rapes, this whole category of rape is systematically excluded from the media picture (Table 7.2).

Not only are they excluded from newspapers, but the rape stories that do appear contain many fewer details than do stories about murder or assault, the two crimes that approach rape in their severity and generation of fear (see Table 7.3). Readers are more often left uninformed about the race, age, occupation, condition of victim, use of weapons, and exact location of the crime for rape than for either murder or assault. The reader is then left to extrapolate from the details that do appear (a sort of creative reading) or to rely on her/his own version of the "typical rape" to fill in missing details. Remarks from women and men who read the newspapers analyzed indicate they indeed engage in very creative reading.

TABLE 7.2
Rape Facts by Source

Who	Media	Victimization Survey (LEAA/Census)*	Social Worker Interview‡	Mail Questionnaire (College Population)‡
Race of victim	Black & white: equal frequency	White frequency: 1.8 × black frequency Black rate: ⅓ higher than white race		
Age of victim	00–12 year — 5.3% 13–17 year —12.0% 18–21 year — 8.0% 22–25 year — 5.0% 26–35 year — 9.0% 36–65 year — 8.0% 65+ — 1.6% No mention—50.0%	16–19 year—3 × average rate	Adult—56% Adolescent (13–17 yr.)	
Victim occupation	1. Student 2. Professional 3. Skilled & nonskilled	1. Seeking employment 2. Student 3. Working 4. Housewife		
Victim alone prior to attack	57% alone	95% alone		
Relationship of victim and suspect	Strangers 17% Acquaintances—10%	Strangers—17%	Adult Victim: Strangers—80%	Slight acquaintance—23% Close acquaintance—23%

Continued on page 72

	Media	Victimization Survey (LEAA/Census)*	Social Worker Interview†	Mail Questionnaire (College Population)‡
	Relatives—2.1%		Adolescent victim:	Friend—5%
	Friends—1.4%		Casual acquaintance—45%	Boyfriend—24%
	No mention—68%		Friend—20%	Ex-boyfriend—5%
			Friend—60%	
Age of suspect	13–21 year —17%	Over 21 year—70%		
	22–25 year —10%			
	26–35 year —17%			
	36–65 year —11%			
	66+ —15%			
	No mention—38%			
What				
Weapon	Weapon used—75%	Weapon used—33%	Weapon used—50%	
	Knife—14.7%	No weapon used—50%	Gun—50%	
	Gun—9.4%	Unsure—17%	Knife—30%	
	No mention—67.8%	White victim:	Other—20%	
		Knife—71%		
		Gun—33%		
		Black victim:		
		Knife—40%		
		Gun—60%		
Victim responses	Submission—9.9%	Resisted		
	Resistance—11.2%	(completed rape)—50%		
	No mention—77%	(attempted rape)—80%		

Hospitalization of victim	Hospitalized—5.5% Treated and re- leased—5.7% Minor injury—11% No mention—66%	Medical attention—50% Overnight hospitaliza- tion—7%
When		
Hour of Attack	Midnight-6AM—9% 6AM–noon—3% Noon–6PM—5% 6PM–midnight—5% No mention—77%	Midnight-6AM—17% 6AM–6PM—33% 6PM–midnight—50%
Where		
Crime Site	Victim's home—25.5% Near victim's home —4.0% Suspect's home—4.4% Street—6.0% Car—5.3%	Victim's home—20% Near victim's home—14% Outdoors—65%
Reported to Police		
		Blacks—Yes—84% Whites—Yes—65%

* M. J. Hindelang and B. J. Davis, 1977. LEAA is the Law Enforcement Assistance Administration.
† J. J. Peters, 1975.
‡ E. S. Byers, A. M. Eastman, and B. G. Nilson, 1977.

TABLE 7.3
Percent of Media Stories with Pertinent Facts Omitted
by Crime Type

	Murder % No Mention	Rape % No Mention	Assault % No Mention
Who			
Victim name	20.6	80.7	36.8
Victim address	77.4	92.6	89.3
Victim age	48.8	49.9	33.9
Victim race	77.4	92.2	82.6
Victim/suspect			
relationship	59.2	67.6	56.5
Victim occupation	50.3	69.4	44.6
Condition of victim	7.0	66.2	41.7
Status of suspect	12.8	16.6	15.7
Suspect name	33.4	40.9	33.4
Suspect address	84.1	77.0	85.1
Suspect age	43.0	37.5	52.5
Suspect race	77.9	80.7	78.2
What			
Details of crime	57.3	53.8	37.3
Weapons	35.9	67.8	44.3
When			
Time	78.2	77.0	77.9
Where			
Crime neighborhood	14.5	19.1	17.6
Site of crime	30.5	34.7	23.6
Distance of crime from			
victim's home	66.8	65.5	80.8
Why			
Why this victim?	44.5	60.2	37.3

One older woman said in response to the question about a "typical rape,"

> Oh, I don't know . . . I think it must be like all those stories in the newspapers and on television. A young girl goes out at night with her friends and then goes home with a boy from a party. . . . But I read one the other day and the woman was my age! She must have done something wrong.

Another factor affecting women's reading of rape stories is the "risk cues" that newspaper articles give or don't give regarding rape.

For example, rates, frequencies, and other statistics give readers the information they need to assess their own risks, yet these appear to be missing in almost all news articles (see Table 7.4). Fewer statistical indications of crime danger appear for rape stories than for stories about murder or assault. Yet these are precisely the details readers say they want to know. When asked what information she thought ought to be in news stories about rape, Maria said:

> Where it happened, how badly she was hurt, what precipitated it, what she did or didn't do . . . so that I can avoid the area . . . if it wasn't in a bad area it would mean I'd have to be more cautious with strangers which I am anyway. There's the possibility if she accepted a ride that it's her fault. It's not the area, it's her. She was not cautious, that's all.

When confronted with newspaper portrayals of rape containing few details, a woman may react in one of three ways. She may form her impression of rape based on the details that *are* present in the articles, if any. Alternatively, she may form only a general picture, and therefore be unable to establish social distance between herself and the victim. This inability to differentiate herself from the victim could result in increased fear of rape and more restrictive self-protective measures. If she is unable to establish any one place

TABLE 7.4
Percent of Media Stories with Danger Cues, by Crime Type

	Murder	Rape	Assault
Court Evaluation			
No mention	96.3	90.3	96.6
Doing good job	.8	.9	1.2
Doing bad job	1.9	7.1	1.8
Mixed evaluation	.9	1.4	.4
Crime Danger			
Serious crime up	1.8	5.1	1.9
Serious crime down	.3	.2	.4
Crime stable	.2	.2	.3
All crime up	—	.2	.1
No mention	97.3	93.6	96.3
Crime Rate			
High	1.4	2.5	2.1
Medium	.1	.5	.3
Low	.3	.7	.1
No mention	97.8	96.3	97.2

as particularly dangerous, she is also unable to identify any one place as particularly safe.

If the crime is presented as totally uncontrollable, happening at random to totally innocent victims, the effect on levels of female fear can be expected to be much greater (particularly if the crime is presented sensationally) than if the crime were somehow controllable. If readers or viewers could somehow convince themselves that the victim got herself into the situation and that they (the readers/viewers) can avoid such situations, the effect on female fear would be much lower.

A third effect of this lack of details in most rape stories is a reinforcement of whatever stereotype a woman had before. Her original view of rape would not be refuted by conflicting information.

If a woman reacts by adopting the view of rape presented by the few details available, she comes away with a somewhat biased view of rape. If she forms only a vague, general picture of rape, she concludes that no place is safe and limits her life more than necessary. If she finds no new information about rape, she is likely to retain her misperceptions.

Magazines also shape women's perceptions. In a study of magazine portrayals of rape since 1900, researchers found few articles before 1956.[6] Between 1956 and 1980, however, the portrayal of rape changed in several ways. First, the absolute number of articles dealing with rape took a dramatic swing upward in the 1970s. In addition, the style of coverage changed. Rape articles appearing in 1970 and earlier focused on the suspect, while post-1970 articles focused on the victim or on rape as a societal problem.[7] Earlier articles discussed the disproportionate number of black men who were convicted of raping white women, particularly when convictions resulted in death sentences.

After 1977, reports about rape focused on a number of topics, such as whether victims' names should be reported in the newspaper and the subject of rape in marriage. As with newspapers, unusual and bizarre rapes got magazine attention. And it was not unusual for the same topic to be treated from differing points of view. For example, early articles discussing the death penalty focused on the suspect and raised issues about the appropriateness of that punishment for committing rape. Articles discussing the death penalty after 1970, however, focused on the victim and raised questions about her safety. Would not the rapists be driven to murder their victims if the punishment were the same in either case?

In a similar vein, discussions of the role of race in rape shifted focus from the suspect to the victim. Most of the articles dealing with racial issues before 1971 discussed the racial bias in rape convictions. But of the articles that have dealt with racial issues since 1971, the vast majority have discussed the prejudice against victims, particularly minority women, by the criminal justice system. Similarly, stories considering legal change before 1971 concerned the fairness of statutory rape laws and capital punishment, whereas post-1971 articles focused on the corroboration rules, publishing names of rape victims and discussing reforms in the Michigan statutes.

The topics of women's anger and the psychological portrait of rapists provide interesting examples of the cyclical nature of rape presentation in magazines over the past thirty years. Only three articles concerned women's anger before 1970, and they were all unusual case history reports. The first appeared in 1956 and described a woman who became pregnant as a result of rape and placed the baby for adoption. The other two dealt with Italian women who refused to "redeem their honor" by marrying their rapists. In both instances, the articles disapproved of the women's defiance of tradition. In one article, the young women of the town were said to be confused by the victim's defiance because the rapist, the bashful Guappo, "was so charming"!

Post-1970 women, on the other hand, are reported to be angry about police treatment of rape victims, the corroboration laws, and the lack of attention to rape as a social problem. Articles reported women organizing speak-outs, lobbying to change laws, and securing federal funding.[8] Only in 1977 is there a return to the case history approach, personified by "Courageous Claudia," an Italian gang-rape victim who pressed charges against her assailants and saw the case through to conviction. Claudia was abducted, raped again, and slashed repeatedly with a razor blade as a result of her testimony.

A similar cycle in types of articles is evident in stories about the psychological profile of rapists. Early articles on this topic described rapists as victims of squalid environments, orphans, sons of sadistic fathers and suicidal mothers. Articles in 1972 described rapists as sexually inhibited, inadequate men who needed to rape their mothers symbolically, but found other victims. By 1973, stories were beginning to differentiate among rapists. Some offenders were seduced by their mothers, others had cold, ungiving mothers, and some were seen as simply hostile and sadistic. The 1975 articles gave more insight into the rapists' (rather than their mothers') motivations, but by that year, articles were concentrating again on case histories of individual rapists whose fathers had committed suicide or seduced them, and even one who had ten personalities. In 1979, studies of convicted rapists began to appear, giving more scientific credence to the belief that there are different types of rapists who require different types of treatment and necessitate alternative prevention strategies.

The magazine presentation of the social reality of rape has changed from one of rape as an unusual event (both in terms of the number of articles and of the particulars of the rape) to a common, serious social problem. The frequency of articles throughout the 1970s probably facilitated the placement of rape high on the political and social agendas of that decade. Data from the last few years suggest that magazine presentations of rape may change yet again to focus on its bizarre characteristics.

Certain spectacular crimes capture the attention of the media, and are given continuing coverage for days or weeks. Often they involve a famous person (Patricia Hearst or Connie Francis, for example) or are freakish or unusual in some way. Continued and widespread media attention makes it more likely that large numbers of people will become aware of these cases and, given that many people have no firsthand experience with rape, the stories will not only remind women of their vulnerability, but also serve as a psychological reference point for readers who will compare themselves to the victims.

Two such rapes were reported by the media in San Francisco and Philadelphia, and greatly affected women there. The San Francisco rape was one in a series which police believed were being committed by the same man—a person described as brutal and smelly. The victims appeared to be selected at random, a factor that seemed to increase fear since it made it more difficult psychologically to "distance" oneself from previous victims and there seemed to be no clear way to protect oneself. The rapes came on the heels of what San Francisco papers dubbed the "zebra killings," also apparently at random. The rapes were reported in all the papers in the city and heightened female fear for most women living there.

The Philadelphia rape involved a black teenage victim who was killed and left with a hot dog placed in her vagina and her body covered with potato chips. The story was printed in only one of the three Philadelphia dailies (the *News*), but because of the bizarre nature of the case, both readers and nonreaders of the *News* knew about the case and talked about it for weeks. Perhaps because it was so bizarre, it did not seem to be associated with increased fear except among black women who had teenage daughters, or among women who lived within a mile or two of where the rape-murder took place. These women viewed either themselves or their daughters as similar to the victims, and felt vulnerable because they lived or traveled close to where the rape took place.

Other, more recent "spectacular" cases have captured the attention of the media and the public and have heightened female fear. One involved a multiple rape, in front of witnesses, of a woman on a pool table in a bar in New Bedford, Massachusetts. The second rape case received considerable media attention because the victim, six years after the conviction of her supposed assailant, recanted and said she had lied at the time of the original trial.

The New Bedford case took several unusual turns, and illustrates the role of cultural differences and social perceptions in reactions to rape. The victim, the assailants, some of the jurors, and several of the legal personnel involved in the case were all Portuguese—a fact that became important in the trial. There were two major waves of immigration of Portuguese men to New Bedford, and those who had been there longer had assimilated and become more established in town. They were somewhat embarrassed by the more recent arrivals, believing that they didn't behave with appropriate decorum. The more middle-class, assimilated group made defensive comments to the press indicating that media portrayals were making it appear that the Portuguese and their way of life were on trial, rather than the particular Portuguese men accused of the crime.

Further, there was evidence of many traditional values and myths about rape. People questioned why the woman was in the bar in the first place; some suggested that she might have flirted with one of the men who became assailants. Feminists from all over the country came to the defense of the victim, vociferously arguing that such behaviors were not an invitation to rape. References were made to the possibility that the crime had been prompted by a fictional account of a pool-table rape in *Hustler* magazine. The trial was covered live on television, and from the first day the victim's identity became known far beyond the confines of the small Massachusetts community. Raped women in other cities notified lawyers and prosecutors that they were unwilling to proceed with their own cases, afraid to risk exposure and publicity. In the end, some of the six defendants were found guilty and others were found innocent. There were protests, and soon after the verdict was announced, news reports indicated that thousands of people had taken to the streets. But careful reporters noted that the people in the streets were there for different reasons. It was not a unified march. Some were protesting the verdict because they thought the victim "asked for it." Some were protesting because they thought the verdict was an indictment of (all) "the Portuguese." Some thought all six of the accused should have been found guilty; others thought they should all have been found innocent.[9]

Weeks after the trial was over, there was some soul searching among the journalists. Some had the courage to wonder about the extent to which they had created the story, played up the sensational aspects. One of the more unusual aspects of the case was that there were said to be several witnesses, yet none of them came to the aid of the victim, who was said to be screaming for help. Early press reports gave the impression that there were many witnesses, perhaps a barroom full of them. Later reports seem to indicate that the initial numbers were grossly exaggerated, and that there may have been only two witnesses—the bartender and a "drunk asleep in the corner"—in addition to the six accused. Reflective journalists admitted that the large number of witnesses was an important element of the story, and that once it had been publicized, it was not in the interests of other reporters to seek information which would correct the misperception.[10]

In the other case, Cathleen Crowell Webb in the spring of 1985 recanted her testimony and said she had lied about Gary Dotson's raping her in 1977. Crowell Webb said a religious conversion had prompted her to recant, and that she had lied originally because she feared she was pregnant following sexual relations with her boyfriend. She said she made up a description of an alleged assailant and then picked Dotson out of a police lineup because he looked like the drawing made by police artists. In 1985, she urged that Dotson be freed from prison. The bizarre nature of that case also captured the attention of the media and the public. Every aspect of the case—from comparisons of details of testimony in 1977 and in 1985, to interviews with feminist activists about the impact for other victims—received painstaking attention from the entire media world. Illinois governor James Thompson, a former state's attorney, personally conducted the hearing held to decide whether Dotson should be freed, and television stations covered it live for the entire three days. The case was the subject of talk shows and nighttime analyses; there were pictures on the front pages of all the major newspapers and cover stories in the newsmagazines.

In the end, Thompson commuted Dotson's sentence. Nonetheless, and despite the results of lie detector tests "passed" by both Dotson and Crowell Webb, many believed she lied in 1985, not earlier. The Monday after the commutation, Dotson and Crowell Webb—like media stars—were each flown to New York in separate, private jets to meet face-to-face with only their lawyers present and to appear together on all the network morning news shows. They were whisked by limousine from one television station to the next. Crowell Webb stated that her goal was then the same as Dotson's, that is, to get his record completely cleared. During this media blitz, the cohost of the now defunct *CBS Morning News,* Phyllis George, asked the pair to shake hands (which they did) and then to hug (which they did not). The next day, media critics lambasted the media's performance, noting that the push for ratings points must have prompted the circus.

These spectacular stories have two major effects. One is to keep the focus of attention on the bizarre and unusual. Such a focus means there is less time and attention given to the day-to-day, more ordinary issues and concerns affecting the majority of women—including more typical rapes, attempted rapes, and sexual harassment. A second effect is to keep the possibility of rape close to the forefront of womens' minds.[11]

The media may affect attitudes toward rape in another way. Researchers working in universities throughout the country have produced consistent findings which seem to partially support feminist contentions of a link between pornography and rape.

In a 1978 review of the work on pornography, researchers concluded:

> There is no doubt . . . that the increase in crime, violence and vandalism, and what might be called unorthodox or unusual sex practices, over the past twenty or thirty years has been paralleled by an increase in the portrayal of violence in the media, particularly in films and TV, by a similar increase in the number of pornographic publications, films and books, and by the greater explicitness of portrayal of sexual behavior in the media and literary publications. The existence of such a correlation over time does not necessarily argue a causal connection; it may be that the changes in the cultural patterns related to violence and sex have produced the greater permissiveness in the media, rather than the other way about. Possibly there has been a reciprocal interaction between these factors.[12]

and

Our major conclusions are that the evidence strongly indicates that the portrayal of sex and violence in the media does affect the attitudes and behavior of viewers; that these effects are variable depending on the details of presentation and the personality of the viewers; and that the recommendations for action depend in part on a person's value system.[13]

Other, more recent studies by teams of researchers in the United States are producing more consistent findings about the effect of pornography on attitudes and behavior.[14] After viewing pornography, both males and females think rape is a less serious crime. Males are more likely to say they would rape or force sex if they were sure they wouldn't get caught or punished; they become more aggressive, especially if the victim in the pornography is shown apparently enjoying abuse; and both males and females tend to degrade women. Finally, there seems to be a "satiation effect" among viewers such that it requires larger and larger dosages of more extreme and bizarre—and perhaps more violent—pornographic behavior to produce the same aggressive and titillating effects.

These researchers and their colleagues, it should be noted, reached their conclusions based primarily on work with undergraduates who agreed to participate in psychological and sociopsychological experiments conducted in controlled settings on university campuses. Their findings may not be generalizable to the larger population. Further, the authors note differences in effects by sex and certain personality characteristics, and it is likely that the settings and previous activities of the subjects also affect the degree of impact. Despite these caveats, it is clear that what the average person sees in pornography is a picture that does not enhance respect, dignity, equality, or empathy for women. Its availability and display on newsstands are daily reminders to women of how they are viewed. It provides an additional parcel of evidence, an additional reminder to women that the social institutions of this country do not always operate fairly or in their favor.

Legal scholars, judges, bookstore owners, feminists, teachers, parents, and many others have been trying for years to define pornography. A dictionary (*Webster's*) definition is that it is "the depiction of erotic behavior designed primarily to cause sexual excitement." Legal scholars discuss it in terms of "prurient interest," with no redeeming social value. Social scientists have used the term "in connection with practices which are believed to be harmful either to the victims or to the people engaged in them."[15] A model statute used as the basis for proposed legislation in several cities says,[16]

1. Pornography is the graphic sexually explicit subordination of women through pictures and/or words that also include one or more of the following: (i) women are presented dehumanized as sexual objects, things, or commodities; or (ii) women are presented as sexual objects who enjoy pain or humiliation; or (iii) women are presented as sexual objects who experience sexual pleasure in being raped; or (iv) women are presented as sexual objects tied up or cut up or mutilated or bruised or physically hurt; or (v) women are presented in postures or positions of sexual submission, servitude, or display; or (vi) women's body parts—including but not limited to vaginas, breasts, or buttocks—are exhibited such that women are reduced to those parts; or (vii) women are presented as whores by nature; or (viii) women are presented being penetrated by objects or animals; or (ix) women are presented in scenarios of degradation, injury, torture, shown as filthy or inferior, bleeding, bruised, or hurt in a context that makes these conditions sexual.
2. The use of men, children, or transsexuals in the place of women in (1) above is pornography for purposes of the law.

In the past, those opposed to the banning of pornography—usually on the grounds that to do so is an abrogation of the constitutional right to free speech guaranteed by the First Amendment—argued that it was difficult to apply the definitions since what was pornographic to one person might not appear so to another. The explicit and detailed definitions in the model law should enable policymakers to reach agreement in more cases.

Many of those opposed to pornography have differentiated between erotic pornography and violent pornography. In the former, mutually consenting partners explicitly portray sexual acts which they seem to be enjoying and which they know will be viewed by people they do not know. Violent pornography adds elements of threat, pain, or torture—usually directed at the women involved. The women may be shown as either enjoying the pain or genuinely hurt and afraid. In the most extreme versions, women are mutilated (and perhaps in undocumented instances, killed) in a sexual context, sometimes at the point of sexual climax.

The role of pornography in rape—and therefore its link to female fear—continues to be widely debated. In 1986, the U.S. Attorney General's Commission on Pornography released a 211-page report on pornography calling for government action against the pornography industry, including stricter penalties for violations of obscenity laws. At the same time, the researchers who provided the key data for the report denied that the task force preparing the final report had established a direct, causal link between most sexually explicit material and any act of sexual violence.[17] The researchers emphasized that the issue is violence associated with sex, not simply the sex. They argued further that these messages are everywhere in our society—in advertising,[18] record jackets, video games—not just in pornography.

Other data support their conclusions. In part because media are ubiquitous in our society, nearly everyone is exposed to these messages, and people are therefore frequently exposed to news and other information about violence. Further, media seem to be the best source of information for a variety of crime-related attitudes and activities.

Most women (83 percent) interviewed reported reading a daily newspaper "in the last few days"; 57 percent said they read newspapers daily or at least "regularly," spending an average of thirty-one minutes per day. More than four-fifths (82 percent) said they usually watch the news on television and 65 percent said they had watched television "last night"—for three hours on the average. Of those, 64 percent said they watched local news, 41 percent reported watching national news, and 42 percent watched a crime or police drama.[19] All in all, only about 5 percent of women avoided both newspapers and television news.

Given the number of crimes reported in the papers and on TV news, and the number of violent crimes "committed" in TV crime dramas, it is reasonable to assume that nearly everyone is exposed regularly to a substantial number of crime stories.

In fact, 68 percent of women remembered reading, seeing, or hearing about a particular crime "in the past two weeks," and 51 percent remembered a crime story from "yesterday." Nearly two-fifths (39 percent) remembered reading or hearing about rapes or sexual assaults. Of the 39 percent who remembered a sex-related crime, about one third (38 percent) said they learned about it from a newspaper. A little less than a third (30 percent) said they learned about it from TV, a fifth (20 percent) said they learned from a friend, and 2 percent said they learned from the radio. Thus, for sexual assaults, the news media together were by far the most common source of information.

The media, *taken together,* were also the best source of information for nearly half the women (46 percent) on crime in the neighborhood. The best *single* source of this information was neighbors (38 percent); many of whom were thought to have learned about crime from the media. Media were also frequently cited as the sources of information about where victims can get help (72 percent), tips or strategies for preventing attacks (30 percent), and identification of "dangerous" places (5 percent).

Although 70 percent of our respondents thought the media do at least an average job in both accuracy and completeness of their crime reporting, 60 percent said they thought crime in their own city was more serious than reported by the daily newspapers and 55 percent thought it was more serious than reported on TV news.

In short, it appears that most Americans are exposed to a considerable amount of media-reported crime, and much of that is atypical crime. Further, people tend to blur the information they get from crime news with information about crime from other sources, for example, from televised crime dramas.[20]

What impact does all this crime information have? One effect is to influence women's perceptions of rape. Comparisons of the details (or lack of them) of the "typical rape" described by women who do not know a rape victim parallel the details (or lack of them) most often available in the news media.

Do media rape stories contribute to women's fear? Unfortunately, there is no easy or simple answer to this question.

First, although the amount of crime served up to women by the media can be ascertained, as can how much women say they attend to those media, it is not known exactly which articles or how many news articles individual women read. Some women told us they make an effort to *avoid* reading crime stories because to read them increases their fear; others said they read every crime story in order to assess their own safety.

Second, the stories women remember may not necessarily be the most frightening to them. Third, there may be "accretion" effects such that one or two rape stories will have little impact, but the effects of reading or watching such stories over a period of weeks and years—especially if the events reported are increasingly bizarre—may accumulate until there is an apparently sudden impact on female fear.

And finally, there are many other factors related to the psychological effect of media reports, some having to do with the journalistic portrayal and many others related to the media consumer. The impact of the crime report depends on its treatment, its placement, the number of details included (especially those that allow distancing), and the proximity and severity of the crime.[21] Consumer-related factors include whether or not the reader has already been the victim of any crimes and, if so, what crimes; the extent to which she believes people "get what they deserve," and the extent to which the world is perceived as "mean" or "just." A few women believe that they are invulnerable, they simply cannot be victims. These women seem unaffected by reading or hearing about crime.

Moreover, there are differences in exposure to media. Reported readership of newspaper crimes is related to the accuracy of people's perceptions about crime *rates* and their concern about these crimes. Greater concern is related to increased readership. *Within* cities, women who read the city paper that devotes the greatest proportion of space to violent crime report feeling less safe when out alone at night.[22] But women's sense of safety is also related to many other factors. Thus, the data about the impact of crimes reported by the media are not as consistent or as compelling as we might wish.[23]

Further, media-reported rapes affect some respondents but not others, and the effects are not entirely consistent from city to city. However, nearly all women *believe* the news media have an impact. Perhaps the truth lies somewhere in between. That is, perhaps there is little or no effect for some women, while for those women who are affected, the impact is great.

Whether that impact is great or weak, women believe the media are not providing them with the information they say they want with respect to violent crime.

More than 90 percent of women's responses to "What is most important for you to know?" concerned information they could use to assess and manage their own risks: whether the rapist has been caught (often not mentioned in the news stories); details about the perpetrator's appearance; where and when the rape occurred; what the victim was doing and wearing; what defensive tactics the victim had tried and whether or not they worked. The women were often very explicit that the reason they wanted to have the information was so that "I can avoid that area" or in some other way use it to decrease risk. Some respondents also wanted to know if the victim had been able to get help, and if so, from where or whom. Many were concerned that bystanders would not intervene, even if they heard calls for help.

What Irma, from Wicker Park in Chicago, wanted to know when she read a rape story is what kind of a person she [the victim] was, what was she doing, how did it happen, and where was she? I'd like to know why because if she wasn't doing anything wrong, like if she was in a bar, it would give an idea to me so I would know how to protect myself. Or I won't go there because it could happen to me. So it would give me an idea not to do it for my protection.

When she reads a newspaper story about rape that happened locally, Julie wants most to know where it happened, the conditions under which it happened, whether or not the victim and rapist knew one another, whether it was in the victim's home or on the street, and the age of the victim. She wants to know these things because

> If it's in my neighborhood . . . that would be important basically only if it was like something that happened more than once . . . it was a pattern thing. You would want to know so that for, you know, you could avoid these conditions if possible. Yeah, something that was a pattern probably or an occasional chance thing.

Sara recalled reading recently about rapes on the San Jose and San Francisco State campuses and in Pacific Heights (in San Francisco). Two of the alleged rapists were caught by decoy police and "it did my heart good." When she reads a news story about rape she wants to know whether or not the victim was hurt, where it happened, and a description of the attacker. She wants to know these things

> for my own protection. It doesn't make sense now that I think about it. Thinking in terms of my own protection. I feel less threatened if it occurred in a high-crime area than if it occurred in my own neighborhood. Of course the most important thing is whether the victim was hurt or not. I'm not happy about the way I answered that question—it sounds very selfish.

If a story about rape appeared in the papers or on TV, Patty wanted to know how the woman reacted, what she did to try to prevent it, her age, "her resemblance to me," and how the police acted. She added:

> I always watch [on TV] to see if the policeman is sympathetic—if he's accepting it as a fact that happened, or if he's kinda ridiculing her. Sometimes you can almost hear scorn in their voices, and then others report it as a fact.

Patty says these things are important to her in a story

because I try to relate to her [the victim], try to imagine what I could do [in order] not to have it happen to me. I try to relate to her and find out . . . what mistake was made . . . if she made one—to see if there was some way I could prevent it from happening to me.

When asked about crime stories she'd read or heard about, Rebecca recalled newspaper articles involving rape and sexual assault. When she reads an article about rape, she wants to know if there is a pattern of rapists doing it in the neighborhood as a regular thing, the age of the victim (if she's a child), whether the victim knew the rapist, and whether or not he was caught. She wants to know about pattern and neighborhood because

if there's a ten percent reporting rate, and they assume he's raped three women in the neighborhood, that means he's probably hit about twenty [women], which doesn't make me feel real safe.

Some people, in order to distance themselves, avoid reading about crime. Mary, for example, thought crime was more serious than reported by the Philadelphia papers, but generally avoided reading about it. She said it just made her more concerned, and she justified her reactions by saying, "What's in the papers doesn't interest me."

Editors and publishers believe Mary is unusual, and that rape stories do interest most people. When Rupert Murdoch bought the Chicago *Sun-Times* in 1983, many Chicagoans predicted that the paper would soon feature more crime, and feature it more sensationally, in the belief that crime sells. Observers went on to predict that in order to compete, the Chicago *Tribune* would also print more crime stories and perhaps give them more sensational treatment.

Content analyses of the *Sun-Times* and *Tribune* a year before the Murdoch takeover and for the two months following support those predictions. That is, both papers increased their coverage of violent crimes—including rape. The *Tribune* increased its crime coverage so much that the space devoted to rapes was nearly double what it had been before Murdoch.[24]

Newspaper stories about crime may heighten women's feelings of fear and encourage them to limit their behavior in order to protect themselves. While these reactions are adaptive and keep women safe in some cases, they may be counterproductive by giving them distorted impressions, producing exaggerated fear and passivity if they are later attacked. The relationship between fear of crime and media coverage of crime calls into question the adequacy with which news media fulfill their functions of informing and edifying the public. Perhaps a more important question is whether what's good for the news business is necessarily good for society.

Such commercial use of crimes against women as that made by the Chicago papers to increase readership contributes to a general climate of violence and fear—and their acceptance as a simple fact of life. Although this state of affairs may be an unintended consequence of the news business in this country, it needs to be confronted. News personnel should be encouraged to take into account the consequences of how they portray crime; that it is a responsibility which comes with the freedom of expression guaranteed by the First Amendment.

8

———◆———

Coping Strategies

GIVEN the lessons from childhood, urban life, the legal system, and the media, what options do women think they have for protecting themselves from rape and for coping with the fear it breeds? In this chapter, seven women disclose, in their own words, the ever-present nature of female fear and the costs of that fear. They illustrate how race, education, religion, and lifestyle interact with fear, affecting the ways they cope and the choices they make about day-to-day activities.

We have selected women who represent a range of experiences: the victims of rape, attempted rape, or other sexual assaults; nonvictims who nonetheless have been affected by the rapes of others; women who work outside the home, women who work only at home, and women on welfare; single, married, and divorced or separated women, with and without children; educated women and women with little formal education; and women from each of the six selected neighborhoods.

These women also include some whose lives seem completely shaped and controlled by fear, and others who admit to no fear at all. Some are very articulate and able clearly to describe these feelings and responses. Others are much less so. While each woman is, of course, unique, these responses to rape and the fear it provokes are not unusual. Their stories are derived from their responses to interview questions (see Appendix A).

PATTY

Patty is thirty-five years old, of Irish descent, and a homemaker. She has lived in the Visitacion Valley neighborhood of San Francisco for six and a half years. Patty went to college for a year and once had a part-time job as a teacher's aide, but quit to become a full-time homemaker and care for her two children.

She thinks of her neighborhood as relatively large, about eight square blocks, and having lived there as long as she has, she finds it easy to recognize people who are strangers to the area. She says she would avoid any stranger who approached her on the street asking her for directions, and she would not let a man into her home to make an emergency phone call.

Patty says the biggest neighborhood problems are crime-related: burglary, purse snatching, and rape. She says the neighborhood is not as safe as it used to be and that now, because of crime, she never goes out after dark. She says more lights, more patrols, and "keeping the teenagers off the streets and busy at something constructive" would make her feel safer. "Teenage boys really make me nervous," she says.

She thinks neighbors would call the police if they thought she was threatened, because she herself called the police when she heard screams of a woman living up the street.

Patty is quite protective of her daughters and encourages them to take safety precautions.

Patty thinks any anti-crime campaign ought to focus on juvenile delinquency and drug abuse because these people "seem to be the ones doing the purse snatching and breaking into houses."

Although she has never been the victim of any crime, Patty rates her own chances of being victimized as quite high—eight on the zero-to-ten-point scale for daytime burglary, nine for nighttime burglary, nine for purse snatching, and seven for neighborhood or downtown rape.

Patty says there is a "superdangerous" place in the neighborhood—a local park where any crime could take place, especially murder, rape, and robbery. She completely avoids the area, even in the daytime. A neighborhood anti-crime organization had warned her against it.

Patty does think that people would deliberately try to harm her, and she feels that way especially when she has to go out "to pick up the girls at night," or walk by the park in the daytime "when those teenage boys are there drinking."

She estimated worry levels of nine or ten (on the ten-point scale) for every item on our scale, and says she simply refrains from doing day-to-day activities, such as going downtown alone or going out alone in her neighborhood after dark (see Tables 2.3 and 2.4).

She does not think she could successfully defend herself against an attacker because

> I'd probably be so scared; I don't have any training. . . . I guess that's why the girls take karate; I'm not a very physical person; I carry a whistle. I'd probably just panic, or I may try to talk them out of it.

She estimates that she is weaker than both the average man and the average woman, about as fast as the average woman but slower than the average man.

She said she didn't think she would fight back if sexually assaulted because

> I'd be afraid of being hurt physically. And the way my husband and I have talked about it, I know he would be understanding. He's always told me, "I'd rather have somebody rape you than kill you or hurt you." I don't really know what I'd do.

When asked what she does to avoid unpleasant situations in the city, she said,

> I change [raise and lower] the shades frequently and try not to follow any patterns. . . . I try not to take my walk at the same time every day—I don't do anything on a regular schedule. . . . Just being aware that it can happen to you and reading everything available on it.

She takes a few extra precautions that she thinks help to prevent sexual attacks: "Wear bulky clothing, don't carry a purse, don't flirt, and don't make eye contact with men."

Patty's obvious fears and worries are reflected in other day-to-day precautions she takes, which correspond with thirty-three of the thirty-eight precautions asked about in the interview (see Appendix A, questions 32 and 33). She thought the most important precautions were "being alert and careful on the street" and "being very careful before opening the door to anyone at home."

When asked to describe what she imagined to be a typical rape, she was readily able to do so, and her depiction contained some of the elements of a rape a friend had experienced and later told her about. Her descriptions of both the typical rape and an actual one she knew about also contain many elements of stereotypes and myths, provoking a lot of ambivalence on her part. She said of the actual rape of her friend:

It happened downtown. This guy just grabbed her as she was walking in the back entrance of the Emporium [a San Francisco department store]. It was lit. He just grabbed her arm and started talking to her. She said she sorta halfway went along with him trying to figure out what he was saying, and then he shoved her into his car. . . . She was so stunned. He was nice-looking and well-dressed. He just shoved her in the passenger side of the car and it didn't have a handle—so he had planned it. She couldn't open the door. At first the way he was talking was normal, so she wasn't really panicked. She said, "I wasn't really terrified enough when he first started driving to really scream and yell to attract attention." . . . Then he drove her to the Third Street tracks someplace . . . and that's when she panicked. But it was too late to get away.

And the police kept asking her, "Weren't you looking? Was it lit? Why didn't you fight right then instead of going into the car?" But she said she was so scared. Mostly she said she didn't think it could happen to her. She hadn't been flirting with him; she was dressed nicely . . . but everybody made her feel like she had done something wrong . . . to bring it on. She was afraid to tell her husband; later they ended up getting a divorce. He halfway blamed her even though he tried not to.

Patty's ideas about the typical rape included some notions that she derived from the rape of her friend. She said the typical rape

would be scary. . . . The actual sexual attack part would be less [scary] than the fear for your safety and the mental damage afterwards. The physical harm, bodily harm, during it would scare me. The concept of it, and the worry about it is what keeps me in. The idea of walking in the street and worrying about it. . . . It could happen anywhere on the street, anywhere that you are walking that you are exposed, I guess, if you are not careful. Even if you are home if you don't lock the doors or let somebody in without checking. I suppose it could happen anywhere. I really only worry about it on the streets in the daytime because that's the only time that it could happen to me [since she stays in at night]. I think it crosses all barriers—income barriers, racial barriers. When I have nightmares I imagine a big, tall, scary, dirty-looking person; but in reality, from what I've read, it could be anybody. She was very nervous and jumpy after that. She was really warning all of us. She was the first person that made me really aware that it could happen to us.

It's not surprising that Patty thought the single worst aspect of rape would be the "mental aftereffects, the mental anguish, feeling dirty and guilty." Patty said that because of her friend's rape she herself did "everything" differently now. "I totally stopped going out at night. I became alert and aware of people around me. I think she was unlucky, and not paying attention."

Patty thought that if there were a campaign to reduce the amount of rape in the city, the best thing to do would be to teach people to be "alert and aware, to wear a whistle, tell them not to go out after dark, and to wear bulky clothes, don't make eye contact, and go everywhere with a friend."

Patty thought crime was more serious than reported in the San Francisco newspapers, but that they do an average job in the accuracy and completeness of their crime reporting. If a story about rape appears in the papers or on TV, she'd want to know how the woman reacted, what she did to try to prevent it, her age, "her resemblance to me," and how the police acted. Patty says these things are important to her in a news story

> because I try to relate to her [the victim], try to imagine what I could do [in order] not to have it happen to me. I try to relocate to her and find out . . . what mistake was made . . . if she made one—to see if there was some way I could prevent it from happening to me.

Patty says she really feels part of her neighborhood, and plans to stay there. She says she favors the women's movement and efforts to strengthen and change women's status in society. She gave fairly nontraditional responses to questions asking about a woman's roles—except that she agreed with the statement that "it's best for everyone in a family if the man is the achiever outside the home." She also indicated that she thinks success is the outcome of one's own hard work and has little to do with luck or fate.

SARA

Sara also lives in San Francisco, in a middle-class neighborhood called the Sunset. She is better educated than Patty and has a job as a social worker. She earns about $30,000 per year, is fifty-five years old, Jewish, and has lived in the Sunset for twenty-one years. Now that her children have grown up and moved away, Sara lives alone with her husband.

Despite her years of living in the Sunset, Sara now finds it difficult to differentiate strangers from people who live there. She says that she would speak to someone on the street who approached her asking for directions, but she would refuse to let someone come into her home to make an emergency call. She thinks the biggest problem in the community is the lack of communication among residents, the lack of a sense of community. She describes herself as feeling "somewhat unsafe" at night, and says she thinks the neighborhood has gotten more dangerous in recent years. She says it would make her feel safer if there were more people on the street. A sense of alienation is reflected in her conviction that the neighbors would do "nothing" if they heard her screaming for help, because of the "lack of community feeling."

When her daughters were young, the kinds of warnings she gave them were related to their going out alone. She says she advised them to "take a cab, or go with someone else; don't let anyone unknown into the house or car, and don't hitchhike." She says she didn't worry about her son being personally attacked, but that she warned him about the company he kept and worried that he'd get into an accident while driving. Sara thinks that muggings and rape ought to be the targets of any neighborhood anti-crime campaign because "they are more likely to occur than other crimes" and because elderly, helpless people are most often victims. "Crimes against people should have a higher priority than crimes against property," she says. Sara rates her own risks as relatively high—five on the ten-point scale for daytime or nighttime burglary when she is away, three for burglary when she is there, seven for purse snatching, four for a rape in her neighborhood, and slightly higher (five) for a downtown rape.

Indicating some ambivalence, Sara says she doesn't think there are any dangerous places close by and that she never fears that anyone would deliberately try to harm her. Then, when asked how much she worries about a series of common activities, Sara indicates she worries most about walking alone on the streets in her own neighborhood, especially when walking by city parks, or if she has occasion to go to a laundromat.

Sara doesn't think she could defend herself effectively against an attacker "because I'd be terrified; I'd freeze; I don't know the fundamentals of self-defense." She reports feeling weaker and slower than she imagines the average man and woman to be. Nonetheless, she thinks she would be somewhat likely to fight back if sexually assaulted because it would "be instinctive to fight back, particularly in that very personal, intrusive kind of assault."

When asked what she does to avoid "uncomfortable situations," she says she tries "to physically avoid getting into dangerous situations" or anyplace she feels unsafe or uncomfortable. She adds, "If I have to be there I try to make myself as inconspicuous and unobtrusive as possible, and I try to get out of the situation as quickly as possible." She also always or often takes about half of the precautions she was asked about, for example, locking the doors and windows, asking service people for identification, and carrying her keys in a manner so that she could use them as a weapon (see Appendix A, questions 32, 33).

Sara rates rape as "something of a problem" in the Sunset and says that it has increased as a problem during the last year. When asked to describe what she thought to be the typical rape, Sara said,

> It occurs most often out on the street. A woman is jumped by someone she doesn't know. I don't think there are any general characteristics I could identify by passing someone on the street. A stranger would be the only way it could happen to me. I think that in most instances the pain is psychological. I know that women can get badly beaten. I think that these days the police treat women more sensitively. This might vary with the area, but I think in this neighborhood it would be true, more than in a ghetto area.

The only rape Sara knows about personally is one that happened to a much younger friend four or five years ago.

> She was on a date and he raped her. She didn't know him before. It happened in Berkeley, in his car. She resisted the attack. She reported it to the police and the guy was arrested, but I don't know if he was convicted. She is still fearful, very fearful of going out, particularly with someone she doesn't know *very* well. . . . You don't expect it on a date.

> It has increased her general anxiety. She was very depressed and self-derogatory. The situation—being out of control—elevated her general sense of low self-esteem and reinforced it. Anxiety, fear and lowered self-esteem.

Sara thinks she would fight back if she were sexually attacked because she'd be afraid of being hurt or killed. She thinks the "single worst aspect" of rape is the "intrusion, the violation of oneself." She estimates that 5 percent of victims get killed, and another 30 percent get seriously injured in addition to the rape.

Sara, isn't sure how best to prevent rape. She seems to believe that prevention is at least partially a collective responsibility.

Rape is a very complicated crime. Women should avoid situations where they might be raped, but that isn't fair. Men's feelings about themselves . . . helping little boys to increase their self-esteem. More cops, better lighting on the streets, better community organizations, neighborhood groups learning to protect themselves, knowing who's in trouble.

When asked if anything like a sexual attack had ever happened to her when she was a child or teenager, Sara recalled,

The one I thought of first occurred when I was fourteen. This old man was in a store. He turned and opened his coat and said, "Here, look at this!" He had his pants unzipped and his penis hanging out. That's all that happened, but it really shook me up . . . I avoided that store after that!

She also says that she was attacked once while dating—not during her teenage years, but after a divorce.

Someone I was seeing occasionally—he literally almost raped me. He got far enough that he had my panties shoved to one side and his penis against me. I gave him a bloody nose and he stopped. It [the bloody nose] ruined the upholstery in his car. I felt good afterwards; I didn't know I could fight back that effectively. It *still* makes me feel angry.

When asked about what kinds of sexual assaults should be considered rape, Sara said she thinks everything on the list in Table 6.1 except "whistling or rude remarks" should be classified as rape and be covered by laws on rape.

Sara also thinks that crime is "about as bad" as reported by the San Francisco newspapers and on television, but that the newspapers do a pretty poor job in terms of their accuracy and completeness in covering crime. She recalls reading about rapes on the San Jose and San Francisco State college campuses and in Pacific Heights (an upper-middle-class neighborhood in San Francisco). She is pleased that two of the alleged rapists were caught by decoy police. When she reads a news story about rape she wants to know whether or not the victim was hurt, where it happened, and a description of the attacker, for her own safety.

Although she has lived in the Sunset area for more than twenty years, Sara doesn't really "feel a part" of her neighborhood, and describes it as "just a place to live" and adds that if she could, she would move to another part of the city.

She generally favors the women's movement and all efforts to strengthen women's status in society, and in other ways indicates that she has nontraditional views of women's roles. She also answers questions about her dependence on herself, as opposed to others or fate or luck, which indicate that she believes very strongly that she is in control of her own destiny.

MARY

Mary is black, forty years old, Catholic, and a high school dropout. She is separated from her husband, unemployed, and living with her two children in the predominantly black neighborhood of West Philadelphia in federally subsidized housing. She reported an income of $15,000 a year. Her answers to interview questions reflect ambivalence: On the one hand, she was unwilling to admit to fear. On the other, she accepted and accommodated to the local crime problem.

Mary has lived in West Philly almost all her life (thirty-five of her years). Although she thinks of her neighborhood as a one-square-block area, she says she finds it difficult to tell strangers from people who live in the area. She thinks the most serious problem in the area is armed robbery and burglary. Yet she said she feels "very safe" both day and night, and "never" worries about her safety in the neighborhood. She has little faith in the neighbors, saying they would do "nothing" in response to her scream or whistle for help, "because that's the way the neighbors are . . . they don't want to help anybody . . . they are too scared to help." Yet Mary maintains she is *not* scared.

She warns her daughter to "be careful how she acts and carries herself," and "don't trust strangers." But she tells her sixteen-year-old son to fight back.

Mary is worried about robbers and burglaries because "that's what's going down now" in her neighborhood.

> On the twenty-fifth floor [of my apartment building] crooks broke into a vacant apartment and then drilled a hole into the next apartment and took everything that could be sold. The guards at our building aren't interested. It's a job. People are always getting their places broken into or robbed on the elevators.

Nonetheless, Mary estimated her risks of rape, burglary and several other crimes as zero on the zero-to-ten-point scale. And she said there were no dangerous places in the neighborhood. At the same time, she said she worries more than once a week about most of the items on the worry scale (see Tables 2.3, 2.4).

Mary said she would be very likely to fight back if attacked "because I don't want to get killed or laid by someone who's sick and dirty." She said she protects herself primarily by avoiding dangerous situations:

> I don't put myself in situations where that will happen. I don't put myself in no dangerous situations . . . the company that you keep is important. I have nice friends and people to protect me from harm.

Mary has an unlisted phone and locks the door at night, but said she takes none other of the thirty-three precautions to protect her home. She also said she makes a point of being "alert and careful" on the street.

Mary doesn't think rape is much of a problem in the neighborhood, even though she herself was attacked there on her way to work. She had avoided being raped by using a pair of scissors in her purse as a weapon. Her attacker was arrested and convicted. Mary's view of the typical rape bore some resemblance to her own experience.

> I feel as though a man will announce a rape. If a woman gets raped the man has been watching her. The way she acts, looks, or the way she dressed. The company you keep. The rapist knows the victims, but she doesn't know the rapist. A policemen sizes you up, too. I gave details when a white man tried to rape me and the cops know I wasn't lying. I went through something, but the cops was trying to do their job. Most women are stupid if they get raped in the street. It happens 'cause they too busy trying to look good and that how they attract a rapist's attention.

Mary thought the single worst aspect of being raped would be the "shame of letting some man take me." She estimated that 90 percent of victims get killed and 10 percent get hurt. She also estimated that in about 25 percent of cases, men are falsely accused.

Mary said that since she was assaulted and her attacker jailed, she never worries about sexual assault, but at the same time, she said the last time she worried about it, she was "very frightened."

Although Mary had prevented her own rape by counterattacking with a pair of scissors, when asked about ways to prevent rape, she said, "Nothing. You can't stop rape."

Mary thought crime was more serious than reported in either the Philadelphia newspapers or on TV, and that newspapers do a "poor job" of reporting crime. She added that what's in the paper doesn't interest her, and she "doesn't think about it."

Mary has very traditional views of women's roles and believes primarily in fate and luck as controls over her destiny.

JULIE

Julie is in many ways stereotypical of the residents of Chicago's Lincoln Park neighborhood—young (twenty-seven), single, and self-confident. She has lived there alone for five years in an apartment in the area known as Lakeview. She works as an accountant in the Loop (Chicago's downtown business section), earning about $35,000 a year. She has some postgraduate education and has attitudes commonly associated with being a "modern woman."

Julie thinks of her neighborhood as a relatively large area (seven blocks by six by one by two), and says it is difficult for her to tell strangers from people who live there.

Although she feels "reasonably safe" in the neighborhood both day and night, she says she would be wary of a stranger's stopping her on the street to ask directions, and that she would definitely not let a stranger come into her home to use the phone. She thinks better street lighting and more police on the street would make her feel safer. But still her safety is something she only seldom thinks about. She thinks "congestion" is the greatest problem facing the neighborhood, but when asked specifically about crime, Julie said "breaking and entering," a property crime of which she had been a victim, was a big problem in that area. She attributes the crime to youths "looking for drug money." She has a rather pessimistic view of her neighbors and says they would "do nothing" if they heard her scream for help, explaining that the people in the area "don't know each other and really don't want to get involved— they are afraid."

She thinks the chances of her home being broken into are high, eight on a ten-point scale, reflecting her actual victimization. She estimates her chances of being raped in the neighborhood as somewhat lower (five)—still a relatively high estimate—but appears to regard her neighborhood as more dangerous than the Loop as she estimates her chances of being raped there as lower still (three).

Julie says there is a park in her neighborhood she regards as a dangerous place, "especially at night because it's dark and empty then." She says she doesn't know it's a dangerous place, but "it just feels unsafe." If she ever has to go through there she says she "surveys" the area, and then walks quickly through, usually on the grass so her high heels won't make noise on the pavement. She says "there's no good reason to be there at night," and she thinks "things like assaults, purse snatchings, and rape are likely to occur there."

Julie says she does sometimes feel afraid that someone might deliberately try to harm her. Two situations which tend to make her feel that way are "meeting teenage boys on the street who are obviously gang members" and whenever she thinks someone might be following her. Julie is least worried when she is home alone, and most worried when she is using public transportation alone after dark, walking by vacant lots or parks, or walking past groups of young men. Even though she thinks she is stronger and faster than the average women, and about as fast as the average man, she thinks she would fight back if attacked because "it might scare them off, you're in a bad situation already . . . it probably won't make it any worse."

When asked what she does to prevent uncomfortable situations from happening, she says,

> take a cab, walk in the middle of the street . . . where the traffic is supposed to be . . . lock my door, don't buzz anyone into the building unless I'm expecting them and know who they are, don't even answer my door if I don't know the person standing there . . . I mean I don't even ask, "Who is it?"

When asked if there were additional things she did to protect herself from sexual assault, Julie indicates several street-smart behaviors.

> That's *why* I walk in the middle of the street . . . they have to come at you from some direction. Oh, I always carry my keys in my hand, like between my fingers you know so you could slug somebody with them. I do that most all the time. I always survey the street before I walk down it; if I don't like the looks of it, I go in another direction . . . it was probably something I read at some point, probably a magazine or newspaper, but I've been doing those things almost ever since I've lived in the city.

Although Julie clearly does quite a bit to protect herself from harm, she has taken only a few of the commonly used precautionary measures (see questions 32 and 33 in Appendix A). She always keeps her door locked and has an unlisted phone, but she didn't care if her full name was on the mailbox nor did she make sure there were special locks or bars on the windows.

Though she estimates her chances of being raped as five on the zero-to-ten scale, Julie doesn't think rape is "much of a problem" in Lincoln Park. She estimates that she worries about it herself "about once a month." She doesn't know anyone who has been raped but has some pretty clearly defined notions about what the crime is like. When asked to describe what she imagined to be the "typical" rape, she said:

> I don't think the appearance of the victim has anything to do with it . . . not even their age . . . not what they're wearing, nothing. They're in the wrong place at the wrong time. Of course, I think your best chance of getting raped is in your own home by somebody that you let in for whatever reason or that possibly even knows you . . . more likely to be younger rather than older, like thirty-five or under. In this neighborhood, likely to be white middle-class kind of thing. I would assume [victims] are almost always hurt unless they're too scared to fight. It's a crime of violence. I wouldn't expect it to be too good. I would assume that they would have many of the common male attitudes, or what I attribute as common male attitudes about rape, i.e., that maybe you were asking for it in some way, especially depending on like what the circumstances are, especially if it was in your own house, but even if you were on the street depending on what you were wearing and the time of day. They're as likely to blame you, at least in their own mind.

Julie thinks the single worst aspect of rape is that it's a violent crime, that a victim is likely to be physically hurt and wind up in the hospital. She thinks about 5 percent of victims get killed, and another 50 percent get beaten or physically hurt in addition to the rape. She estimates that in about 20 percent of the cases men were unjustly accused, that is, that women had agreed, or led men to believe, they would have sex and then changed their minds.

Julie's most frequent worry was not about physical harm, but when she did worry about rape she describes herself as "very frightened." She knows there are places in the city to turn for help in the event of rape, but knows no specific names or locations.

When asked what she thought would help to prevent rape she said:

> Education of women . . . try to teach them what the most likely scenarios are for rape and what they might be able to do in the situation. Public education in terms of trying to change attitudes is of some value. Trying to get people to think beyond the "lay

back and enjoy it concept" . . . that's not an uncommon thing to hear. Try to get people to understand what it is in terms of being an assault. . . . I personally can't think of anything else I think would be effective. I'm not an optimist.

When asked about personal incidents that might be considered sexual assaults, or things that made her feel uncomfortable, Julie talked about a man exposing himself to her. When she called the police to report him, they said, "So?" She also reported being "pushed to go farther than she wanted to" by a "blind date" and then being hit by him when she resisted.

Julie thinks six of the ten items listed in Table 6.1 should be considered legal rape. She also thinks crime in the city is less serious than the newspapers report, but more serious than TV depicts it. She thinks the Chicago newspapers do an average job in both accuracy and completeness of their crime reports.

REBECCA

When we asked Rebecca, another inhabitant of Lincoln Park, if she knew a victim of sexual assault, Rebecca said, "Yes, me." It turned out Rebecca had been assaulted at least twice, in both cases by people she knew.

Rebecca lives alone, is twenty-eight, earns less than $10,000 a year while working part-time as a paralegal, and is in her second year of law school.

Rebecca's view of the typical rape has some elements similar to her own experience. For example, she thinks the crime happens most often "in the home with someone the victim knows."

It matters very little how she looks or what she's wearing. Usually it's planned. Most women wouldn't report it. If they did, I'd say at this point the police would be somewhat sympathetic. . . . They've improved a little bit, but as far as competency in catching the man, I don't think she should expect too much. And prosecutions, at least in Chicago, it's pretty useless, especially if she knows him. . . . I don't think they'd get too hurt—just a few bruises— no serious injury. I think most women are too afraid to resist. I imagine rapists to be between twenty-five and thirty. He doesn't respect women a lot. He's able to objectify them enough to do it. It's something that in ninety percent of the cases he could control. He may have some pressures in his life that make him need to dominate someone else.

Rebecca generally does quite a bit to protect herself—always carrying her keys through her fingers to use as a weapon. She worries a lot about her safety, and unlike most people, feels safer after dark on public transportation than in her own home alone, perhaps as a result of the recent attack on her.

If attacked, Rebecca says she would fight back because she feels "fairly confident it would do some good." She adds, "It's such an insult to me that I couldn't ignore it."

When asked about other things she does to keep herself safe, she emphasizes being aware of what's going on around her:

> Well, I walk on the outside of the sidewalk. If I see a group of men or a tavern up ahead I would cross the street. If I thought someone was following me I'd cross the street. If a car were to slow down next to me I would either ignore it or run away. I walk against the traffic so someone can't follow me in a car. When I get on the el[evated train] I get in the car with a conductor with other people. And I carry my keys in my hand.

Rebecca thinks the worst aspect of rape is that it "takes the woman's self-control away from her, makes her feel helpless." Rebecca, however, says she worries most about money, not about something related to her own safety. When asked about the best ways to prevent rape, Rebecca said:

> I think patrolmen on the streets. What I think would help would be a special task force in the police department, just to handle rape . . . ultimately, you will increase the conviction rate and act as a deterrent. And self-defense classes being mandatory for children in school, women in school, I think better education on rape prevention. There's a number of things you can do to prevent it, such as always having your door locked, not letting someone in the car. Passing the Equal Rights Amendment, that's a long-term thing. Anything that would place women on an equal basis with men so that they are not as easily objectified, made into objects.

Much later in the interview, when asked if she had ever been "pushed farther than she wanted to go" on a date, Rebecca said:

> Well, that's when I was nineteen and I was raped that time. . . . I met him at an extra job I'd taken at a modeling boutique. He worked there also. We went to an outdoor concert afterwards and then had something to eat and I went to his apartment. I was going to school and I was very naive. And his roommate left. And he started, you know, making advances which I didn't

like. I was willing to go so far, and I told him that I didn't want to get pregnant, and I'd never had sex before, I wasn't protected and I just—I didn't know him that well. And he just basically ignored it.

After that she never went to any man's apartment. She also says it was hard for her to deal with emotionally and that she'd "pretty much blocked the event out of her mind."

Rebecca has very modern views of women's roles, and a strong sense that she is in control of her own life.

IRMA

Irma also lives in Chicago, but in a different neighborhood from Julie and Rebecca, called Wicker Park. Irma is a thirty-nine-year-old clerk for the Chicago Board of Health. She was born in Puerto Rico. She has completed some high school, is Lutheran, and earns between $20,000 and $25,000 per year.

Irma has lived in Wicker Park for five years. She lives in a single-family house with her husband, two daughters, a son, and a son-in-law. She feels it is "pretty easy" for her to recognize a stranger in the area. Irma says she would talk to a strange man who approached her on the street for directions, but if he came to her door and asked to use the phone she would make the call for him instead of letting him in. She thinks that "teenagers, fighting" are the most serious problem in the neighborhood. She says she feels reasonably safe in the neighborhood both day and night, but would feel safer if there weren't "so many crimes in the street." She tries "not to go out after dark unless it's necessary, but I'm not afraid to go out after dark." She warns her daughter to be careful. "I always say to her, 'Say hello to everybody and if somebody stops you, be very careful' in how she acts, what she says . . . be very careful about people." Irma advises her son, "Don't get into trouble, don't get into a fight, don't drink, don't smoke, don't stay out too late, travel safely."

Irma thinks the worst crime problems in the neighborhood are "drug abuse and sexual child abuse." About drugs she said,

That's a big problem now. Even kids are taking drugs these days. It's very easy to buy . . . there's a lot of buyers and sellers in the streets. And little children—you will see five- and six-year-old children smoking. I'm not talking about marijuana, I'm talking about cigarettes; that's the way to start.

Irma estimates her risks of victimization as quite high—six for daytime burglary, eight for nighttime burglary and nine for nighttime robbery at home, ten for being pickpocketed, and ten for chances of being raped on the street in her neighborhood (higher than Patty and Julie). Irma said she did not know of any recent instances of child sexual abuse or molestation in the neighborhood. At the same time, she feels reasonably safe in her neighborhood. Irma thinks her chances of being raped in her own neighborhood are lower than being raped downtown. She also indicates considerable apprehension for her children, estimating the chances that they'd be physically harmed and/or raped at ten out of ten.

Irma's worry about being home alone after dark is considerably higher (five out of ten) than the women living in Lincoln Park, and her worry about other things is about the same as her fear of being home alone. In other words, she doesn't feel her home is a very safe place to be. She rates her worry about "walking by groups of young men" at eight. Irma also said she simply never does any of several common activities such as going on rides, to movies, to bars, or to laundromats alone at night.

Irma thinks she would try to defend herself if attacked, although she describes herself as weaker and slower than the average woman and average man. She says she protects herself by trying to prevent things before they can happen, by "not doing them," that is, by isolating herself from the danger. She also has an unlisted phone and a dog for protection. She always locks the doors, checks to see who's there before opening, leaves on the lights and/or radio when not at home, avoids poorly lit streets or alleys, and crosses the street when she sees someone "strange or dangerous-looking."

Although Irma estimates her chances of being raped as ten out of ten, she nonetheless says rape is "not much of a problem" in her neighborhood. When asked to describe a typical rape she reflects a belief that it can happen to anyone, anywhere, anytime.

> I could say [it happens] at night, but say daytime too . . . it doesn't have to be any particular place, it just happens . . . most of the time it's outside; well not most of the time . . . I think it's half and half, inside the house and outside the house . . . rapists are just men, it could be good-looking, ugly. The victim could be an ugly woman, a beautiful woman. . . . A man is not looking for a beautiful woman to rape her; he just wants to rape a woman, that's all. . . . Most of the time they do hurt the person, beat her up . . . the victim doesn't have to be attractive.

Irma knows of a rape victim in the neighborhood, and she learned about the crime from her son who saw the police at the victim's home and later told her the story.

> The guy got inside the house and beat up the lady and then he raped her and stole whatever he could find. It was an old lady who probably lived alone. It must have been a stranger.

When asked what she would do if someone tried to sexually assault her, Irma said,

> I would like to kill the person really. I think I would if I had the chance. It's very hard to say because this person could have a gun or knife. . . . So I guess you just say "do it, but don't kill me."

She thinks the worst aspect of rape is the possibility of being killed. She believes 10 percent of rape victims get killed, and another 50 percent are beaten or physically hurt in addition to the rape. She estimates that only 1 percent lie about having been raped.

Despite all her fears and precautions, and her estimate that someday she will be raped (ten on a ten-point scale), Irma says she worries about rape only "once or twice a year," and that when she thinks about it she is only "mildly frightened." Irma thinks the best way to prevent rape is for women to stay inside the house after dark. "If you have to go out at night, take a bodyguard," she advises.

Irma's views about what sexual acts should be covered by rape laws, unlike those of many we talked to, did not include unwanted intercourse between a husband and wife. Irma thought the crime problem was more serious than in newspapers or on TV, and that papers do an "average job" in terms of accuracy. She remembered a recent TV news story about a rape; a woman had been raped, murdered, and left on a "highway edge all naked." When she reads a rape story she wants to know "what kind of a person she [the victim] was, what was she doing, how did it happen, and where was she." Irma seemed to be interested in facts that would give her ideas about situations and places to avoid, and clues about how she might protect herself.

Irma has traditional views about women's liberation, saying that "this women's liberation is ridiculous. . . . A woman wants to do the same things a man does these days. She can do them, but she can do them in a way she don't lower the man so much. A man should be the man of the house and that man should have respect for that woman."

She also believes a great deal in fate and luck, and feels she herself can do little to control her own destiny.

At the end of the interview Irma commented, "It's interesting to find out there's still people that care and that they're willing to do something, being the way the law is, and it would be nice if they could do something for women to prevent this."

MARIA

Maria is a forty-five-year-old Italian woman with a high school education. She lives in the area of Philadelphia known as South Philly. She works full-time as a clerk in the customer service department of a newspaper in Philadelphia and earns less than $20,000 a year. She is separated from her husband and has lived alone since her daughter grew up and moved away.

Maria has lived in South Philly for about three years. Although she thinks of it as a relatively small area, she has difficulty distinguishing strangers from people who live in the area. She says she feels safe enough to talk to someone who approaches her on the street for directions, but would not let a strange man into the house to make a phone call.

Maria thinks the most serious problem in the neighborhood has to do with teenagers—vandalism, disorderly conduct, and general destructiveness. She thinks vandalism and drug abuse should be given the highest priority in an anti-crime campaign "because it's so prevalent in the area." Vandalism "bothers" her more than drugs, because "that's their own business." She characterizes the neighborhood as "somewhat unsafe" both day and night, and thinks it could be made safer if there were more policemen, more people generally, on the street. She thinks neighbors would probably try to help her if they thought she was in any kind of trouble.

When her daughter was younger, Maria "always insisted that she be home at a decent hour and always be accompanied by someone if she went to a girl friend's house, that the parents or someone walk her home to within very close distance of her home." She also advised her not to talk to strangers, take rides from strangers, or invite them home.

Maria describes a dangerous place in the neighborhood—"a street in a business section which was closed in the evening." She says most of the people "traveling there are violence-prone, lower-class blacks." She thinks mugging is the most likely crime to occur there, and that there is a "good possibility of sexual assault and murder."

Maria also says she often feels afraid someone might harm her. When asked about the situations that make her feel afraid she says, "Oh, I don't know. Just some people look like they are violence prone and I try to avoid them. Anybody big and strong is a suspect— teenagers, and men, naturally, are suspects, especially big men." Her worry levels are all five or above on the ten-point scale.

Nonetheless, Maria considers the neighborhood safe from rape, estimating her own chances of being raped as one on the ten-point scale. However, she estimates her chances of being raped in downtown Philadelphia as significantly higher (six). She also thinks she would be able to defend herself effectively against an attacker, by "kicking and screaming and punching and doing whatever is needed to get this person off me." She says she would be very likely to fight back if sexually assaulted because "I just don't want anybody putting their hands on me. It's just something I'd never take."

When asked what she does to protect herself in the city, Maria said:

> Well, I avoid areas where there are suspicious people and I try to stay on well-lit streets if it's late at night. I stand in the middle of the street. I'd rather face traffic than worry about someone jumping out. I always try to be aware of what's happening around me and don't let anybody walk in back of me. If I hear footsteps behind me I turn around and even if it's a woman I'm not going to assume she is not violence prone. So, if I have to cross the street to get away from a person I will. If they cross the street too, I'll know there is something going on. I feel awareness is the most important thing when you are out on the street alone. Also stay out of dangerous areas, some neighborhoods and the subway. In the subway, watch yourself just like on the street, stay away from corners at night when there is nobody there, stay right next to the stairway, or stay by the cashier until the train comes in. . . . When it rains I carry an umbrella with a point on it . . . boots I feel especially good about because they are not only good support and you can walk in them, but if anybody bothered you, you can kick with the boot.

Maria had checked out the neighborhood before moving in. She also says she "always" took nineteen of the thirty-three precautions she was asked about.

Though Maria had never been raped, she, along with the other 97 percent of our sample, was able to describe a "typical rape."

Her description included several stereotypes based on myths, and other nonexperiential sources of information: a stranger accosting a woman in a dark out-of-the-way area, such as a side street or under a subway, and inflicting both physical and emotional pain. Some of the elements of Maria's typical rape story were traceable to actual rapes she knew about.

If attacked herself, Maria says she would "try to fight off the rapist, try to talk him out of it" or say she had "some horrible disease which he could contract." She says she would "try everything in my power not to have this thing happen to me . . . it's a terribly horrible thing. I can't think of anything worse except dying or having cancer." She thinks the worst aspect of rape is "anybody putting their hands on you and the sexual penetration."

She estimates that 10 percent of rape victims get killed, and of those not killed 90 percent get beaten or physically hurt in addition to the rape. She estimates that in about 5 percent of the cases, men might be falsely accused by women "who were trying to get back at them or get them in trouble."

Maria says she worries about rape or sexual assault as often as once a month, and then, when she does think about it, she feels very frightened. But the things that worry her most are unrelated to her physical safety—having enough money and keeping her job.

If there were a campaign to reduce rape in Philadelphia, Maria would urge changes requiring collective action: well-lit streets, more people protecting certain areas, and making people in the community more alert and ready to help or call the police.

When asked if anything had ever happened to her that might be considered sexual assault, Maria talked about having been assaulted by her former husband. Nonetheless, when asked if she thought unwanted sexual intercourse between a husband and wife ought to be covered in laws about rape, Maria said no.

Maria thinks the crime problem is more serious than reported by Philadelphia newspapers or television news, and that in general the papers do a good job of covering crime. When asked what information she wanted in a news story about a local rape, Maria indicated she wants to better assess her own risks and to distance herself from other victims.

Maria thinks all victims should report to the police "so that the person who raped can be stopped after the first time. They should be brought to trial and given psychiatric examinations and therapy."

Maria is not particularly attached to her neighborhood, and says she'd really prefer to live in another part of Philadelphia, but that she can't afford it.

She also believes herself to have been helped by the women's movement, and as having quite modern views. She does not believe much in luck or fate, and depends pretty much on herself.

Maria, Patty, Sara, Julie, Rebecca, Irma, and Mary all had widely ranging amounts of fear and took varying precautions. Yet their stories include similarities which allow us to identify patterns of coping with female fear. Patty was especially afraid and the fear caused her to invoke many precautions that considerably restrict her life and those of her daughters. She seemed to be struggling with the myths and stereotypes she'd grown up with, because she knew how much her friend had suffered after being raped.

Sara lived in a neighborhood with a much lower crime rate, was better educated, worked full-time, and had considerably more self-confidence than Patty. She was less fearful, but nonetheless indicated ways in which unpleasant sexual encounters had influenced the way she lives.

Julie also exhibited a lot of self-confidence and seemed to epitomize the young modern woman. She had never been the victim of a personal attack but had been a victim of burglary. Perhaps as a consequence, she felt reasonably safe and took only an average number of precautions, but at the same time seemed to be very "street smart." She had sophisticated and modern views about rape, disbelieving most common myths. She also had informed ideas about the root causes of rape and possible preventive measures.

Rebecca, a resident of the same area as Julie, had been attacked twice, both times by men she dated. On the first occasion, many years before she recounted her story, she had been raped; but on the second occasion, just a few weeks before the interview, she had been able to prevent the rape by a former boyfriend who attacked her when he came into her apartment drunk and angry. She also was relatively well educated and had a sophisticated view about rape and women's roles. She remained poised and self-confident.

Irma, a resident of the same city as Julie and Rebecca, but living in a different neighborhood, was much less educated than those women and held much more traditional views about rape and women's roles. She had never been attacked by a stranger, although a man had once exposed himself to her. She estimated her risk of rape as very high (ten on a zero-to-ten scale), and also seemed to live a life of fear.

Mary, a less-educated, unemployed black woman, lived in the midst of danger and seemed to cope by telling herself nothing bad could happen to her. Despite the fact she had been attacked, knew of several recent crimes in her neighborhood, and said she worried all the time about crime and her safety, she estimated her chances of rape victimization at zero and said she felt very safe in her neighborhood. She also seemed to accept rape as a fact of life, saying there was "nothing" anyone could do to prevent it.

Maria is a divorced, working-class Italian woman living alone in Philadelphia. She doesn't like all the teenagers hanging around, or the vandalism and drug abuse she associates with them. She tends to think that the troublemakers, and the likely rapists, are black. She said she'd never been a victim of personal attack, but during the interview when rape was defined as "unwanted, forced sexual intercourse" she decided she had been raped by her former husband. She had nontraditional views of women's roles, yet her descriptions of the typical rape incorporated many of the traditional myths and stereotypes.

The stories of these women indicate three major factors which affect their fear, the centrality of rape to their fear, and the degree to which they voluntarily restrict their lives because of it: knowing a victim, education, and working outside the home. Knowing a victim increases fear, but both education and the experience of working outside the home moderate both the fear and the restrictiveness of the strategies used by women to protect themselves.

Are these seven women typical? In a discussion of strategies people use when deciding how to respond to pressures in their environment, researchers distinguish between reactions that call for people to change themselves in some way to make their current situation less stressful (adaptation) and those that call for changing the situation (coping).[1] This distinction is similar to the avoidance and self-protective measures these seven women take in response to the threat of rape. Avoidance behaviors, such as not going out at night or staying out of certain parts of town, limit one's exposure to dangerous situations. In contrast, self-protective behavior, such as self-defense tactics or asking repairmen to show identification, has the goal of minimizing the risk of victimization when in the presence of danger. While avoidance may require changes in one's daily behavior to reduce exposure to risks, self-protection tactics permit the management of risks once they occur.[2] This distinction between avoidance and self-protection, which has been supported through statistical analyses in several studies, also appears in the tactics that women use to increase their safety.[3] (See Table 8.1.)

Analysis of information from all 299 women we interviewed about how they protect themselves from harm indicate that indeed both adaptation and coping mechanisms are used, and that the frequency of their use is related to their fear of rape. The first basic strategy is self-isolation, a type of adaptation. Women said they "stayed inside," "avoided being out on the streets," or "avoided going to certain parts of town" in order to avoid being victimized. This isolating strategy represents a range of tactics designed to prevent

TABLE 8.1
Self-Protective Behaviors*

	Isolation	Street Smarts
How often do you try to wear shoes that are easy to run in, in case of danger?	.156	.677
When a salesman or repairman comes to your home, how often do you ask for identification before opening the door?	.137	.446
When you go to a movie or ride on a bus, how often do you choose a seat with an eye to who would be sitting nearby?	.240	.405
When you walk down the street, how often do you avoid looking at people you don't know in the eye?	.202	.452
When you are out alone, how often do you try not to dress in a provocative or sexy manner?	.090	.449
How often do you restrict your going out to only during the daytime?	.500	.136
How often do you avoid doing shopping, errands, laundry, or other things you have to do because of fear for your safety?	.750	.223
How often do you not do things you *want* to do, but don't *have* to do—like visiting somebody or going to the movies—because of fear for your safety?	.703	.236

* Varimax rotated factor loadings. (Numbers indicate the relative importance of items to the factors.)

victimizations by avoiding risks. Nearly half the women (42 percent) said they relied on these restrictive isolating tactics "all or most of the time" or "fairly often." Those women with fewer financial, educational, and personal resources—the poor, the elderly, blacks and Hispanics, and the less educated—relied even more than the average woman on these especially restrictive tactics to protect themselves (see Table 8.2).

In stark contrast, 90 percent of men living in the same neighborhoods said they never bother avoiding exposure to risk. It seems rarely to cross their minds.

The second basic strategy, street smarts, a coping mechanism, represents a range of tactics women believe will reduce their risks when they do go out on the streets or believe themselves to be in a

TABLE 8.2
Demographic Distribution of the Frequent Use of Precautionary Behaviors by Gender, Age, Race/Ethnicity, Income, and Education

Category	% Often Using Isolation		% Often Using Street Smarts	
	Men	Women	Men	Women
Sample	10.3(68)*	41.5(299)	29.4(68)	73.9(299)
Age				
18–26	5.3(19)	37.3(102)	15.8(19)	74.5(102)
27–33	5.6(18)	35.7 (56)	33.3(18)	75.0 (56)
34–51	16.7(18)	38.8 (98)	38.9(18)	75.5 (98)
52–93	15.4(13)	64.3 (42)	30.8(13)	66.7 (42)
Race/Ethnicity				
Black	9.1(11)	45.0(100)	36.4(11)	78.0(100)
White	4.9(41)	33.3(159)	22.0(41)	68.6(159)
Hispanic	11.1 (9)	69.2 (26)	22.2 (9)	80.8 (26)
Income				
$6000	14.3 (7)	38.0 (50)	28.6 (7)	84.0 (50)
$6000–9999	–0– (9)	40.7 (54)	33.3 (9)	77.8 (54)
$10000–14999	18.8(16)	52.5 (61)	31.3(16)	77.0 (61)
$25000 and over	11.1(27)	38.7(106)	33.3(27)	67.0(106)
Education				
Less than H.S.	15.4(13)	59.1 (66)	53.8(13)	71.2 (66)
H.S. graduate	22.2 (9)	44.3 (88)	33.3 (9)	81.8 (88)
More than H.S.	6.5(46)	31.7(145)	21.7(46)	70.3(145)

* Numbers in parentheses indicate sample sizes.

potentially dangerous situation. Such tactics include avoiding eye contact with men, wearing shoes easy to run in, and asking repairmen to show identification. Nearly three fourths of the women living in the six selected neighborhoods frequently use these street-smart tactics. Poor women, especially Hispanics, rely on them heavily, but the elderly do not, preferring to remain inside.

Again in stark contrast to what women do, 70 percent of the men in the neighborhoods said they never bother with any of these tactics to protect themselves.

Since crime, rape, and fear of crime differ by neighborhood, one might imagine that the use of these precautionary strategies varies by neighborhood also. Women living in West Philadelphia (black, low-income) and Wicker Park, Chicago (heterogeneous, low-income) are high users of both street-smart and isolating tactics, while residents of South Philadelphia (white ethnic, low-income), Sunset, San Francisco (white, middle-income), and Lincoln Park, Chicago (white, middle-income) are relatively low users of both types of precautions. Women living in Visitacion Valley in San Francisco (heterogeneous, low-income) are high users of isolating tactics and low users of street-smart tactics.

What determines the strategy a woman will rely on most? Police-based crime rates (Uniform Crime Reports—UCR) are not related to which precautions women choose, but *perceptions* of risk of rape are, as are women's perceptions of their general safety at night in the neighborhood. These factors also are most important in explaining how often women use each strategy. Also relevant are a sense of physical competence (or its flip side, a sense of physical vulnerability) and the extent to which women feel their neighborhoods are decaying. Women who feel physically competent are less likely to isolate themselves to avoid risk, and very likely to use a lot of street-smart tactics and to use them often. Women who believe conditions are deteriorating in their neighborhoods are more likely to use both kinds of tactics, and to use them more often than women who feel good about their neighborhoods.

Each strategy is useful in different situations. Avoidance allows women to reduce exposure to risk, and street-smart tactics permit the management of risks once they occur.

Analyses examining the relative influence of personal circumstances (e.g., income), psychological attributes (e.g., sense of vulnerability), and neighborhood conditions (e.g., signs of social disorder) on use of the two basic strategies indicate that psychological factors are most important for women's choice of isolation tactics, and neighborhood conditions and psychological factors are about equally important in influencing women's choices of street-smart tactics.[4]

In summary, four basic patterns of response describe women's reactions to fear of rape.

Pattern 1: The Susceptibles

One pattern, typified by Patty, is characterized by a life shaped by fear and a high degree of restrictive and isolating behavior as a precaution. "Susceptibles" believe they are quite likely to be victimized, regardless of the actual crime rate in their neighborhoods. These women tend to have relatively traditional views of women's roles, and to hold women responsible for preventing their own rapes. They tend to know victims and to generalize from victims' experiences to their own lives. They tend to have a moderate amount of education, and not to be employed outside the home.

Pattern 2: The Invincibles

These women, typified by Mary, accept crime and violence as a normal part of everyday life. The "Invincibles" don't admit to a great deal of fear, perhaps because to do so would make the stress unbearable. Nevertheless, they engage in many precautionary behaviors and in other ways indicate that crime and avoidance of victimization are important factors shaping their lives. They tend to be relatively uneducated, unemployed or underemployed, and to know many victims.

Pattern 3: The Realistic Pessimists

"Realistic Pessimists," typified by Irma and Maria, experience considerable fear and estimate their risks of rape as quite high. They have a high school education and perhaps some college, work at semiskilled or skilled blue-collar jobs, and have mixed views of women's roles. They are ambivalent because on the one hand they think women are responsible for preventing their own rapes, but on the other, they think women's self-protective measures are ineffective, and that societal agents and institutions must change if rape is to be prevented.

Pattern 4: The Realistic Modernists

These women, typified by Julie, Rebecca, and Sara, are relatively well educated, tend to have nontraditional views of women's roles, and to work at full-time professional jobs which they regard as important stepping-stones in lifelong careers. They report low to moderate fear and take a moderate number of relatively nonrestrictive precautions to prevent it. They attribute blame entirely to rapists or to societal structures and conditions that they think may support rape. Many know rape victims, and they express anger and frustration at the way rape is treated by our society's institutions.

Whether a susceptible, an invincible, a realistic pessimist, or a realistic modernist, every woman in our society must consider the possibility of being raped and decide how she is going to respond to the threat of it. No woman is free to ignore it.

9

Should Women Fear?

UNTIL society and the major institutions in this country are willing to take responsibility for female fear and do whatever is necessary to reduce both rape and the burden of fear of rape on women, it would be unwise to advocate that women completely stop being afraid. Fear and related behavior may protect some women.

Learning to fear is a process that begins at birth for women and continues throughout their lives. As is shown in Figure 9.1, the fear each woman experiences is the product of her own personal background as it intersects for her—in her own particular time and geographical and social space—with the forces of history and trends of contemporary times. It is striking that women respond so similarly to the threat of rape, both in their fear and in the precautionary strategies they adopt. Female fear has become a social fact.

Unfortunately, there are many good reasons for women to be afraid. Feminist analyses of the effect of the threat of rape on women assert that it operates as an instrument of social control, encouraging women to restrict their behavior and keeping them in a state of continuous stress.[1] A large proportion—much too high for a nation that calls itself the land of the free—of the three hundred or so women who shared their stories for this book reported high levels of female fear. Further, among these women, those with the fewest physical, financial, educational, and other resources are those who bear the heaviest burden of fear. Thus the distribution of fear appears to follow existing social cleavages delineated by gender, age, race, and social class that mark status and power inequalities in our society.

Women also have good reason to be afraid because of the consequences for women who are victimized. Studies of the aftereffects

Figure 9.1
Basic Factors Related to Female Fear

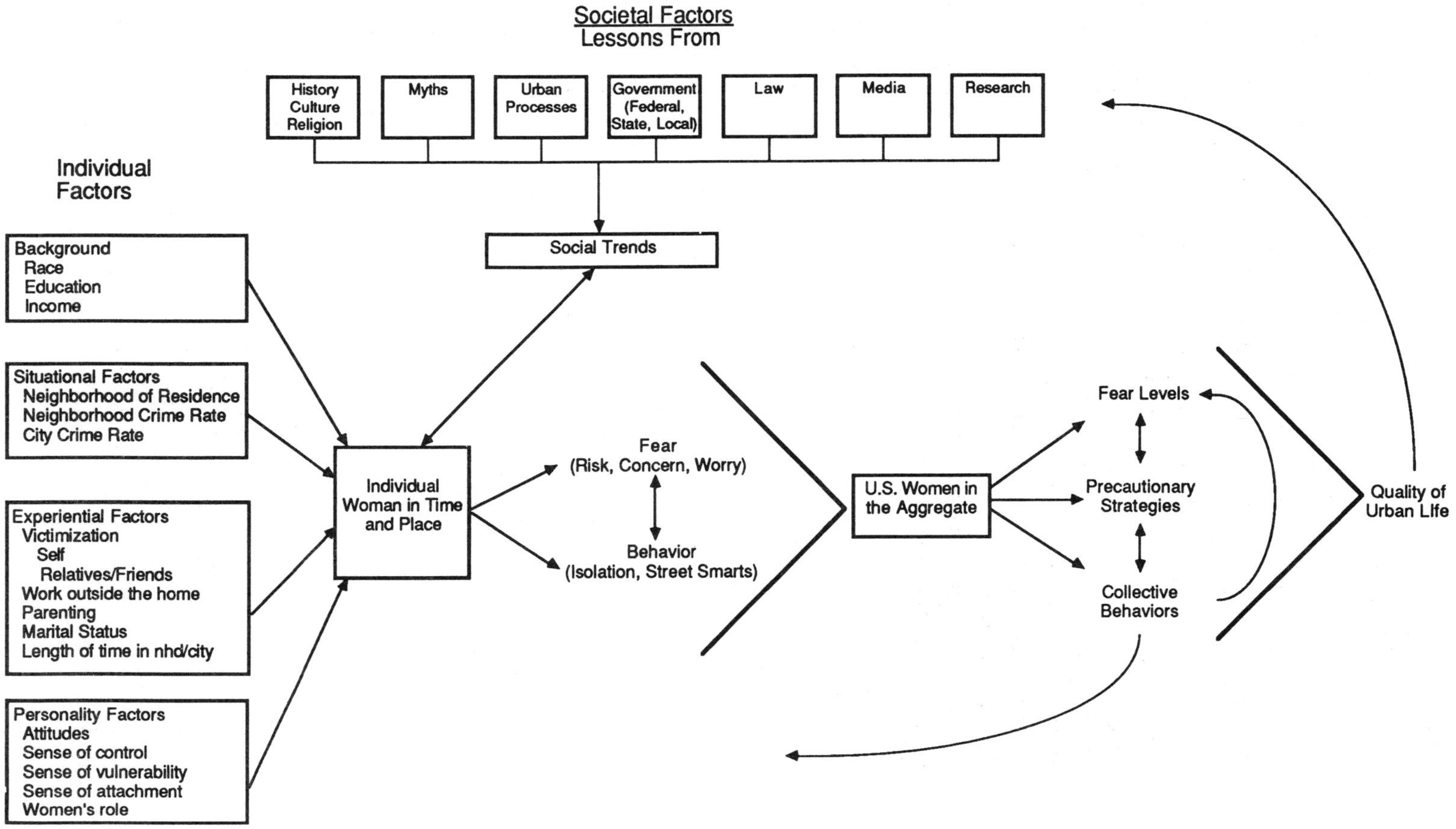

of rape indicate that it is one of the most traumatic of crimes, with many victims developing symptoms of emotional distress that last for several weeks or even years after the attack. For some, the distress increases over the years rather than subsiding.[2] In addition to the damage occurring from the rape itself, attribution of blame to the victim by friends, co-workers, and actors in the criminal justice system may leave women feeling doubly victimized.[3] To some extent this may happen to all crime victims, since most people seem to want to believe in a world where people "get what they deserve."[4] By blaming the victim, people are able to preserve their belief in justice.[5] Such "blaming" reactions are particularly likely to occur in the case of rape,[6] and men are especially likely to attribute responsibility to the rape victim.[7]

Rape may be especially fear-inducing because of widespread belief that it is nearly always linked to gratuitous violence (in addition to the rape itself), and that it is nearly impossible to resist successfully. Both of these positions reflect media coverage but are contrary to fact. The statistical profile of rape derived from the National Crime Survey indicates that despite the common presence of more than one offender or the use of a weapon, most victims actively resist or attempt to escape.[8]

Two recent studies comparing women who were raped with those who managed to deflect an attack found that successful resisters were those *who from the moment they realized they might be in danger* used a combination of self-protective strategies, for example, physical resistance, screaming, and trying to flee, and the like.[9] Active, forceful fighting at the onset of an attack rather than passive pleading or screaming appears to be more successful in warding off attackers.[10] In addition to thwarting the assault, resistance appears to help many women preserve their self-esteem and lessen the psychological damage done by rape.[11] However, in the presence of weapons such as knives or guns, such struggling may be ill-advised, so it is unwise to advocate any specific action as the best for all situations.

A third study of four thousand cases of rape survivors in the National Crime Survey data from 1973 to 1979 differentiates between forceful (hitting, kicking) and nonforceful (screaming, running) resistance in stranger-to-stranger rapes and robberies.[12] In those cases, too, women who resisted were much more likely to avoid being raped than nonresisters. "Women who resisted without force (e.g., screaming) were least likely to be raped and nonforceful resistance had little effect on the risk of other injury. . . . However, women who forcefully resisted were 24 percent more likely than those who offered no resistance to be injured." Most of the injuries take the form of bruises, cuts, scratches, and black eyes, rather than more severe stabbings or capricious beatings that most women imagine.

Rape also may induce greater fear than other crimes because it may be a "bellwether" crime against which people judge the general criminal environment in their communities. When rape does occur it may signal that other crimes are also likely to happen. The high correlation in the FBI Uniform Crime Reports (UCR) between the rates of rape and rates of other violent crimes indicates that this is a reasonable speculation.[13] Women's estimates of their risk of rape are associated with their perceived risk of other violent crimes, and this index of the combined risks of interpersonal violence is strongly related to female fear.[14] This suggests that women's fear of rape may lead them to experience their whole environment as a dangerous place to be.

Although fear appears disproportionate to the actual risks women face as measured by victimization and reported crime data, women's fear is proportionate to their own *estimates* of their own risks. Not surprisingly, women's perceptions of their risk of rape have more impact on how they feel and act than the actual crime rates. The rates do not give an individual woman any comfort with respect to her own chances of being attacked.

The sizable proportion of women who regularly use isolation tactics to protect themselves gives support to the argument that the impact of the threat of crime on many women is restrictive. The work, social, and leisure opportunities lost to women because of the threat of crime seem likely to very much reduce the overall quality of their lives and of urban life in general. Although the precautionary strategies employed by women may not often involve significant monetary expenditures, these strategies are undoubtedly costly in terms of personal freedom. The *sum* of subtle and not so subtle accommodations by women exert a considerable toll on their time, effort, and freedom.

Thirty-four percent of women say they avoid "most of the time" or "fairly often" such ordinary tasks as shopping or running errands because of fear for their safety. When asked about behavior that did not involve necessary tasks but rather things they wanted to do, such as visiting friends or going to movies, 36 percent of women say they "often" avoid engaging in such activities because of fear of harm, and only 30 percent say fear never deters them.

Other data suggest that the price paid by women for safety is greatest in the area of behaviors involving the most discretion, such as visiting friends or going out for evening entertainment.[15] High fear seems to shrink the scope of women's choices about their lives by restricting their movement through time and space.

Despite all these restrictive precautions, women *believe* that more assertive strategies are actually more efficacious. It is as if they behave in a restrictive manner only because that is what they have been taught they *should* do, not because they believe it will keep them safe. Perhaps they believe that if they do what they've been taught and get raped anyway, they are more likely to get sympathy and support.

Whatever the causes of rape and other violence against women, a major effect of these crimes on even nonvictims is self-imposed restrictions. Men are more frequent victims of every violent crime except rape yet they do not react by restricting their behavior, suggesting that something more than crime is implicated. Rarely are men warned not to go out alone at night because they will be victimized, even though they are victimized more often than women. It seems that *crime against women, whatever the motivation of the individual criminal, has the cumulative effect of reinforcing social norms about appropriate behavior for women.* Women who are victimized, especially in rape, are blamed for that victimization.[16] This is not only because of belief in a "just world,"[17] but also because in being victimized women are breaking social norms, and blame acts as a cautionary warning to other women not to do the same.

Too much fear is debilitating and incapacitating. But appropriate fear may promote the use of precautions which may help keep women safe, or at least keep them *feeling* safer. Given the fact that violent crime is still very much a part of the U.S. urban scene, can women afford to reduce their fear before rape has been substantially reduced or eliminated?

What seems most appropriate is a three-pronged approach which aims to (1) reduce rape, (2) educate the citizenry about the facts of rape, and (3) involve them in collective activities that simultaneously will increase their attachment to their communities and reduce female fear to levels appropriate for that community. Perhaps the last—involving people in a way that increases their attachment to community—is the most important because that process may also serve to educate people about rape *and* may even lead to a reduction in rape (and other crime) by increasing neighborhood cohesiveness.

Perhaps more than anything else, the women who shared their stories suggest that egalitarian views of women's roles and education are related to less fear, less isolation, and less restricted behavior. However, egalitarian views and education do not result in greater freedom of action if women perceive that their risk of being raped is high. Therefore, the efforts of feminist activists, who proselytize for more egalitarian views of women's roles while simultaneously organizing urban residents to "take back the night" by marching and demonstrating against rape, may be especially liberating for our nation.

In short, rape is a serious national problem. It is a social problem that must be taken seriously because of the high costs to women and to society. It claims as many victims among women as cancer. Every woman grows up fearing it, and most learn to take precautions to avoid it. The precautions they take result in self-imposed restrictions which cost many, if not all, of them lost work and leisure opportunities, and cost the nation the full participation and involvement of more than half of its citizens. Ironically, although women feel compelled to take so many precautions, they do not think these actions are effective in preventing rape. Nor do men. Effective rape prevention strategies, people say, are not the tactics individual women can use to prevent their own rapes. More effective, long-term strategies are much more difficult to achieve. These include promoting greater equality of the sexes through elimination of sexist language in textbooks and school, and fostering equality of work opportunities and rewards.

The figures available from the United States and other nations, however underrepresentative, show this country to have the highest rate of rape in the world. Analysts attribute the high U.S. rate to a range of causes, from the widespread distribution of pornographic literature and films (particularly violent pornography),[18] to the objectification of and displays of violence toward women in advertising, to the low conviction rates for rapists, to the more general supports in the culture for male aggressiveness toward women. After ten years of operation, the National Advisory Committee to the government-sponsored Center on Prevention and Control of Rape concluded that there is a widespread tolerance of rape in the United States and it is related to an excessively high tolerance of all forms of violence.[19]

This reality of widespread tolerance of rape is apparent in the urban institutions that deal with rape—the police, the courts, the hospitals, and the media. Prodded by the efforts of feminist activists in the 1960s and 1970s, police and medical personnel in the large U.S. cities have greatly improved their treatment and processing of rape victims to the point that many more women are willing to report the crime and press charges against assailants. However, because these *are* the institutions that deal with rape it is assumed that legal and medical issues are the most important. The political, economic, psychological, and emotional consequences of rape are largely ignored or left to increasingly weary volunteers in rape crisis centers, women's centers, and churches.

This tendency to view rape in legal and medical terms results in emphasizing the *consequences* of a serious social problem, rather than its prevention. Until rape is seen as a product of social interaction in our society, policymakers will never promote the necessary changes to alter the norm of acceptable behavior in our society. And until such changes take place, women will continue to be afraid.

10

Society's Responsibility

WHAT can be done to reduce the burdens of day-to-day female fear for women, and reduce the costs for society? Women, especially women in isolation, cannot do it alone, anymore than they alone can prevent rape. Society as a whole must take the responsibility for female fear, and do what is necessary to alleviate it.

First, there must be changes in how people think about rape—how it happens, who is responsible, and what can be done. Those who think about this topic must shift the emphasis from what individuals can do to what groups, organizations, and institutions can do. Continued emphasis on what individual women can do to prevent their own rapes enhances the likelihood that victims will continue to be blamed for their own predicaments. Rape is no longer only an individual problem for victims to deal with. It is a national social problem, and national policies must be generated for dealing with it. Individualized issues must be merged into social policies for correcting what is now a collective problem.[1] Policymakers must have the courage to promote policies that may be unpopular, but will be more effective at preventing rape and reducing the burdens of female fear.[2]

A well-known researcher in this field argued in 1978 that "there is no more pressing or urgent focus of research . . . than the study of the male prerogative as a social support for rape and other abuses of women because they are women," and that "in the sphere of social problems possibly no subject is more complex [than rape]: because of legal, ethical, political and administrative difficulties involved, and because of the cultural supports for aggression against females. Research on rape and strategies for its utilization call for the utmost in ingenuity, resources and persuasiveness."[3]

Despite these difficulties, research and activism over the last ten years have suggested several socially responsible approaches to the problem of female fear.

In part because it is regarded as primarily a women's issue, one of the "trivia" of women's everyday lives,[4] but also because it has been more generally a taboo topic,[5] the crime of rape received virtually no academic attention until the last ten years. Only since the mid-1970s, when the National Institute for Mental Health established the National Center for the Prevention and Control of Rape and began funding research on rape, has it become a somewhat acceptable academic topic.

Since most rape research concerns itself with the study of victim outcomes, it is difficult to make research-based policy recommendations that do not focus on actions victims can take, rather than on what societal agents or institutions must do to prevent victimizations.[6] Yet to make such recommendations seems to be inadvertently "blaming the victim."[7] One feminist has suggested that this approach could be corrected if we referred to "survivors" of rape rather than to rape "victims."[8] Yet to do so seems particularly distracting or strident to others.

Other problems also make this topic a difficult one for researchers. We found that many clerical and support staff who worked with us on studies of victims reacted to the data with intense fear for themselves. This required extra sensitivity on our part, and in some cases, shifting staff members to other research projects. On two occasions, different secretaries burst into tears while typing scholarly papers based on our data. In the course of our trying to calm them, we learned for the first time that they had been rape victims. Coders developed coping mechanisms for dealing with their horror at reading countless stories of victimizations by, for example, posting the "best" (i.e., most gruesome) violent crime story of the week on the project bulletin board. In addition, in the early months of the project, we, too, experienced greatly increased fear.

We found that interviewers had to be selected and trained more carefully than in many other types of research in sensitively dealing with respondents, who often became upset. Also, some service providers resent the time and resources used by researchers, pointing out that many more victims could be offered services for the cost of the research.

In the mid-1970s the National Organization for Women's Task Force on Rape led to a lobbying effort to establish a National Center for the Prevention and Control of Rape (NCPCR) in the National Institute of Mental Health (NIMH).[9] The Center was mandated to provide funds for research and demonstration projects, compile and publish training manuals, and develop and maintain an information base in the area of sexual assault. Yet activists had expected to receive money for operating rape crisis centers from NCPCR, and often did not have research skills necessary to conduct and evaluate demonstration programs. Further, they objected to placing NCPCR within NIMH because they thought it implied that rape victims have something wrong mentally. When the NCPCR funded several research projects, it became the target of bitter attacks by activists.

The Center also had a difficult time within the Institute. Much like an unwanted stepchild, it was shunted from one part of the Institute to another, never receiving solid, long-term administrative support. Personnel cuts during the early Reagan years greatly impacted the Institute, resulting in a 100 percent turnover twice in a four-year period for the Center. Eventually, it was folded into a new division on Violent and Anti-Social Behavior and its National Advisory Committee eliminated.

In the course of our work, we talked to many victims. As our work began to become known in the Chicago area, we were contacted more and more frequently by victims seeking solace or guidance. But as academics, we were not trained to provide the kinds of emotional, economic, or legal help these victims sought. As human beings, we offered whatever comfort we could. With time, we found ourselves with an increasingly strong sense of obligation to victims, a feeling that our research must do something to prevent victimizations or alleviate the plight of victims. We cannot ignore what others have said: "that the decision to study an issue implies the willingness and responsibility to do something about it."[10] We have experienced skepticism about whether social research can offer lasting solutions, and a sense of helplessness because of the magnitude of the problem in the United States.

From all that has been said above, it should come as no surprise that researchers, along with service practitioners, suffer from burnout. One researcher has defined burnout as involving emotional exhaustion and the development of "detached concern."[11] She adds, "A common response to burnout (among social service practitioners) is to get out, by changing jobs, going into administrative work, or even leaving the profession altogether." Many academics doing research on rape and related topics respond over time by simply changing topics.

Despite these problems, however, research has shown that many positive steps can be taken to allay female fear.

1. Educate the Public About Rape

Evidence from a wide variety of sources indicates that public education about rape can help to dispel myths and stereotypes.[12] It also could provide information on services for victims, as well as help potential victims assess their risks.

From the NCPCR's inception, personnel have been committed to research and dissemination of educational and other materials—all based on a wide range of research studies—which could, in the long run, help to prevent rape and/or improve the care and treatment of victims.

In 1985, the NCPCR was advised to place particular emphasis both on the perpetrator, to understand how to effect better prevention strategies,[13] and on long-term effects on victims, to deal with those whose symptoms increase rather than decrease with time.[14]

2. Examine the Role of Pornography

In the midst of the widespread controversy described in Chapter 7 about the role of pornography in violence toward women, many feminists believe that the objectification of women in pornography and advertising perpetuates myths and sex-stereotyping which contribute to a culture of rape. Others limit their objections to the portrayals of *violence* toward women, as opposed to eroticism. Some researchers believe that most viewers of pornography are subject to a "saturation effect," which means that more and more violence is required to produce a thrill or satisfaction.[15] They note further that viewers of pornography, especially violent pornography, regard actual rapes as less serious crimes than do nonviewers. However, even nonviolent or erotic pornography has negative consequences for women. Since in erotic pornography women are shown enjoying "standard" and "unusual" sex with a number of different types of partners (male, female, animal), viewers are left with the impression that women are insatiable sexually, and willing (and eager) to have sex under a variety of demeaning conditions. Viewers of such pornography—male and female—rate rape as less serious than nonviewers, and would impose shorter sentences in convictions than before seeing the films.

Given the possible link to rape and, therefore, female fear, there should be further examination of the role different types of pornography may play with respect to violence against women and the perpetuation of a cultural climate which condones (or at least accepts) high rates of violence and crime.

3. Promote Campus Rape Education and Prevention Programs

Given the apparently increasing incidence of date and gang rape among acquaintances on U.S. college campuses, there is a widespread need for programs designed to educate students about rape, its consequences, and its prevention. Model programs have been instituted on several university campuses.

One program at Northwestern University begins with a one-hour presentation to first-year students during orientation week in the fall. The presentation includes a film on date rape, discussions by researchers and rape crisis counselors, and a demonstration of self-defense techniques. Students are advised where they can go for more information or, if needed, counseling or other (e.g., legal) help. They are also given the opportunity to enroll in self-defense classes offered free or at rates subsidized by the University. This hour-long program is supplemented throughout the year by informal discussions available in all living units, where films or other dramatic portrayals are followed by discussions led by teams of students and experts in the field. In addition, there are three University-sponsored browsing libraries at strategic locations on campus where students, faculty, and staff can find academic and popular books and articles on rape, sexual harassment, pornography, spouse abuse, child abuse, and other related topics.

The Northwestern rape education and prevention program is coordinated by a student women's coalition with the help and support of interested faculty and the financial support of the University. Activists have noted that the University is wise to have offered such support since, in the event of any lawsuits, it would be helpful to the University if it could demonstrate that it has been making every effort to prevent rapes on campus. There are also active programs at the University of Michigan, the University of California, Duke University, and many others.

4. Promote Reform in the Law and the Legal System

Our examination of the laws and legal system (see Chapter 6) suggests the need for reform and monitoring of laws and procedures for dealing with rape cases.[16]

In recent years, the American Bar Association (ABA) has become concerned more generally with the plight of all victims. ABA staff designed the Omnibus Victim's Rights Bill and outlined for members of the bar better procedures for dealing with victims.

If adhered to, these procedures can greatly improve the treatment of all crime victims. The law requires a written Victim Impact Statement specifying the impact of the crime and subsequent processing of the case. It also requires that prosecutors consult with victims before entering into any plea bargaining.

The Victim's Rights Bill attends to compensating victims for physical injuries and expenses related to medical care or loss of work. In the case of rape, long-term emotional damage is frequent and may require more medical care and therapy than the physical injuries. Therefore, compensation boards should be empowered to compensate rape victims for emotional damage, too. Rape victims have the right to the aid and comfort of rape crisis counselors and other supports often provided by rape crisis centers. This implies the need for financial support for those centers, which now often exist only through the efforts of increasingly weary volunteers.

Victims also should have the right to sensitive and adequately trained prosecutors and judges, conversant with the nuances of handling rape cases.

It may also be useful to monitor the effects of victim compensation statutes at the state level. Enforcement and benefits currently vary widely for rape victims.

In nearly all states there has been interest in revising the statutes as they apply to rape, and many states have new codes. The effectiveness of the new statutes should be monitored, and legal professionals made to understand the underlying concerns and interests of those who worked for reform.

Professors involved in training new lawyers or writing texts to be used in law schools should ensure that young lawyers are learning up-to-date versions of the laws covering rape and the intent of the reform efforts.

Prosecutors should push for the creation of special units to deal with rape cases. This has been very effective in large cities where the number of cases merits a special unit. The prosecutors in such a unit can then get special training, and establish working relationships with local rape crisis centers. Such interunit cooperation has been found to aid in the success of prosecutions and in diminishing stress for victims.

One excellent example can be found in Philadelphia's District Attorney's Office. The unit there has worked cooperatively with a local group, Women Organized Against Rape (WOAR). In addition to increasing rape prosecutions, the team developed a program complete with videocassettes for training new prosecutors. The leader of the Philadelphia unit was invited to use these program materials to train prosecutors in Chicago, and in a workshop for district attorneys at an annual conference. Judges would benefit from such training, too.

Many women think rape might be deterred by judges meting out harsher penalties to convicted rapists. Several have suggested castration. Studies of the effects of castration on the relatively few rapists who have suffered this penalty indicate that although a castrated man may be unable to rape, he is no less prone to violence.[17] The history of the changes in rape law shows that in places where the penalty for rape is death, the very harshness of the penalty seems to make juries less likely to bring a verdict of guilty. In fact, reformers often argue for *reduction* in the severity of such penalties because they believe this would increase the likelihood of convictions. Nevertheless, evaluations of the reform law passed in Michigan in 1978 indicate that even when the rate of convictions increased, it did little to deter rapists. Victims, however, were reported to be less traumatized by the judicial system experience and more willing to follow through on prosecutions. This willingness to push for prosecution may also be attributable to a general increased awareness which resulted from media coverage of the legislative debate when the reform law was being written and passed.[18]

Analyses of the processing of rape cases, as well as papers by scholars and prosecutors, indicate that the handling of cases is strongly influenced by power struggles on several levels.[19] Electoral politics affects the way rape is treated by elected district/states attorneys and by legislators during battles over legal reforms. Bureaucratic politics can be seen in the maneuvering and manipulating of caseloads and scheduling in courts, and interpersonal politics can determine the degree of cooperation or conflict between prosecutors and doctors over client rights. The path taken by a rape case through the legal system is determined by a great degree of discretion practiced at every level from police to judges. It is affected by the race and social class of victims and offenders, and by the suspicion raised by requirements of corroboration and proof of resistance. All of this together distinguishes rape cases from other crimes.

These analyses suggest there may be bases for a class action suit on behalf of victims (particularly poor black victims) against prosecutors and the courts, raising the issue of whether the civil rights of victims are being violated by these very laws about rape, the unequal application of the laws, and the general processing of rape cases. Prosecutors consulted about the possibility of such suits feel there may be some merit in considering them, but they would be difficult to win.

5. Reform Media Coverage

Current news coverage of rape enhances women's fears and leaves misleading impressions of both the crime and how it might be dealt with. Women need information in rape stories that will help them to calculate their own risks. The press could also play an important role in informing the public about the careless and inconsistent treatment of rape by the criminal justice system—from police (who may "unfound" a case), to prosecutors (who may drop or plea-bargain less "winnable" cases), to judges (who vary in their instructions to juries and their sentences)—and in publicizing the types of evidence needed in most cases to win a conviction against the accused, which is sometimes unwittingly destroyed.

Journalists should carefully consider whether or not to name the victim in their reports, and try to present good, current information on rape and its consequences. Most media do not name rape victims unless they are murdered. Some name the woman if the alleged assailant is acquitted; some name her if she is a public figure or wants her name used (as did Connie Francis).

By law, a journalist can use the name of a rape victim when it becomes part of the public court record. Although no law stops a reporter from trying to get the name of a victim sooner, many police departments and state prosecutors adhere to in-house rules or state laws that prevent them from revealing the names of victims before a case reaches court. Nevertheless, for media personnel, the question is whether the name of the victim should be used at all. It is an ethical question, not a legal one.

Every media agency should establish a policy in this area, and the reporting staff should be informed. Prosecutors and police must know what to expect from local media so they can adequately inform victims.

Those who favor naming the victims argue that the crime should not be treated differently from any other crime because to do so implies that rape victims are different from other crime victims. They believe that naming a rape victim, as one would name a burglary victim, will eventually help to eliminate the stigma associated with having been raped. Furthermore, naming the defendant and not the victim implies that a rape has actually occurred and that the accused is guilty, when by law it is an alleged rape and the defendant is innocent until proven guilty. There is a social stigma attached to being accused of a rape as well as to being a rape victim. Some therefore argue that the accused has a constitutional right to confront his accuser in public and in the media as an extension of the public domain. Finally, some victims *want* their names publicized because they hope that public awareness of the crime will prompt actions to eliminate rape.

Those who oppose use of the victim's name argue that victims will not report rape to the police or be willing to prosecute if they know their names will be made public. Victims should be able to control who knows about the crime; often they do not want family and acquaintances to know because reactions are too often patronizing or critical. Reporting the victim's name may add to the guilt, shame, or sense of loss of control she may already feel.

Those opposed to reporting names argue that, in fact, rape is not like other crimes. A sexual assault is more personal than any other form of attack and the psychological damage is often greater and usually longer lasting than the physical damage. A victim must also be the key witness in a trial that forces her to relive her ordeal and face her assailant again. Because of the social stigma against rape victims, they are subject to more public scrutiny than robbery or assault victims. Proponents of this argument believe that newspapers have a moral and ethical responsibility to protect the victim from further pain by not reporting her name.

At the least, journalists have a responsibility to know how rape is perceived in their communities. Rape reporting policies should be defined with the advice of prosecutors, defense lawyers, doctors, rape crisis center workers, and victims. By listening to the community before setting policy, a media agency can better serve the public and improve its own image as well.

Journalists should also make an effort to include details that allow readers to assess their own risks. There should be follow-up stories when assailants are arrested and released or convicted. And in stories about bizarre rapes, there should be indications that these are indeed atypical cases.

Journalists need to pay more consistent attention to rape reporting. Too often after a feature story, the issue is dropped for weeks, months, or even years.[20] Yet rapes continue, and there is a continuing need for ongoing, thoughtful analyses.

More responsible treatment of rape by the media would concentrate on dispelling myths concerning the victim (her clothing, age, occupation, etc.), the location of the crime, or her relationship with the assailant. Maps could identify areas of the city where recent rapes have occurred, and stories could discuss the relationship between fear and actual crime levels in neighborhoods. Attempts could be made to present the actual number of rapes, relying not only on police reports but also on victimization surveys and information from rape crisis centers. Changes in rates of rape, in reporting rates, and in the frequency with which police unfound or prosecutors downgrade a case could be identified. Laws and sentencing patterns could be analyzed. Rape prevention efforts could be highlighted. Support services for victims could be profiled. Long-term follow-ups could be done describing the impact of rape on victims and their families and friends, and ways to cope with the stress of rape long after the attack has taken place. Finally, stories about those who have successfully resisted and avoided rape could be presented.

6. Involve Legislators and Other Policymakers

Well-informed policymakers can play several roles with respect to educating the public about the incidence and consequences of rape, preventing and eventually eliminating it, and providing services to victims. They can campaign to pass new, needed laws and can support implementation of existing laws. They can support activities to educate the public in order to dispel myths about rape and inform the public of the realities, and support provision of services needed by victims and their families. And they can support research and demonstration programs needed to identify the best models of service and prevention.

National-level policymakers can sponsor requests for funds to create model/demonstration programs for provision of services to rape victims and their families. State-level policymakers can examine state laws applicable to rape and sexual assaults, and consider needed reforms. On the local level, policymakers can identify, assess, and publicize local services available to victims and their families through police, hospitals, volunteer programs, churches, and others. They can improve reporting procedures and increase prosecutions. They can conduct workshops to sensitize police, prosecutors, judges, and hospitals to the preferred treatment of victims. Finally, they can support or sponsor self-defense classes for women and girls.

7. Encourage Community Involvement

Collective community effort in the late 1970s moved the issue of rape onto the political agenda. Throughout the country, women (and men) marched through city streets with chants of "Take back the night" accompanied by cries of "Stop rape now!" These marches heralded women's refusal to accept the restrictions on their lives advocated as protection against the threat of rape and other forms of criminal victimization. Unwilling to go out alone only in daylight, to hide behind locked and barred windows and doors, or to live in a constant state of anxiety, women acted together to change the situation.

Although it is impossible yet to determine if such actions have had an impact on rates of rape and other crimes against women, they may have increased many women's sense of control of their lives. Such active resistance may be critical to maintaining a sense of well-being and self-esteem. For unless women feel safer in proportion to increased actual safety, the full potential of an effective rape prevention program will not have been reached.

8. Consider New Situation-Centered Policies

Situation-centered policies concern activities or strategies which could be enacted by social institutions such as police or neighborhood groups to prevent an attack from occurring.

Many of the women we interviewed indicated that improved lighting in streets, alleys, and parks and/or more police on the streets would help to prevent rape, or at least make them feel less frightened.

In a report about the relationship of architecture to crime, one researcher noted that many crimes take place in "undefended" space.[21] Designing buildings, especially apartment buildings, with as little as possible of this "undefended" space would seem to be a useful strategy. Of particular relevance may be the location of women's rest rooms in public establishments such as hotels and restaurants. Many public buildings are required by law to have rest rooms that can be used by customers and noncustomers alike. One professional woman, Jill, observed that most women's rest rooms are located near entrances from the street, and that simply moving them to more central spots where perpetrators are more likely to be noticed would reduce the incidence of rape. The day after Jill made this observation, notices appeared in a large hotel in Detroit warning women not to go to hotel rest rooms alone. Two women had been raped in the public rest rooms near the outside doors of the hotel.

9. Encourage Nonrestrictive Individual Tactics

Until there is widespread institutional responsibility for female fear, women will—and probably should—continue to take a range of self-protective measures.

One tactic that seems to promote a sense of competence and control among women is enhancing one's physical ability. There are at least four reasons why this is important. First, women who feel physically competent report less fear.[22] Second, women who are less fearful use fewer restrictive precautions, thus limiting their lives less.[23] Third, women who feel more physically competent are more likely to resist a rapist, if attacked, and more likely to avoid being raped.[24] Finally, believing that there is something they can do to prevent future rapes may make it easier for women to cope with the effects of rape.[25] These positive results suggest that we should begin training girls while they are young to feel strong, swift, and physically competent.

A second tactic useful to many women is to simply learn more about rape, going beyond the myths and stereotypes pervasive in the United States. Women can take steps to learn the facts, especially as they pertain to their own communities, including what services are available for victims, and where they are located.

The freedom to walk safely through city streets should be a right enjoyed by every citizen in this country. This freedom is denied to too many women through the use of self-imposed restrictions. The threat of rape limits women's opportunities to be active participants in public life. It is destructive to the social fabric of our nation. We believe most Americans want to live in a society in which women and men are united against rapists, a society in which men will not want to rape, or think women want to be raped. Until the full weight of social institutions can be brought to bear against the conditions that cause rape, the burden of fear and its consequences will fall disproportionately on women and, among women, on those with the fewest resources for coping with it. Until collective action wipes out violence against women, widespread female fear will continue to be the legacy of rape in the United States.

Afterword

Susan, the thirty-three-year-old minister from Chicago who was raped while five of her colleagues were tied up in her living room, was able to share the story of her ordeal with friends. They learned a great deal about rape, as well as being a great comfort to Susan.

About a year after the rape, Susan gathered her friends for a rite of passage—a ritual marking an end to her year of anxiety, mourning, grief, and anger. She began the ceremony by playing music which portrayed the revival of the human spirit after tragedy and pain. After the music stopped, Susan explained to the ten women and two men gathered there that each had been for her like the water in the song—rushing again, persistent, comforting, and faithful. She said it had been a difficult year, but that she felt at the end of it like a *survivor,* not a *victim.* She told how she remembered each person with respect to her rape and its consequences during the year. Then Susan invited the participants to share their own thoughts about her experience, or about sexual assault and violence more generally.

One friend spoke of her sense of anger and injustice upon hearing of Susan's rape, and of wishing only evil for the unapprehended rapist. Another said she believed that Susan had suffered for *her,* and that if she were now to be raped herself she knew she would be able to survive since Susan had taught her how, and had led her through the suffering. Another, a black man, told how he had prayed on hearing of the rape, "Oh, God, don't let him be black!" Another guest said Susan's experience had caused her to further question the existence of God: "At the very least, God must have been on vacation," she said. Another said that the irrationality and clearly unprovoked nature of Susan's rape caused her to feel even more determined to attack the causes—which she believes are the generally high tolerance of violence in the United States, the inequitable distribution of wealth in our society, and sexual child abuse.

After a few moments of silence, a woman who had until then remained silent read a poem from a book called *Women in Transition*. She noted that each guest had been asked to bring to the gathering symbols of hope and healing, and that now was the appropriate time to discuss them. She then presented Susan with a small glass filled with apricot tea and said that it symbolized the times she and Susan had shared a cup of warm and comforting tea, and the similar, healing times she had shared with other women. Another woman gave Susan a plate of brownies she had made that afternoon, and said she wanted to *give* Susan something, and it was all she could think of at the time.

Susan's new roommate said she thought it was a sign of hope and healing that the two of them could laugh about encounters with men they were dating, and especially about Susan's newly re-emerging sexuality. Another friend brought three symbols: a note of love and healing that Susan had written to her, a daisy to accompany a poem, and a brass bracelet she'd been wearing for the year since Susan's rape and wanted her to have. Still another read a passage from *Color Me Purple* that was especially meaningful to her, and then gave Susan her well-worn and marked-up copy of the book.

Another woman, a minister, read a message of hope from a collection of religious passages and then gave Susan the booklet.

One of the two men present, also a minister, brought bread and wine to the center of the room and consecrated them for Communion. When he had finished, he passed the bread, and asked Susan to offer the wine to each. As she did so, she said softly, "The cup of healing." When each person had been served, the group stood with arms encircled and sang "Amazing Grace." At the conclusion of the hymn, those who wished offered prayers for Susan's future, and expressed determination to work toward the elimination of rape from our society.

About two years after her rape, Susan took a position as pastor of two small rural churches about eighty miles from Chicago. She had to live alone in a relatively isolated area, and initially she often felt very uncomfortable and sometimes afraid. She dreaded the second anniversary of the rape, and made sure she spent it with some of her new (and unknowing) acquaintances. She survived it, but realized that her life would never be the same. The third anniversary was a bit easier, and the fourth easier still. Early in 1988, Susan got married.

Susan's willingness to share her ordeal brought comfort from her friends, and perhaps speeded the healing process.

It has also permanently changed the lives of those friends. Most of them had not before known a rape victim, and they understood, for the first time, the depth of the devastation wrought by the crime. They saw how important it was to express their caring to Susan and to one another. They shared Susan's pain, and learned that Susan's rape and its aftermath were not just Susan's problems, but also theirs. They saw that rape is not only a problem for victims, but for our entire society.

Appendix A: In-person Interview Schedule

APPENDIX A

IN-PERSON INTERVIEW SCHEDULE
FEAR OF RAPE PROJECT

© CENTER FOR URBAN AFFAIRS AND POLICY RESEARCH
NORTHWESTERN UNIVERSITY

Hello, I am _____ from Northwestern University.   I talked to you earlier to set up this appointment.

Participation in this interview is strictly voluntary on your part. No one will be able to link your name to anything you say. I want to assure you that you can end the interview at any time, or refuse to answer any of the questions. You will be paid $10 for your time.

Before we get started, I'd like you to read this consent form and ask me any questions you have.

[IF NECESSARY, MOVE TO ANOTHER ROOM TO ASSURE PRIVACY]

[ASK EACH RESPONDENT TO SIGN CONSENT FORM AND PAY (HER/HIM) $10]

CARD 1

I.D. #: [   ] [   ] [   ] [   ] [   ] [   ]   1-6/

INTERVIEWER #:   [   ] [   ]   7-8/

NEIGHBORHOOD:

PHILADELPHIA	West Philly...11	9-10/
	South Philly..12	
CHICAGO	Lincoln Park...21	
	Wicker Park...22	
SAN FRANCISCO	Sunset...31	
	Visitacion Valley...32	

Time: [   ] [   ] [   ] [   ]   11-14/

A.M...........1

P.M...........2   15/

NORTHWESTERN UNIVERSITY
CENTER FOR URBAN AFFAIRS AND POLICY RESEARCH

CONSENT FORM

I consent to participate in the study described to me by the interviewer. I am at least 18 years old, and I give this consent freely.

The research project and my participation in it have been explained to me. I have had an opportunity to ask questions.

I understand that at any time during the course of the interview I am free to refuse to answer any of the questions. I also understand that no one outside the project staff will be able to link my name to anything I say; that is, my identity will be fully protected. I consent to participate in this study.

I understand that the information from this interview must be very accurate in order to be useful. This means that I must do my best to give accurate and complete answers.

I have received $10.00 for my participation.

Signature: _____

Interviewer: _____

Date: _____

Time: _____

(This form will be retained by the investigators and filed separately from the interview forms.)

[INTRODUCTION]

As you know, we are talking to people about how crime affects their lives, especially their day-to-day lives in their communities.

[WOMEN ONLY]

We are particularly concerned about crimes against women, and how women protect themselves from harm.

---

1. First, how long have you lived in your neighborhood?

    [INTERVIEWER: CODE MONTHS LATER]   # Months [   ] [   ] [   ] [   ]   16-19/

    Months: _____

    Years: _____ **[MULTIPLY BY 12]**

    All my life **[PROBE FOR YEARS]**.....................................9998

---

2. A lot of the questions I will ask you have to do with your neighborhood, so we need to understand what area you think of as your neighborhood.

    When you think of your neighborhood, what streets form the boundaries for you? How far away is each one?

    [ROUND UP TO NEAREST WHOLE BLOCK]

    1st Street   _____   # Blocks: [   ] [   ] 20-21/

    2nd Street   _____   # Blocks: [   ] [   ] 22-23/

    3rd Street   _____   # Blocks: [   ] [   ] 24-25/

    4th Street   _____   # Blocks: [   ] [   ] 26-27/

---

3. *In general,* is it pretty easy for you to tell a stranger in your neighborhood from someone who lives there, or is it difficult to recognize a stranger?

    > Easy or pretty easy 1
    > Difficult or pretty difficult 2   28/
    > DK...8

---

4.   What if a man you didn't know approached you on the street some day in your neighborhood and asked for directions? Would you talk to him and give him directions, or would you avoid him?

           Talk to him, give directions............................1
           Give him directions, but not
                converse [VOLUNTEERED]..........................2   29/
           Avoid him..3
           ....Depends
     [SPECIFY]_____4
           DK [VOLUNTEERED]..8

---

5.   What about when you are at home alone? If a man you didn't know asked to come into your home to use the telephone, would you let him or would you refuse?

           Yes, let him...1
           I'd offer to make the call, but leave
                him outside the door [VOLUNTEERED] 2   30/
           No, refuse...3
           Depends [SPECIFY]_____4
           DK [VOLUNTEERED]..8

---

6.   Now think about problems in your neighborhood. By neighborhood in this question, we mean the 5 or 6 blocks around your home. What do you think is the most serious problem in your neighborhood at this time?

     [IF MORE THAN ONE MENTION] "I see. Of those mentioned, which *one* do you think is the most serious?"

     [NO MENTIONS] "Perhaps if I ask the question again you might think of some things."
     [IF ANY MENTIONS] "O.K., thanks. This is the kind of information we want."

     [RECORD VERBATIM]   _____

     [INTERVIEWER CODE]

           Crime-related...1   31/
           Not crime-related 2

---

7.   Think about safety here. In general, would you say that for you, your neighborhood is very safe, reasonably safe, somewhat *un*safe, very *un*safe.

           Very safe..1
           Reasonably safe 2   32/
           Somewhat *un*safe...3
           Very *un*safe..4

8. Would you say that since you've first lived here, your neighborhood is...
    [READ FIRST 3 CATEGORIES]

    Not as safe as it used to be...........................1
    About the same as always, or.......................2   33/
    Safer than it used to be? 3
    DK [VOLUNTEERED]..8

---

9. What about after dark? How safe do you feel when you are out alone in your
    neighborhood after dark? [PROBE: READ FIRST 4 CATEGORIES]

    Very safe [GO TO Q.11]................................1
    Reasonably safe [ASK A].............................2   34/
    Somewhat *un*safe [ASK A]..........................3
    Very *un*safe [ASK A] 4
    Never goes out
        after dark [VOLUNTEERED] [ASK A].........5
    DK [VOLUNTEERED]..8

    A. What would make you feel safer after dark? _____

---

10. Is fear for your own safety something that you think about... [READ FIRST 4 CATEGORIES]

    All or most of the time,.................................1
    Fairly often,..2   35/
    Seldom, or..3
    Never? 4
    DK [VOLUNTEERED]..8
    NA..9

---

11. If you were attacked on the street at night in your neighborhood and screamed or used a
    whistle, what do you think the neighbors would do?
    [PROBE: READ FIRST 4 CATEGORIES]

    Nothing 1
    Call the police..2   36/
    Shout, try to scare off the
        attacker, but stay inside 3
    Come outside, try to help.............................4
    "Depends", or other [SPECIFY] _____5
    DK [VOLUNTEERED]..8

    A. What makes you think that? _____

12. [DO NOT ASK IF KNOWN] By the way, do you live in an apartment or a house?

> Apartment [ASK A] 1
> Duplex [GO TO Q.13] 2   37/
> House [GO TO Q.13] 3

A. [IF APARTMENT] Hi-rise or lo-rise?

> Hi-rise (More than 5 stories) 1
> Lo-rise (1-5 stories) 2   38/

   1) Do you live on the 1st floor or higher up?

> 1st floor (including ground floor) 1   39/
> Higher up 2

---

13. How many people live in your household altogether including you?
   [IF MORE THAN ONE, ASK A]
   [IF ONLY ONE, ASK B]   Code #   [   ] [   ]   40-41/

A. [IF MORE THAN ONE] Who else lives here? I don't need names, just their
    relationship to you. [CIRCLE ALL MENTIONED]

> Husband/boyfriend/male companion?
> Yes 1   42/
> No 2

> Parents?
> Yes 1   43/
> No 2

> Other adults?
> Yes 1   44/
> No 2

> Children?
> Yes 1   45/
> No 2

B. Do you have any children living elsewhere?

> Yes [ASK C & D] 1   46/
> No   [IF NO, BUT HAS CHILDREN
>   AT HOME, ASK C]
>   [IF NO, BUT LIVES WITH
>   OTHER ADULTS, ASK E]
>   [IF NO, AND LIVES ALONE,
>   GO TO Q.16] 2

C.   [IF HAS CHILDREN AT HOME OR ELSEWHERE] Do you have any daughters?

           Yes...1   47/
           No [ASK D]..2

D.   [IF HAS CHILDREN AT HOME OR ELSEWHERE] Do you have any sons?

           Yes...1   48/
           No 2

E.   [IF LIVES WITH OTHERS] Do you fear for the safety of others who live at home with you?

           Yes [ASK E1]..1   49/
           No 2
           NA..9

    1) For your (daughters, sons, husband/boyfriend, parents)?

       Daughters?
           Yes...1   50/
           No 2

       Sons?
           Yes...1   51/
           No 2

       Husband/boyfriend?
           Yes...1   52/
           No 2

       Parents?
           Yes...1   53/
           No 2

---

14. [IF HAS DAUGHTERS] What warnings about safety (do/did) you give your girl(s)?
     [PROBE: "What sorts of things did you tell your daughters to keep (her/them) safe?"]

           NA...99   54-55/

_____

What else? _____

---

15. [IF HAS SONS] What warnings about safety (do/did) you give your son(s)?
     [PROBE: "What sorts of things did you tell your sons to keep (him/them) safe?"]

           NA...99   56-57/

What else? _____

_____

16. Suppose there was a campaign to wipe out crime in your neighborhood. Of the crimes listed on this card [HAND CARD], which one do you think should be given the highest priority?

	Code #	[ ] [ ]	58-59/
	Code #	[ ] [ ]	60-61/

   A. Which should be given the next highest priority?

   01. Drug abuse
   02. Breaking & entering houses
   03. Robberies & hold-ups
   04. Juvenile delinquency
   05. Mugging, assaults on the street
   06. Theft
   07. Murder
   08. Rape & sexual assault
   09. Arson
   10. Vandalism
   11. Child abuse & neglect
   12. Sexual child abuse
   13. Other [SPECIFY] _____

   B. Why do you rank [HIGHEST CRIME MENTIONED] above the others?

   _____

   C. What have you read or heard about [HIGHEST CRIME MENTIONED] in the past couple of weeks?

   _____

_____

17. Now, I want to know what you think the chances are that some crimes will happen to you in your neighborhood. [PROMPT: "You answered some questions like this one on the telephone interview."] Here's a card with a row of numbers from zero to ten. [HAND CARD] Let "0" stand for "NOT AT ALL" and "10" stand for "VERY LIKELY TO HAPPEN SOMETIME." If it has *actually* happened to you in your neighborhood, tell me and I'll mark that down. Then, tell me what you think the chances are that it would happen *again* here.

[SHOW CARD: POINT OUT 0, 10, AND 5]

	"Has Happened?" Yes No		
A. What do you think the chances are that someone would try to break into your home during the *daytime* when you are away?	1 2	[ ] [ ]	62/ 63-64/
B. What about at *night* when you're not there? What do you think the chances are that someone would try to break in then?	1 2	[ ] [ ]	65/ 66-67/
C. What about at night when you *are* there?	1 2	[ ] [ ]	68/ 69-70/

How likely do you think it is that:

D. Someone will try to rob you, snatch
your purse or pick your pocket in the
streets in your neighborhood at night?   1   2   [ ] [ ] 71/ 72-73/

E. [FOR FEMALE RESPONDENT, use "you"]
[FOR MALE RESPONDENT, use "a woman"]
What do you think the chances are that
someone would try to rape [YOU/
A WOMAN] in your neighborhood at night?   1   2   [ ] [ ] 74/ 75-76/

F. Do you think [YOUR/A WOMAN'S] chances
of being raped here are higher, about
the same, or lower than the chances of
being raped downtown in the city?

Higher 1
About the same 2   77/
Lower 3
                                                                          SKIP 78-79
                                                                               80/1
                                                                          CARD 2 DUP 1-6

G. What rank on the 0-10 scale would you
give the likelihood of [YOU/A WOMAN]
being raped when downtown at night?   1   2   [ ] [ ] 7/ 8-9/

---

18. ASK ONLY IF HAS CHILDREN *LIVING AT HOME* (SEE Q.13A(4))
    [IF 0 CHILDREN, CODE 99 IN BOXES.]

    How likely do you think it is that: "Has Happened?"
                                                            Yes   No

    A. Someone would try to harm your
    (child/ren) while (he is/she is/they are)
    in the streets around your neighborhood
    in the daytime?   1   2   [ ] [ ] 10/ 11-12/

    B. Someone would try to harm your (child/ren)   1   2   [ ] [ ] 13/ 14-15/
    while at or near school?

    C. Someone would try to sexually assault,
    molest, or rape your (child/ren) in the street
    around your neighborhood in the daytime?   1   2   [ ] [ ] 16/ 17-18/

---

19. Is there one certain *place* in your neighborhood that you consider especially
    dangerous? That is, where you are likely to be robbed or harmed in some way?
    [IF MENTIONS MORE THAN ONE, ASK ABOUT THE *MOST DANGEROUS*]

    Yes [ASK A-G]...1   19/
    No [GO TO Q.20]....................................2
    DK...8

A.   Where is that place? _____

B.   About how many blocks from your home is it?   # Blocks   [   ] [   ]   20-21/
     [PROBE: "Just a guess will do."]

C.   [OMIT IF KNOWN] What *type* of place is it, like a park, or alley or train station?

                              [INTERVIEWER, CODE LATER]   [   ] [   ]   22-23/

01. School or school yard	14. Public housing project
02. Church	15. Hi-rise residential (not a project)
03. Home	16. Sports facility
04. Street or alley	17. Bank
05. Outdoors, fields	18. Hotel/motel
06. Park(s)	19. Retirement home
07. Factory, warehouse	20. Gas station
08. Store, restaurant	21. Theater
09. Government building,	22. Museum
office building	23. Train station
10. Bus, car, truck	24. Subway station/platform
11. Prison or other	25. Other [SPECIFY] _____
correctional facility	
12. Tavern/bar	
13. Shopping center	

D.   What makes that [PLACE] dangerous? _____

[INTERVIEWER, CODE LATER]	1st mention	2nd mention		
Kids hanging out	01	01		
Drugs, addicts	02	02	24-25/	26-27/
Drunks, bums	03	03		
Fences/bushes where people could hide	04	04		
Darkness	05	05		
Deserted area	06	06		
Crimes happen there [CODE BELOW]	07	07		
Proximity to certain groups,				
[SPECIFY] _____	08	08		
Other [SPECIFY] _____	09	09		
Not ascertained	99	99		

E.   And what kinds of crimes do you think are likely to happen at [PLACE]?

_____

[INTERVIEWER, CODE LATER]	1st mention	2nd mention		
Drugs [ANYTHING INVOLVING]	01	01		
Breaking & entering houses	02	02	28-29/	30-31/
Robberies & hold-ups				
[VICTIM IS PRESENT]	03	03		
Attacked, mugged, beaten up	04	04		
Delinquency among youth/				
neighbborhood gangs, toughs	05	05		
Theft [VICTIM ELSEWHERE]	06	06		
Murder	07	07		
Rape & sexual assault	08	08		
Arson	09	09		
Vandalism	10	10		
Child abuse & neglect	11	11		
Sexual child abuse	12	12		
Other [SPECIFY] _____	13	13		
Not ascertained	99	99		

F. If you have to go through the area where [PLACE] is, do you do anything special to protect yourself?

                Yes [ASK F(1)] 1   32/
                No [ASK G]..2
                Avoid area [VOLUNTEERED, ASK G] 3
                Other [SPECIFY] _____4
                Not ascertained...9

  1) What do you do?

                Walk quickly 1
                Bring an escort 2   33/
                Drive..3
                Carry a weapon..4
                Keep alert..5
                Pray 6
                Stay on lit streets, walk in
                     the middle of the street............................7
                Other [SPECIFY] _____8
                Not Ascertained...9

G. Did you learn that [PLACE] is a dangerous area from your own experience, because someone   told you, or in some other way?

                Own experience, way area looks
                and other [SPECIFY] _____01

[IF "SOMEONE TOLD ME" ASK: "Who was that?"]
[PROBE: READ CATEGORIES; CODE FIRST MENTIONED]

Victim [ASK G1]...02   34-35/
Friend from neighborhood [ASK G1] 03
Friend [ASK G1]..04
Relative [ASK G1]...05
Co-worker [ASK G1]..06
Police [ASK G1]...07
Shopkeeper [ASK G1]..08
Other person [SPECIFY & ASK G1] _____09

[IF "SOME OTHER WAY" ASK: "How was that?"] [READ]

TV/Radio..10
Newspaper...11
Something else? [SPECIFY] _____12
Not ascertained...99

1) [IF "SOMEONE TOLD ME"] As far as you know, (does that/do those) person(s)
                              usually pay more attention to crime news
than you do?

Yes...1   36/
No 2
DK..8

---

20. Do you regularly go into some other neighborhood in this city?

Yes [ASK A-C]..1   37/
No [GO TO Q.21]...2

A. [IF YES] What neighborhood is that? [NAME] _____
    [IF MORE THAN ONE, USE ONE MOST FREQUENTLY GOES TO]

    How far away is it? # Blocks _____ Miles _____   [   ] [   ] 38-39/

[INTERVIEWER, CODE MILES. ASSUME 8 (CHICAGO), 10 (PHILADELPHIA) OR 10 (SAN
FRANCISCO) BLOCKS TO ONE MILE. ROUND TO NEAREST WHOLE MILE]

B. Do you usually go there in the daytime or at night?

    Daytime..1   40/
    Nighttime 2
    Both 3

C. Do you generally feel less safe there, about as safe, or more safe there than in your
    own neighborhood?

    Less safe 1   41/
    About as safe..2
    More safe..3

21. Do you ever feel afraid that someone might deliberately harm you?

    Yes [ASK A]...1   42/
    No 2

    A.   What kinds of situations make you feel that way most often?

    _____

    _____

22. Now I am going to read a list of situations, and I would like you to tell me how worried or uneasy you feel in each one *after dark*. Tell me the amount of worry or uneasiness in each situation. We are going to use the card again that we had before. This time, "0" means "NO WORRY AT ALL" and "10" means "VERY WORRIED OR EXTREMELY UNEASY." The middle means "SOMEWHAT WORRIED."

    [IF REPLY IS "I DON'T DO IT," CODE 99 IN "HOW WORRIED" COLUMN AND "NEVER" IN FREQUENCY COLUMNS]

	More than once a week	More than once a month	Once a month	More than once a year	Never	
How worried?						
A. How worried, or uneasy do you feel after dark on this scale from 0 to 10 when you are at home alone? [ ] [ ]						43-44/
1) How often are you at home alone after dark?	1	2	3	4	5	45/
B. How worried or uneasy do you feel walking alone on the streets in your neighborhood after dark? [ ] [ ]						46-47/
1) How often do you do this after dark?	1	2	3	4	5	48/

	More than once a week	More than once a month	Once a month	More than once a year	Never	
C. How worried do you feel using public transportation alone after dark? [ ] [ ]						49-50/
1) How often do you do this after dark?	1	2	3	4	5	51/
D. How worried do you feel being downtown alone after dark? [ ] [ ]						52-53/
1) How often do you do this after dark?	1	2	3	4	5	54/
E. How worried are you walking by vacant lots or parks anywhere in the city after dark? [ ] [ ]						55-56/
1) How often do you do this after dark?	1	2	3	4	5	57/
F. How worried or uneasy are you walking past hang-outs, bars, poolrooms after dark? [ ] [ ]						58-59/
1) How often do you do this after dark?	1	2	3	4	5	60/
G. How about when walking by groups of young men or boys after dark? [ ] [ ]						61-62/
1) How often do you do this after dark?	1	2	3	4	5	63/
H. How worried are you when accepting rides from men you don't know after dark? [ ] [ ]						64-65/
1) How often do you do this after dark?	1	2	3	4	5	66/

	More than once a week	More than once a month	Once a month	More than once a year	Never	
I. How worried are you when going to movies, plays, or other entertainment alone after dark? [ ] [ ]						67-68/
1) How often do you do this after dark?	1	2	3	4	5	69/
J. How worried or uneasy do you feel going to social bars or clubs alone after dark? [ ] [ ]						70-71/
1) How often do you do this after dark?	1	2	3	4	5	72/
K. How uneasy or worried are you when giving rides to strangers after dark? [ ] [ ]						73-74/
1) How often do you do this after dark?	1	2	3	4	5	75/
L. How uneasy are you when going to laundromats or laundry rooms alone after dark? [ ] [ ]						76-77/
1) How often do you do this after dark?	1	2	3	4	5	78/

SKIP 79
80/2
CARD 3   DUP 1-6

23. Do you think that you would be able to defend yourself effectively against an attacker?

Yes [ASK A]...1
No [ASK B]...2   7/
Depends [SPECIFY] _____3

A. What would you do? _____

B. [IF NO] Please tell me why not? _____

---

24. Now I'd like to know how physically strong you think you are. Do you see yourself as stronger, equally as strong, or weaker than the average *woman*?

Stronger..1
Equally as strong 2   8/
Weaker..3

---

25. And compared to the average *man*, do you think you are physically stronger, equally as strong, or weaker than the average man?

Stronger..1
Equally as strong 2   9/
Weaker..3

---

26. What about speed? Would you say you can run faster than the average *woman*, about as fast, or not as fast?

Faster 1
About as fast 2   10/
Not as fast..3

---

27. Would you say you can run faster than the average man, about as fast, or not as fast?

Faster 1
About as fast 2   11/
Not as fast..3

---

28. [WOMEN ONLY]

If you were sexually assaulted, how likely do you think you would be to fight back?
[READ FIRST 3 CATEGORIES]

Very likely [ASK A] 1
Somewhat likely, or [ASK A].......................2   12/
Not at all likely? [ASK B] 3
Depends ["on what"] _____4
NA..9

A. Why would you fight back? _____

B. Why wouldn't you fight back? _____

---

29. Sometimes when people live in the city they have ways of trying to prevent uncomfortable situations from happening. There are certain things they do to avoid unpleasant or dangerous situations. I would like you to tell me what things *you* do to avoid dangerous situations.

_____

_____

[PROBE] What other things do you do? _____

_____

---

30. Other than what you just told me you do to keep yourself safe generally, are there any things you do specifically to protect yourself from sexual assault?

Yes [ASK A-B]..1
No [GO TO Q.32] 2   13/

[PROBE FULLY]

B. Where did you get the idea to do (that thing/those things)? From something you saw or read, talking with your friends, or what?

[IF SOMETHING YOU READ] "Was that a..." [READ]

Book, ...01
Magazine,...02   14-15/
Newspaper, or...03
Something else? [SPECIFY] _____04

[IF SOMETHING YOU HEARD] "Was that from..." [READ]

TV,..05
Movie,..06   14-15/
Radio, ...07
Talking with friends,.....................................08
or were you told by authorities
    (police, etc.)? 09
Something else? [SPECIFY] _____10

---

31. [OMITTED]

32. I'm going to read list of things that some people do to protect themselves. Other people don't do any of them. I'd like you to tell me for each one whether or not you have done that since you've lived in your present home.

		Yes	No	NA	
A.	Did you get an unlisted phone number?	1	2	9	16/
B.	Do you use initials instead of first name on the mailbox or would you if you lived alone?	1	2	9	17/
C.	Did you install or make sure there were special locks or bars on the doors?	1	2	9	18/
D.	Did you install or make sure there were special locks or bars on the *windows*?	1	2	9	19/
E.	Did you install or make sure there were bright lights outside the house?	1	2	9	20/
F.	Did you install or make sure there was a burglar alarm?	1	2	9	21/
G.	Do you have a dog for protection?	1	2	9	22/
H.	Do you own a gun for protection?	1	2	9	23/
I.	Did you ever take a self-defense class?	1	2	9	24/

Now, a couple of other things about safety...

		Yes	No	NA	
J.	Have you ever moved because of fear for your safety?	1	2	9	25/
K.	Did you ask the police or otherwise inquire about the safety of your neighborhood before moving in?	1	2	9	26/
L.	Have you ever thought about moving to a place with a guard or doorman at the front entrance because of fear for your safety?	1	2	9	27/
M.	Have you considered the safety of the neighborhood where you would be working when you have thought about taking a job?	1	2	9	28/

33. Some people report that they do certain things, or act in certain ways, in order to increase their safety. We have written those things on the cards I have here, and I would like to know how often you do any of these things. I'd like you to sort the cards into 4 piles or categories. Pile 1, over here, has things that you do *all or most of the time*. Pile 2, over here, has things that you do *fairly often*; Pile 3 here has things that you *seldom* do, and Pile 4 has things that you *never* do.

[INTERVIEWER PLACE CAPTION CARDS FACING RESPONDENT] I can read the cards to you, or you can read them yourself, whichever you prefer. [HAND CARD 1-24 IF RESPONDENT IS TO READ THEM]

Pile 1 Things You Do All or Most of the Time	Pile 2 Things You Do Fairly Often	Pile 3 Things You Seldom Do	Pile 4 Things You Never Do

[IF NECESSARY] "Now, I'll read each card to you; then you put it in the right pile for you." [CODE PILE # LATER]

A. First, think about when you are at home:

01) How often do you turn the lock closed on the outside doors when you are home alone during the day: all or most of the time, fairly often, seldom, or never? [RESPONDENT TO PLACE CARD IN APPROPRIATE PILE]　　[　]　　29/

02) How often do you lock the doors when home alone at night?　　[　]　　30/

03) When someone comes to your door, how often do you check to see who is there before opening it? [PROBE: "Use a peephole or intercom?"]　　[　]　　31/

04) When a salesman or repairman comes to your home, how often do you ask for identification before opening the door?　　[　]　　32/

B. Now, when you are out of your home:

05) When no one will be home for several hours, how often do you deliberately leave on lights or a radio?　　[　]　　33/

06) When no one will be home for several days, how often do you ask a neighbor to watch it, or bring in the mail, papers, and so on?　　[　]　　34/

07) When you go to a movie or ride on a bus, how often do you choose a seat with an eye to who would be sitting nearby?　　[　]　　35/

08) When you go to a movie or ride on a bus, how often do you change seats when someone nearby seems strange?　　[　]　　36/

09) When you walk down the street, how often do you avoid looking at people you don't know in the eye?   [   ]   37/

10) How often do you go out with a friend or two as protection?   [   ]   38/

11) When you are out at night, how often do you avoid using alleys or streets that are not well-lit?   [   ]   39/

12) When you are out alone, how often do you try not to dress in a provocative or sexy manner?   [   ]   40/

13) How often do you try to wear shoes that are easy to run in, in case of danger?   [   ]   41/

14) When out alone, how often do you take something along for protection like a dog or whistle?   [   ]   42/

15) When out alone, how often do you take a gun for protection?   [   ]   43/

16) How often do you restrict your going out to only during the daytime?   [   ]   44/

17) How often do you stay out of parts of town you think are dangerous?   [   ]   45/

18) When you make plans to go out at night, how often do you try to avoid going downtown?   [   ]   46/

19) How often do you get your house keys out so they are in your hand before reaching your door?   [   ]   47/

20) How often do you avoid doing shopping, errands, laundry, or other things you have to do because of fear for your safety?   [   ]   48/

21) How often do you not do things you *want* to do, but don't *have* to do -- like visiting somebody or going to the movies -- because of fear for your safety?   [   ]   49/

22) When you go out, how often do you drive or take a taxi, rather than walk, because of fear of being harmed?   [   ]   50/

23) When you are out walking on the street, how often do you make a point of being alert and watchful?   [   ]   51/

24) When you see someone on the street who seems strange or dangerous, how often do you cross the street?   [   ]   52/

34. Do you own or drive a car?

> Yes [ASK C; HAND CARDS 25-29] 1
> No [GO TO Q.35; LATER CODE 9 IN
>   BOXES FOR Q.25-29] 2   53/

C. When you are in a car:

25) How often do you lock the doors?   [   ]   54/

26) When you are in a car and looking for parking places
at night, how often do you think about safety, for
example by avoiding parking in deserted places?   [   ]   55/

27) How often do you carry keys in your hand when
going to the car, instead of waiting to get the keys
out after reaching the car?   [   ]   56/

28) When returning to your parked car, how often do you
check the back seat for intruders before getting
in the car?   [   ]   57/

29) How often do you lock the car when it is parked?   [   ]   58/

[INTERVIEWER: PUT RUBBER BANDS AROUND "OFTEN," "SELDOM," AND "NEVER" PILES WITH CAPTION CARDS ON TOP OF EACH PILE]

Now, take the pile of "Things You Do All or Most of Time." Please tell me which two are the most important for keeping you safe? Which is most important and which is second?

A. Most important   [   ] [   ]   59-60/

B. 2nd most important   [   ] [   ]   61-62/

---

36. Now, I would like to ask you some questions about the problem of sexual assault, or rape, in your neighborhood. By rape, we mean any type of unwanted sexual intercourse. As far as you know, is rape a big problem, something of a problem, or not much of a problem in your neighborhood?

> Big problem 1
> Something of a problem 2   63/
> Not much of a problem 3
> DK [VOLUNTEERED] 8

---

37. During the last year has the problem of rape in your neighborhood increased, stayed the same, or decreased? [PROBE: "Since you've lived here..."]

        Increased..1
        Stayed the same...2   64/
        Decreased..3
        DK [VOLUNTEERED]......................................8

---

38. People have different ideas about what rape is like. Please try to describe what you think of or imagine to be the "typical rape." I mean things like when or where it usually happens, characteristics of the rapist and the victim, whether or not the rapist and his victim know each other, whether or not the victim gets hurt, police behavior where the victims gets help, attractiveness of the victim, and so on.

        Describes rape..1
        [REFUSES: GO TO Q.39]..............................2   65/

[RECORD VERBATIM; *PROBE FULLY* FOR COMPLETE ANSWER]

_____

_____

39. Do you personally know of anyone who has been raped or sexually assaulted?

        Yes [ASK A]..1
        No [GO TO Q.40]...2   66/

  A.   [IF MORE THAN ONE, CIRCLE 1 IN BOX AND SAY: "Let's talk about the one that made the biggest impression on you."]   Did this happen to you, or to someone else?

                                                            [1]   67/
        Respondent [GO TO Q.41]...........................1
        Someone else [ASK B]...................................2   68/
        Both [GO TO Q.41]..3

  B.   [IF SOMEONE ELSE] How did you learn of it?

        From the victim [GO TO Q.41]......................1
        From someone else [GO TO Q.41].............2   69/
        Media [GO TO Q.41]......................................3
        Other [SPECIFY] _____4

---

40. What about incidents that you know about either because you personally heard about them, or read about them in the papers, or heard about them on TV? Do you remember any reports of rapes or sexual assaults?

        Yes [ASK A]..1
        No [GO TO Q.59]...2   70/
        Not applicable 9

A. [IF YES] How did you first learn of it?
[IF MORE THAN ONE "Let's talk about the one that made the biggest impression on you."]

Newspaper..1
TV..2   71/
Radio...3
Other media 4
From someone else...5
Other [SPECIFY]_____6

SKIP 72-79
80/3
CARD 4 DUP 1-6

41. Please tell me everything that you remember about the incident [RECORD VERBATIM. IF MORE THAN ONE STORY, CIRCLE BOX AND READ: "Let's talk about the one that made the biggest impression on you." [*PROBE FULLY* FOR COMPLETE ANSWERS.]

_____

_____

It's important to get that down in your own words. Now let me check to make sure I have all the information I need about the incident.

[INTERVIEWER, ASK Q.41-Q.59. MAY REWORD, E.G., "You said the attack was six months ago, right?"]

B. How long ago did the attack occur? [PROBE: USE CATEGORIES]

Within the past six months............................1
7 months-1 year...2   8/
More than 1 year-5 years 3
More than 5-10 years.....................................4
More than 10 years...5
DK [VOLUNTEERED]...8
NA..9

42. Did it happen in your neighborhood, elsewhere in this city, or somewhere else?

In your neighborhood......................................1
Elsewhere in this city.....................................2   9/
Somewhere else..3
DK [VOLUNTEERED]..8

43. Where (were you/was the victim) when the attack took place?

       Inside or near own home..............................1
       Other's home 2   10/
       Inside hotel/motel......................................3
       Inside business/school 4
       Outside on the street/public area...............5
       Car/enclosed vehicle 6
       Bar/party 7
       Other [SPECIFY]_____8
       DK [VOLUNTEERED].......................................9

44. How did (you/the victim) react when the attack occurred? [CODE ALL MENTIONED]

       A. No resistance 1   11/
       B. Flight/attempted flight............................2   12/
       C. Verbal measures: screams, pleas,
           threats...3   13/
       D. Physical measures: fought, bit,
           kicked..4   14/
       E. Resisted with weapon............................5   15/
       F. Other [SPECIFY]_____6   16/
       G. DK [VOLUNTEERED, GO TO Q.46]........8   17/

45. What did the attacker(s) do when (you/the victim) did this?

       Released victim...1
       Continued assault (without weapon) 2   18/
       Continued assault (with weapon
           as before)......................................3
       Continued assault, began to
           use weapon....................................4
       Other people interceded.............................5
       Other [SPECIFY]_____6
       DK [VOLUNTEERED].......................................8
       NA 9

46. [CODE] In this incident, was there one attacker or more than one?

       1 attacker [ASK A]...1
       More than 1 attacker [ASK B].......................2   19/
       DK [GO TO Q.47]..3

    A. [IF ONE ATTACKER] Please describe the attacker. For example...

       1) About how old was he? [PROBE: "Just a guess will do."]

                                 # Years: [ ] [ ]   20-21/
                                   DK.............................98

2) What was his race?

```
White ...................................................................1
Black....................................................................2          22/
Asian ...................................................................3
Other  [SPECIFY]_____4
DK [VOLUNTEERED]......................................8
NA ......................................................................9
```

3) What was his ethnic background? [PROBE: "Like Irish, Puerto Rican or Afro-American or something else?"]

```
Cuban ...............................................................01
Mexican/Chicano...........................................02          23-24/
Puerto Rican ...................................................03
Other Hispanic  [SPECIFY]_____04
Polish ...............................................................05
Italian................................................................06
Other European  [SPECIFY]_____07
Afro-American...................................................08
Asian ................................................................09
Other [SPECIFY] _____10
DK .....................................................................98
```

4) What else about him? _____
                                      [GO TO Q.47]

B. [IF MORE THAN ONE ATTACKER] Pleases describe the attackers. For example...

1) Were they... [READ FIRST 3 CATEGORIES]

```
Young men (say under 30) ..........................1
Middle-aged men, or.....................................2          25/
Both?................................................................3
DK .....................................................................4
NA ......................................................................9
```

2) What race were (they/most of them)?

```
White ...................................................................1
Black....................................................................2          26/
Asian ...................................................................3
Other  [SPECIFY]_____6
DK [VOLUNTEERED]......................................8
NA ......................................................................9
```

3) What was the ethnic background of most of them? [PROBE: "Like Irish, Puerto Rican or Afro-American or something else?"]

Cuban 01
Mexican/Chicano...02   27-28/
Puerto Rican 03
Other Hispanic [SPECIFY]_____04
Polish 05
Italian..06
Other European [SPECIFY]_____07
Afro-American...08
Asian 09
Other [SPECIFY] _____10
DK 98

4) What else about them? _____

---

47. Was the attacker someone (you/the victim) knew or was he a stranger?

Stranger [GO TO Q.48]................................1
Known by sight only [GO TO Q.48]..............2   29/
Casual acquaintance [GO TO Q.48] 3
Well-known [ASK A]......................................4
Other [SPECIFY] _____5
          [GO TO Q. 48]
DK [VOLUNTEERED].......................................8

A. Was he a... [READ FIRST 6 CATEGORIES]

Friend..1
Date...2   30/
Neighbor..3
Husband/boyfriend
       or ex-husband/boyfriend......................4
Another relative, or 5
Someone in authority like
       a boss, teacher, or doctor.....................6
DK [VOLUNTEERED].......................................8
NA 9

---

48. Did the attacker(s) have a weapon, such as a gun or knife, or something used as a weapon, such as a bottle or baseball bat?

Yes [ASK A]..1
No [GO TO Q.49]..2   31/
DK [VOLUNTEERED].......................................8

A. [IF YES]   What was the weapon?

                 Gun mentioned..1
                 Knife mentioned..2   32/
                 Other [SPECIFY] _____3
                 DK [VOLUNTEERED].......................................8

---

49. [ASK ONLY IF OWN RAPE]   Did you think you would be killed?

                 Yes..1
                 No 2   33/
                 NA 9

What made you think that? _____

---

50. [OMITTED]

---

51. Where did (you/the victim) first go or who did (you/she) first telephone for help?

                 Nowhere...01
                 Relative...02   34-35/
                 Neighbor..03
                 Other friend (female) 04
                 Boyfriend/lover/husband 05
                 Other friend (male)..06
                 Police 07
                 Hospital...08
                 Doctor..09
                 Rape crisis center/women's group 10
                 Stranger(s) nearby 11
                 Other [SPECIFY] _____12
                 DK [VOLUNTEERED].......................................98
                 NA 99

---

52. Was the incident reported to the police?

                 Yes [ASK A]...1
                 No [GO TO Q.53]...2   36/
                 DK [VOLUNTEERED].......................................8

A.   [IF YES: "Was the rapist arrested?"]
      [IF MORE THAN ONE RAPIST: "Were any of the rapists arrested?"]

                 Yes [ASK B]...1
                 No [GO TO Q.53]...2   37/
                 DK [VOLUNTEERED].......................................8

B. [IF YES: "Was the rapist convicted?"]
[IF MORE THAN ONE RAPIST: "Were any of the rapists convicted?"]

```
Yes....................................................................1
No ......................................................................2        38/
DK [VOLUNTEERED]......................................8
NA .....................................................................9
```

---

53. [OMIT IF VICTIM DIED]
Aside from the police, did (you/the victim) tell anyone else about this experience?

```
Yes [ASK A]........................................................1
No [GO TO Q.54].................................................2        39/
DK [VOLUNTEERED] [GO TO Q.54]...............8
NA .....................................................................9
```

A. Whom did (you/the victim) tell *first*?

```
Spouse............................................................01
Other relative like parent or child...............02        40-41/
Neighbor
        male..........................................................03
        female.......................................................04
Other friend
        male..........................................................05
        female.......................................................06
Doctor/therapist..............................................07
Rape crisis counselor....................................08
Other authority figure
        (minister, teacher, boss)......................09
Other [SPECIFY] _____10
DK [VOLUNTEERED]......................................98
```

---

54. [IF OWN RAPE, ASK A]

Did the victim die as a result of the attack?

```
Yes [GO TO Q.56B].........................................1
No [ASK A]........................................................2        42/
```

A. What about long-term effects of the rape? Were there any permanent physical
injuries?

```
Yes [ASK B].......................................................1
No .....................................................................2        43/
DK [VOLUNTEERED] .......................................8
```

B. What were they? _____

55. Were there any long-term emotional effects?

    Yes [ASK A]...1
    No 2   44/
    DK [VOLUNTEERED] 8
    NA 9

A. What were they? _____

---

56. [IF VICTIM DIED, ASK B ONLY] (As far as you know) Did (you/the victim) do things differently in any way after the attack?

    Yes [ASK A]...1
    No [IF NOT OWN RAPE, ASK B].....................2   45/
    DK [VOLUNTEERED, ASK B] 8
    NA 9

A. [IF YES] What did (she/you) do differently? _____

B. [IF NOT OWN RAPE] After you heard about this rape, did you do things differently in any way?

    Yes [ASK B1]...1
    No 2   46/
    NA 9

1) [IF YES] What did you do differently? [PROBE FULLY]

_____

[PROBE] What else? _____

---

57. Why do you think (you/this woman) became the victim of this attacker? [RECORD ALL MENTIONED]

A.	Unlucky...................................01	47-48/
B.	Just there................................02	49-50/
C.	Wrong place at the wrong time 03	51-52/
D.	Lives in dangerous neighborhood......04	53-54/
E.	Careless, stupid.....................05	55-56/
F.	Seductive, provocative, sexy...............06	57-58/
G.	Attractive..............................07	59-60/
H.	Small, weak...........................08	61-62/
I.	Rapist insane, crazy 09	63-64/
J.	Rapist a sex maniac...........................10	65-66/
K.	Other [SPECIFY] _____11	67-68/
L.	DK [VOLUNTEERED] 98	69-70/

58. [OMIT IF OWN RAPE AND GO TO Q.59]   When you think about the victim, would you say that she is someone very much like you, somewhat like you, or not like you at all?

Very much like me [ASK A&B] 1
Somewhat like me [ASK A&B] 2   71/
Not at all like me [ASK B] 3
NA 9

A.   [IF "VERY MUCH" OR "SOMEWHAT LIKE ME"] In what ways is she like you?

[PROBE FULLY] _____

B.   How is she different from you?

[PROBE FULLY] _____

SKIP 72-79
80/4
CARD 5   DUP 1-6
SKIP 7-18

59. [IF OWN RAPE, ADD "AGAIN"] Have you thought about what you would do if somebody tried to sexually assault you?

No [GO TO Q.60] 1
Somewhat [ASK A&B] 2   19/
Yes [ASK A&B] 3

A.   [IF "SOMEWHAT" OR "YES"] What would you do? [INTERVIEWER, RECORD AND CODE]

_____

_____

[CODE FIRST MENTION FOR Q.59A]

Scream 1
Run, try to run 2   20/
Fight back 3
Try to talk way out of it [GO TO Q.60] 4
Figure out how to avoid injury or death
    and do that [GO TO Q.60] 5
Submit 6
Depends [PROBE: "On what?"] _____ 7
Other [SPECIFY] _____ 8
DK [VOLUNTEERED] 9

B.   Why would you do that?

_____

60. We know that rape is a terrible crime, for many reasons. What do you believe is the single worst aspect of rape?

_____

[INTERVIEWER, CODE LATER]

The possibility of being killed 1
The fear of being permanently
    injured or maimed 2
Emotional damage to the victim.................3
The sexual violation 4
The shame of being a rape victim..............5
The fear of men that results.........................6
Other [SPECIFY] _____7
DK [VOLUNTEERED]......................................8

21/

---

61. What percentage of rape victims in the United States do you imagine get killed?
[PROBE: "Just a guess will do."] [ROUND UP TO NEAREST %]

    % killed [ ] [ ]   22-23/
    DK............................98

---

62. Of those not killed, what percentage do you think get beaten or physically hurt in addition to the rape? [PROBE: "Just a guess will do."]

    % hurt [ ] [ ]   24-25/
    DK............................98

62a. Some people think that many rapes are times when a woman has agreed to have sex, or led a man to believe she would, and then changed her mind. In what percentage of rapes do you think men are unjustly accused?
[PROBE: "Just a guess will do."]

    % [ ] [ ]   26-27/
    DK............................98

---

63. We know some people worry more than others, and they worry about different things. Some people worry about keeping their jobs, not having enough money, divorce, their children's behavior, and so on. Others worry about getting mugged or even murdered. We are trying to understand how fear or worry about rape fits in with other things people fear or worry about.
When you worry about things, do you worry about being physically harmed, or is your most frequent worry *not* about physical harm?

Related to harm...1
Not related to harm...2
Doesn't worry [VOLUNTEERED] 3
DK [VOLUNTEERED]..8

28/

64. How *often* does rape or sexual assault worry you? Would you say...
[READ FIRST 5 CATEGORIES]

    More than once a week, ...1
    Once a week, ...2
    Monthly, ...3
    One or two times a year, or 4
    Never? [GO TO Q.66] 5
    DK [VOLUNTEERED].......................................8

29/

---

65. The last time you worried about rape, how afraid or scared did you feel?
[PROBE: READ FIRST 4 CATEGORIES]

    Absolutely terrified...1
    Very frightened...2
    Mildly frightened...3
    Not scared at all 4
    Never worried [VOLUNTEERED] 5
    NA 9

30/

---

66. Have you heard of any organizations in this city that help victims of sexual assault?

    Yes...1
    No [ASK D]..2

31/

A. [IF YES] What organizations? _____

                           # of organizations named: [   ] [   ]   32-33/

[INTERVIEWER, CODE LATER ALL APPLICABLE]

Type of Organization	Yes	No	
01) Hospital.....................................1	2		34/
02) Rape crisis center...............................1	2		35/
03) Other women's groups.........................1	2		36/
04) Police rape unit 1	2		37/
05) Victim/witness program.......................1	2		38/
06) General anti-crime program.................1	2		39/
07) Don't know names...............................1	2		40/
08) Know whom to ask to get names 1	2		41/
09) Other [SPECIFY] _____1	2		42/
10) Incorrect responses (named agency refers rape victims to other agencies)..1	2		43/

B. [IF MORE THAN ONE] "Which one organization do you know best?"

                                                    [   ] [   ]   44-45/

[IF ONE OR MORE THAN ONE, CODE APPROPRIATE NUMBER
FROM Q.66A]

C. How did you hear about that organization?

Someone else:

Victim...01
Friend in neighborhood..............................02   46-47/
Other friend 03
Relative...04
Police 05
Other [SPECIFY] _____06

Media:

TV 07
Radio...08
Newspaper..09
Leaflets/flyers/advertisements....................10
Other [SPECIFY] _____11
Other [SPECIFY] _____12
DK [VOLUNTEERED]......................................13

D. [OPTIONAL: INTERVIEWER, ASK WHEN APPROPRIATE]

List was shown...1
List was not shown 2   48/
NA 9

Here is a list of organizations in this city that help rape victims and those close to rape victims. Which of these have you heard of?

[RECORD NUMBER OF ORGANIZATIONS. LATER, YOU MAY LEAVE LIST WITH RESPONDENT]

List was left with respondent.......................1
List was not left..2   49/
NA 9

67. Suppose there was to be a campaign to reduce the amount of rape in the city. What do you think would help to prevent rape? [INTERVIEWER, CODE LATER]

_____

[PROBES]
  [4 OR MORE MENTIONS]   O.K., thanks. You've mentioned _____ things. Is there
                                                                   anything else?

  [3 OR FEWER ITEMS MENTIONED] That's _____ thing(s). Is there anything else?

  [NO MENTIONS] Perhaps if I ask the question again you might think of something.

  [IF ANY MENTIONS] O.K., thanks. This is the kind of information we need.

[INTERVIEWER CODE LATER]

Item	Order of Mention	No mention	
A. Stronger security measures at home, like better locks or alarms	1 2 3 4 5+	6	50/
B. Increasing the number of police on the street	1 2 3 4 5+	6	51/
C. Having a man go with a woman to protect her when she goes out	1 2 3 4 5+	6	52/
D. Stiffer penalties for rapists	1 2 3 4 5+	6	53/
E. Increasing men's respect for women	1 2 3 4 5+	6	54/
F. Women not going out alone, especially at night	1 2 3 4 5+	6	55/
G. Women dressing more modestly, or in a less sexy way	1 2 3 4 5+	6	56/
H. Women staying out of certain parts of town	1 2 3 4 5+	6	57/
I. Providing psychological treatment for rapists	1 2 3 4 5+	6	58/
J. Encouraging women to take self-defense classes, like judo or karate	1 2 3 4 5+	6	59/
K. Public education about how to prevent rape	1 2 3 4 5+	6	60/
L. Neighborhood anti-crime programs, like block clubs or neighborhood watch groups	1 2 3 4 5+	6	61/
M. Women carrying weapons for protection, like guns or knives	1 2 3 4 5+	6	62/
N. More vigorous prosecution of rape cases	1 2 3 4 5+	6	63/
O. Newspapers publicizing names and pictures of known rapists	1 2 3 4 5+	6	64/
P. Eliminating poverty and bad environments that produce rapists	1 2 3 4 5+	6	65/
Q. Reducing sex and violence on TV	1 2 3 4 5+	6	66/
R. Stopping the push for women's rights and women's liberation'	1 2 3 4 5+	6	67/
S. Rape victims fighting back against attackers	1 2 3 4 5+	6	68/
T. Women not hitchiking	1 2 3 4 5+	6	69/
U. Women refusing to talk to strangers	1 2 3 4 5+	6	70/
V. Other **[SPECIFY]** _____	1 2 3 4 5+	6	71/

68. We've been talking about the problem of rape or sexual assault. We are concerned about other things that happen to people that may or may not be considered sexual assault. Has anything *ever* happened to you that might be considered sexual assault? That is, anything from actually being attacked, being hugged or touched in a way that made you uncomfortable, having someone expose themselves to you, or anything else?

> Yes [ASK A-D]...1
> No [GO TO Q.69]..2　　　　　　72/

[IF MORE THAN ONE INCIDENT, ASK FOR "one that made the biggest impression on you."]
[PROBE FULLY]

A. What happened? _____

B. How did you feel about this when it happened? [PROBE: READ THE FIRST 6 CATEGORIES]

[PROBE FOR STRONGEST FEELING:　　"On looking back on the incident, which feeling would you say is strongest?"]

> Flattered, positive reaction..........................1
> Shocked, surprised, disconcerted..............2
> Revolted, disgusted.....................................3　　　　73/
> Annoyed, angry, irritated 4
> Worried or apprehensive..............................5
> Actually afraid..6
> Other [SPECIFY] _____7
> DK [VOLUNTEERED]......................................8

> SKIP 74-79
> 80/5

CARD 6　DUP 1-6

C. Would you look at this card and tell me the relationship of this person to you? You can just tell me the number. [HAND CARD]

> Stranger...01
> Casual acquaintance.....................................02　　　7-8/
> Friend...03
> Date..04
> Person in authority, like a boss,
> 　　teacher, or doctor...................................05
> Husband/boyfriend..06
> Wife/girlfriend...07
> Father...08
> Mother..09
> Brother..10
> Sister..11
> Other relative 12
> Someone else [SPECIFY] _____13
> Refused..97
> NA 99

D. Did you change what you usually do because of this?

    Yes [ASK 1] 1

    No 2   9/

1) What did you do differently? _____
   [PROBE FULLY]

69. During your dating years (has/did) anyone ever pushed you to go farther sexually than you wanted to? This happens a lot. Did this ever happen to you?

    Yes [ASK A]..1

    No [GO TO Q.70]...2   10/

    Same incident as Q.68 [GO TO Q.70].........3

A. Please tell me about an incident you remember. [PROBE FULLY]

B. How did this make you feel? [PROBE FOR STRONGEST FEELING: "Looking back on it, what would you say was your strongest feeling, overall?"]

    Flattered, positive reaction...........................1

    Shocked, surprised 2

    Revolted, disgusted......................................3   11/

    Annoyed, angry, irritated 4

    Worried or apprehensive..............................5

    Actually afraid...6

    Other [SPECIFY] _____7

    DK [VOLUNTEERED].....................................8

C. After that, as a result of that incident, did you do anything differently?

    Yes [ASK D]..1

    No 2   12/

D. [IF YES] What did you do differently? [PROBE FULLY]

70. The laws about what is considered rape differ from state to state. We need to know what kinds of incidents you think should be covered by the laws on rape. **[PLEASE READ EACH STATEMENT]**

Situation	"Rape?" Yes	No	Assault or "Sexual Assault" [VOLUNTEERED]	Incest [VOLUNTEERED]	DK
A. What about unwanted sexual intercourse on a date? Would you call that rape?	1	2	3	4	8 13/
B. What about someone whistling or making rude remarks? Would you call that rape?	1	2	3	4	8 14/
C. A stranger pinching or grabbing in a sexually suggestive way?	1	2	3	4	8 15/
D. A stranger exposing his genitals?	1	2	3	4	8 16/
E. Sexual intercourse with someone without consent. Is that rape?	1	2	3	4	8 17/
F. Unwanted sexual intercourse with someone when physically forced or overpowered?	1	2	3	4	8 18/
G. Unwanted sexual intercourse between a husband and wife? Is that rape?	1	2	3	4	8 19/
H. A relative having sexual intercourse with a child?	1	2	3	4	8 20/
I. A relative having sexual intercourse with a teenager under age 18?	1	2	3	4	8 21/
J. Is there anything else you would call rape? **[IF YES, ASK K]**	1	2	3	4	8 22/

K. **[IF YES TO J]** What?_____

---

71. Now I would like to know what you think about the way the newspapers and TV shows treat crime in general.

Do you think that the crime problem in the city is more serious, less serious, or about the same as reported by the *newspapers*?

More 1
Same..2   23/
Less...3
DK 8

72. What about TV news? Is crime in the city more serious, about as serious, or less serious than reported by TV newscasters?

> More 1
> About as serious 2   24/
> Less..3
> DK 8

73. About how many minutes a day, on weekdays, would you say you spend reading the newspaper?

> # Minutes: [   ] [   ] [   ]   25-27/
> NA: 9   9   9

   A. How about on Sunday? How many minutes do you spend reading the paper then?

> # Minutes: [   ] [   ] [   ]   28-30/
> NA: 9   9   9

74. Do you think the newspapers usually do a good job, an average job, or a poor job in the accuracy and completeness of their reports of crimes?

> Good..1
> Average 2   31/
> Poor..3
> NA 9

75. Thinking about crime, in general, is there anything in particular that you remember you read, heard, or saw in the last two weeks?

> Yes [ASK A-B]...1
> No [GO TO Q.76]...2   32/
> NA 9

   A. [IF YES] What crime was involved in the one incident you remember most?

   _____

   B. What did you read or hear about it?

   _____

76. Did you watch TV yesterday?

> Yes [ASK A-C]...1
> No [ASK C]..2   33/
> No TV [GO TO Q.78].......................................9

A. [IF YES] For about how many hours? [ROUND UP TO NEAREST HOUR]

Hours: [ ] [ ]   34-35/
NA: 9 9

B. Did you watch an evening news show?

Yes [ASK C]...1
No [ASK C]...2   36/

C. Do you usually watch the news?

Yes 1
No 2   37/

---

77. I'm going to read the names of some TV shows, and I'd like you to tell me if you watch them "usually," "occasionally," or "not at all."

Program	Usually	Occasionally	Not at all	Never heard of it [VOLUNTEERED]	NA	
A. Six Million Dollar Man	4	3	2	1	9	38/
B. Bionic Woman	4	3	2	1	9	39/
C. Police Woman	4	3	2	1	9	40/
D. Kojak	4	3	2	1	9	41/
E. Baretta	4	3	2	1	9	42/
F. Charlie's Angels	4	3	2	1	9	43/
G. Barney Miller	4	3	2	1	9	44/
H. Hawaii Five-0	4	3	2	1	9	45/
I. Barnaby Jones	4	3	2	1	9	46/
J. Rockford Files	4	3	2	1	9	47/
K. Quincy	4	3	2	1	9	48/
L. Starsky & Hutch	4	3	2	1	9	49/
M. Switch	4	3	2	1	9	50/

---

78. When you read a newspaper story about a rape that happened locally, what facts do you think are most interesting or important?

[PROBE 1: "What are the things you're interested in knowing about?"]
[PROBE 2: "Like facts about the victim or attacker, where it happened, and so on."]

[RECORD BRIEFLY, PRESERVING ORDER; PROBE FULLY]

_____

_____

79. Now, please tell me which of the things you mentioned is the most important (#1) for you to know, and which is second most important (#2).

    A. #1 _____

    B. #2 _____

    C. Why is #1 important to you? [PROBE FULLY]

        _____

    D. Why is #2 important to you? [PROBE FULLY]

        _____

We are trying to learn about people's reactions to the way newspapers treat stories about rape. I would like to read parts of a couple of news stories that are about issues we haven't discussed yet and ask you a question or two about them. [SHOW CARD ON BRITISH PAYING VICTIMS] "Shall I read them to you, or would you rather read them yourself?" [HAND CARD FOR Q.80].

> [A London newspaper story described the British government policy of compensating rape victims for their physical and emotional injuries. A spokesman for the Criminal Injuries Compensation Board said a victim could expect a minimum of 1,000 pounds ($1650) for "no significant physical injuries and average psychological reaction," and up to twice that amount depending on the seriousness of the outcome. Many rape victims, however, elect to forego compensation in order to forget their trauma, he said.]

> [A U.S. newspaper story recounted the views of a Wisconsin county judge, who angered feminists by declaring that women are "sex objects" and provoke rape by wearing provocative outfits and teasing men. The judge was responding to a case involving a 16-year-old girl who was raped by three boys in a high school stairwell. He said the rape was a young boy's "normal reaction" to sexual permissiveness and sexy clothing. The victim was wearing sneakers, jeans, and a blouse over a turtleneck sweater. The judge claimed nationwide support for his opinion.]

80. **[SHOW CARD]**

"What Britain Pays Its Rape Victims"

A. Did you know before you read this that the British pay rape victims?

    Yes 1
    No 2   51/

B. Do you think it would be a good idea to do that here in the United States?

    Yes 1
    No 2   52/

C. Why (do/don't) you think so?

    _____

    1) **[IF YES TO B]** What amount of payment do you think would be appropriate here?

    [IF RANGE, CODE HIGHEST AMOUNT]
        $: [   ] [   ] [   ] [   ] [   ] [   ] [   ] [   ]   53-60/

D. Do you think rape victims should be encouraged to report and prosecute their attackers?

    Yes 1
    No 2   61/

E. Why (do/don't) you think so?

    _____

F. Some newspapers print names of victims and others don't. Do you think names of victims should be printed in the paper?

    Yes 1
    No 2   62/
    Up to victim **[VOLUNTEERED]** 3
    Other **[SPECIFY]** _____4

_____

81. **[SHOW CARD WITH STORY ON JUDGE]** "Judge Stirs Outcry Over Rape Views"

A. Did you know before you read this about the judge's decision?

    Yes 1
    No 2   63/

B. Do you agree or disagree with his views?

      Agree 1
      Disagree 2   64/

C. Why or in what ways?

    _____

82. I have asked you a lot about safety in your neighborhood. In order to understand your answers better, I need to know some more about your experience with people in your neighborhood.

    First, do most of your close friends live in your neighborhood or in other parts of the city, or not in this city at all?

      Here [ASK A] 1
      Other parts of this city 2   65/
      Not in this city..3
      Other [SPECIFY] _____4

A. [IF "HERE"] Did you know them before you moved here, or did you get to be friends after you or they moved here?

      Before...1
      After 2   66/

I'm going to read a list of activities. I'd like to know whether or not you've done them in the last two weeks, and if you did them alone, with a relative or someone who lives in your household, a neighbor, a friend from outside the neighborhood, or someone you've worked with. [HAND CARD] If you've done them more than once, be sure to tell me all the different types of people you've done them with. [CODE ALL MENTIONS]

		Yes No [ASK A]		A. Who did you do this with?							
				Alone	Relative/household	Neighbor	Friend	Co-worker	Someone Else	NA	
83.	Did you go out for entertainment in the past two weeks, like to a movie or restaurant or something like that?	1	2	1	2	3	4	5	6	9	67/ 68/
84.	Did you go to someone's house to visit, or have someone visit at your home?	1	2	1	2	3	4	5	6	9	69/ 70/
85.	Did you do a favor for someone, like water plants, swap recipes, loan tools or something like that?	1	2	1	2	3	4	5	6	9	71/ 72/
86.	Did you talk to somebody about a personal problem, or ask for or give advice to somebody?	1	2	1	2	3	4	5	6	9	73/ 74/

SKIP 75-79
80/6
CARD 7   DUP 1-6

87. Now I would like to get some idea of how you use your neighborhood. I will read a list of activities, and you tell me if you usually do your things in your neighborhood, downtown, or somewhere else.

Where do you usually go:	Your neighborhood	Downtown	Somewhere else	NA	
A. For weekly grocery shopping -- your neighborhood, downtown or somewhere else?	1	2	3	9	7/
B. To buy everyday items like soap or Kleenex?	1	2	3	9	8/
C. To your bank?	1	2	3	9	9/
D. Movies or other entertainment?	1	2	3	9	10/
E. To see your regular doctor?	1	2	3	9	11/

F. Are you working now?

        Yes [GO TO G] 1
        No [GO TO H] 2   12/

	Your neighborhood	Downtown	Somewhere else	NA	
G. Is your place of work in your neighborhood, downtown or somewhere else?	1	2	3	9	13/

H. Do you go to church?

        Yes [GO TO I] 1
        No [GO TO J] 2   14/

	Your neighborhood	Downtown	Somewhere else	NA	
I. Is your church	1	2	3	9	15/
J. [IF CHILDREN 5-18 AT HOME, ASK FOR YOUNGEST CHILD] Is your child's school	1	2	3	9	16/

88. Now I would like to get an idea of how you feel about your neighborhood.

Would you say that you think of your neighborhood as just a place to live, or that you really feel a part of it?

        Just a place to live 1
        Really feel a part of it....................................2   17/

89. Do you feel less attached to your neighborhood than to the city as a whole, about as attached, or more attached?

Less attached 1
As attached 2   18/
More attached..3

---

90. If you could, would you like to stay in your neighborhood permanently, or would you rather live in another part of the city?

PHILADELPHIA

West Philly...11   20-21/

South Philly...12

CHICAGO

Lincoln Park...21

Wicker Park...22

SAN FRANCISCO

Sunset..31

Visitacion Valley...32

Other [SPECIFY] _____01

DK...98

---

92. Now I'd like to know your opinion on some other things so that we can better understand your point of view.

There has been much talk recently about changing women's status in society today. On the whole, do you favor or oppose most of the efforts to strengthen and change women's status in society today?

Favor 1
Favor some,
    Oppose some [VOLUNTEERED]................2   22/
Oppose 3
DK [VOLUNTEERED].......................................8

I have a few statements that are commonly made about women. Would you tell if you agree or disagree with them? There are no right or wrong answers; we just want to know what you think.

93. I want to know if you strongly agree, agree, disagree, or strongly disagree with these statements. **[HAND CARD]**

Statement	Strongly Agree	Agree	Disagree	Strongly Disagree	
A. It is much better for everyone involved if the man is the achiever outside the home and the woman takes care of the home and family.	4	3	2	1	23/
B. Women should be encouraged to seek elective and appointive posts at local, state, and national levels of government.	4	3	2	1	24/
C. A working mother cannot establish as warm and secure a relationship with her children as a mother who does not work.	4	3	2	1	25/
D. It is more important for a wife to help her husband than to have a career herself.	4	3	2	1	26/
E. The movement for women's rights has helped you personally.	4	3	2	1	27/

94. Now I have some other general questions. Tell me "Yes" or "No" in answer to each of them. **[PROBE FOR "YES" OR "NO" ANSWER]**

	Yes	No	
A. Is your own hard work more important for getting ahead than knowing the right people?	1	2	28/
B. Do you believe that most problems will solve themselves if you just leave them alone?	1	2	29/
C. Does your success depend more on your own efforts than on luck or fate?	1	2	30/
D. Most of the time, do you find it easy to change another person's opinion?	1	2	31/
E. Is getting ahead for you mostly a matter of getting the right breaks?	1	2	32/
F. Do you think that good luck charms are a waste of money?	1	2	33/
G. For the most part, do you think that your success depends largely on the help of powerful people?	1	2	34/
H. Are you the kind of person who believes that planning ahead makes things turn out better?	1	2	35/

Now, finally, I need to know some other things about you so that your answers can be compared with those of other people in this survey.

95. What is your principal occupation? [PROBE: "What is the name of your job?"]

Homemaker/housewife 1
Student 2
Unemployed/laid off 3
All others [SPECIFY] _____ 4
Retired (what was your occupation
    before you retired?) _____ 5

36/

96. [FOR WOMEN ONLY] Which of the following patterns of work and being a homemaker best describes your adult life since finishing your formal education. [IF STUDENT, CONSIDER AS WORKING]. [HAND CARD]

Have worked outside
    the home continuously 1
Worked, then became
    full-time homemaker 2
Have been homemaker
    continuously 3
Have combined working and
    being homemaker at same time 4
Have alternated working and
    being full-time homemaker 5
Other [SPECIFY] _____ 6
NA 9

37/

97. Are you *currently* employed in a job outside the home?

Yes, full-time [GO TO Q.98] 1
Yes, part-time [GO TO Q.98] 2
No [ASK A] 3

38/

A. Have you *ever* been employed outside the home?

Yes 1
No 2

39/

98. What is your age? [INTERVIEWER CODE]   Age: [·] [ ]   40-41/

[IF REFUSES, PROBE: "I'll read some categories, and you tell me when to stop." CODE ABOVE]

[IF:]	[CODE IN BOXES]
18-20	[1] [9]
21-30	[2] [5]
31-40	[3] [5]
41-50	[4] [5]
51-60	[5] [5]
Over 60	[6] [5]
Refused	[9] [8]
NA	[9] [9]

---

99. What was the last grade in school you completed?

[PROBE: READ CATEGORIES]

8th grade or less 1
Some high school...2   42/
High school graduate.....................................3
Business/trade school....................................4
Some college 5
College graduate 6
Some post-graduate work............................7
Post-graduate degree obtained.................8

---

100. Would you call yourself: [READ]

Protestant 1
Catholic...2   43/
Jewish...3
Muslim...4
Buddhist..5
Agnostic..6
Atheist (no religious beliefs) 7
Other [SPECIFY] _____ 8

---

101. What is your current marital status? [PROBE: READ CATEGORIES]

Never married..1
Currently married...2   44/
Separated 3
Divorced 4
Widowed..5
"Living with someone"...................................6
Common-law marriage.................................7

102. About what was the total combined income last year before taxes of all the people living in your household?

$[ ][ ][ ][ ][ ][ ]   45-50/

[PROBE: "O.K. Here's a card with some categories; could you just tell me the number of the right category?"] [HAND CARD] [FEEL FREE TO HELP RESPONDENT CALCULATE APPROXIMATE INCOME]

Below $6,000...1
$6-9,999 2   51/
$10-14,999...3
$15-19,999...4
$20-24,999...5
$25-29,999...6
Over $30,000..7
Refused..8
NA..9

---

103. A. What is your race/ Are you: [READ]

White 1
Black...2   52/
Asian 3
Other [SPECIFY] _____ 4
Refused...7

Besides being an American, what ethnic background are you? [PROBE: "Like being Irish, Puerto Rican or Afro-American?]

Cuban 01
Mexican/Chicano.....................................02   53-54/
Puerto Rican 03
Other Hispanic [SPECIFY]_____04
Polish 05
Italian..06
Other European [SPECIFY]_____07
Afro-American..08
Asian 09
American only..10
Jewish...11
Other [SPECIFY] _____12
Refused 97

B. Were you born in the United States or somewhere else?

Born in U.S...1
Born elsewhere...2   55/
DK 3
NA 9

104.   [IF RESPONDENT IS *MALE*, GO TO Q.105]

[IF *FEMALE* RESPONDENT LIVES IN HOUSEHOLD WITH HUSBAND OR BOYFRIEND (SEE Q.13), ASK THIS QUESTION]

We are interested in finding out about how men who are important to women we interview feel about a lot of the same issues.

We would like to ask your (husband/boyfriend) if he is willing to be interviewed.

We would ask him a lot of the same questions we asked you, but of course all your answers will remain confidential. We do ask that you do not discuss any of the questions with him until after we have had a chance to interview him.

Is it O.K. with you if we ask him if he is willing to be interviewed?

> O.K., up to him [ASK A]..................................1
> Not O.K. [GO TO Q.106]................................2   56/
> NA 9

A. I need to call him to arrange a time convenient for him, so I need his name and telephone number.

_____

[GO TO HUSBAND TEARSHEET]

---

105.   [IF RESPONDENT IS FEMALE, GO TO Q.106]

Was your wife/girlfriend already interviewed as part of this survey?

> Yes (husband sample)....................................1
> No (phone sample)..2   57/
> DK 8
> NA 9

HUSBAND TEARSHEET

Name _____ Phone number _____

ID# of Wife   [   ] [   ] [   ] [   ] [   ] [   ]

Husband ID #   [   ] [   ] [   ] [   ] [   ] [   ]

For husband's ID, last 4 digits should be the same as the wife's. First 2 digits should be selected from among the following:

If Residence is:	First 2 Digits in Husband's ID Are:
West Philly..16	
South Philly..17	
Lincoln Park...26	
Wicker Park..27	
Sunset...36	
Other Hispanic [SPECIFY]_____37	

106. [END] That's all the questions I have. Thank you very much for participating. Do you have any comments you want to make about this interview?

        Yes [SPECIFY] _____1
        No 2   58/

_____

107.   Time: [   ] [   ] [   ] [   ]   59-62/

                            A.M...........1
                                                                            63/
                            P.M...........2

_____

INTERVIEWER SHEET

INTERVIEWER: WHEN EDITING, BE SURE CODING IS COMPLETE.
INTERVIEWER REMARKS: Fill out after completion of interview.

108. Length of interview (# minutes): [   ] [   ] [   ]   64-66/

109. Date of interview: [   ] [   ]   [   ] [   ]   [   ] [   ]   67-72/
      Day   Month   Year

110. Place of interview

      Respondent's home 1
      Office 2   73/
      Restaurant...3
      Public Library..4
      Other [SPECIFY] _____5

111. Privacy?

      Yes, entire time..1
      Most of the time 2   74/
      No [WHO ELSE WAS THERE?]_____3

                                                          SKIP 75-79
                                                               80/7
                                                  CARD 8 DUP 1-6

112. Understanding of questions:

      High...1
      Medium..2   7/
      Low...3

113. Ability to articulate answer:

      High...1
      Medium..2   8/
      Low...3

114. Cooperativeness:

      Cooperative 1
      Suspicious...2   9/
      Hostile...3
      Uncommunicative..4

I have reread this completed questionnaire and certify that all questions requiring answers have been recorded in the respondent's exact words, and that all boxes and spaces requiring an "x," a number, or a letter are filled in. This interview has been obtained according to all interviewing specifications. I agree to keep the content of questions, respondent's answers, and the subject of this interview confidential.

Interviewer's Signature   _____

Supervisor's Name   _____

Appendix B:
Methodological Notes

THIS appendix briefly describes the methods we used to obtain data on women's fear and coping strategies from women living in selected neighborhoods in Philadelphia, Chicago, and San Francisco. These three cities were selected by the Reactions to Crime Project[1] and Fear of Rape Project[2] (both being conducted at the Center for Urban Affairs and Policy Research at Northwestern University) for a variety of theoretical, geographical, and practical reasons. At the time of site selection, San Francisco had a high crime rate but generally low fear of crime; Philadelphia had a high crime rate and crime had been an important political issue; Chicago had relatively moderate levels of both crime and fear. Within each city, neighborhoods were selected for systematic study according to differences in race, degree of organized response to crime, social class (as defined by median income), and official crime rate. We examined the relationship between attitudes and rape-prevention behavior in six (two in each city) of the ten communities included in the Reactions to Crime study.

In conjunction with the Reactions to Crime Project, we conducted a telephone survey in 1977 of 1,620 people living within the city limits of the three cities.

In each city, we interviewed 540 adults living in households selected through random-digit dialing. The sample was weighted to correct for the number of telephone lines per household, since that affected people's chances of being contacted. The weighted sample

(N) equaled 1,389. (This sample is referred to hereafter as the three-city aggregate sample.) More complete discussions of the methodology of the telephone interview are given elsewhere.[3]

An additional 3,533 women and men from randomly selected households in ten neighborhoods in the three cities (West Philadelphia, South Philadelphia, and Logan in Philadelphia; Woodlawn, Back of the Yards, Lincoln Park, and Wicker Park in Chicago; and Sunset, Visitacion Valley, and Mission districts in San Francisco) were also interviewed by telephone. At the end of these interviews, all respondents in *six* of the *ten* neighborhoods (West and North Philadelphia, Wicker Park, Lincoln Park, Sunset, and Visitacion Valley) were invited to participate in an in-person interview about fear of crime, including sexual assault. We deliberately oversampled women so that the causes and consequences of their greater fear of crime could be explored in depth. Respondents were paid $10 each to cover expenses incurred by participation in the in-person interviews.

Of the 472 in-person interviews, 71 pairs, or 142 persons, were part of a spouse subsample in which both husband and wife were interviewed in person (but only one in each couple had been previously interviewed by telephone). In addition, 34 Hispanic women were added as a snowball sample of Hispanic women living in Chicago; they had not been interviewed previously by telephone but their names were given to us by people who were part of the random sample. The number of persons participating in *both* the in-person and telephone interviews (excluding spouses and the Hispanic snowball sample) was 367, of which 299 were women; the 299 women and 68 men interviewed both on the phone and in person made up the *core* sample for our study.

Interviewers and respondents were matched on language and racial and ethnic characteristics (black, white, Hispanic) whenever possible; however, males were interviewed by females.

A comparison of the 367 persons interviewed in person with the three-city aggregate sample indicated no statistically significant differences in their area of residence or race. However, the in-person respondents were younger, better educated, and wealthier than the randomly selected telephone sample. Two percent of the women in the three-city aggregate sample reported having been raped or sexually assaulted. Among the women who were interviewed both in person and on the telephone, 6 percent reported on the phone that they had been raped or sexually assaulted, whereas nearly twice as many (11 percent) mentioned such an assault when interviewed in person. (Note that this incidence data is considerably higher than that reported in UCR data or by other victimization surveys; this may be because the question asked about sexual assault as well as rape, and because the time frame was not limited to the past six or twelve months, as is typical of most victim surveys.) These data raise serious questions for epidemiological studies of rape, since methodological artifacts may contribute considerable error to rape rates reported in such studies.

Since the three-city aggregate sample fairly well approximates the demographic profiles of the cities from which it was drawn, we used that sample to determine the distribution of levels of fear and perceived risk of criminal victimization. However, questions were added to the in-person survey to examine determinants of fear and coping strategies.

The in-person sample has the following characteristics: the average age is thirty-five years (standard deviation = 12.52); the modal (most typical) education level is high school graduate; the modal income, between $10,000 and 15,000 in 1977–78; 53 percent of the sample is white; and 45.5 percent of the sample was married at the time of the interviews.

THE NEIGHBORHOODS

The six neighborhoods in which we conducted our interviews were selected to provide a mixture of economic and ethnic groups. At the time the interviews were conducted, South Philadelphia was characterized by pockets of black residents mixed in with the estimated 75 percent white residents, many of whom were Italian, and open tensions existed between the black and white residents. It is a primarily blue-collar, working-class area. West Philadelphia is similar economically but is predominantly black. It is a stable area, with most people living in single-family homes.

In Chicago, most people in our study from the Lincoln Park area are white, with higher income and education levels than those from Philadelphia. Part of the area has been designated an historic district and has been subjected to considerable "gentrification" in recent years. The other Chicago neighborhood, Wicker Park, is populated by lower working class people, with a high percentage below the official poverty level and many families on public aid. The rapidly changing population is estimated to be about 40 percent Hispanic, with black and white (predominantly Polish) groups each about 30 percent.

In San Francisco, the Sunset district is a white, middle-class, conservative neighborhood described by neighbors and police as having the lowest crime rate in the city. Many skilled tradesmen, city workers, and police live there. Visitacion Valley, in southern San Francisco, is an area with a diverse population made up of many different ethnic groups in addition to blacks and whites. Most people who live there are working-class and live in single-family homes, with the exception of a substantial portion of black residents who live in two large low-income housing projects.

THE INTERVIEW PROCESS

Insofar as possible, in-person interviews were conducted in respondents' homes. In each city there was also a project office where some interviews were conducted; this occurred when the respondent requested that the interview not be at home or when the interviewers were fearful of going to certain areas. Most interviews lasted approximately 90 to 100 minutes, but some ran as long as three hours. All interviews were tape-recorded, but respondents were told they could choose to have the recorders turned off at any time. Interviewers also recorded answers on forms prepared in both English and Spanish.

Interviewers were concerned that respondents—especially if they happened to be rape victims—would become upset during the interview sessions and that interviewers would be put in the role of counselor. We did two things to deal with this.

First, during the interview training sessions we brought in specialists from the crisis intervention teams at the local hospital and police department to teach the interviewers how to recognize the less obvious signs of emotional upset and post-rape trauma.

Second, we added a question near the end of the interview which the interviewers *at their own discretion* could decide to use or omit:

> Here is a list of organizations in this city that help rape victims and those close to rape victims. Which of these have you heard of?
>
> CAN LEAVE LIST WITH RESPONDENT

Interviewers chose most often to ask the question and leave the list (as a service to the respondent). There were no reports of extreme distress on the part of any respondents.

The interview schedule contained questions in the following areas:

- Household composition, including demographic data on race, religion, income, education, age, and work experience.
- Perceptions of neighborhood, including ability to differentiate

neighbors from strangers; neighborhood problems, including crime, dangerous places.

- Precautions taught to children.
- Childhood and dating-years experiences.
- Victimizations of crimes, estimates of risks of victimizations, fear and worry while engaging in day-to-day activities.
- Precautionary strategies for protecting oneself from crime in general and rape in particular.
- Assessments of physical competence and responses to actual or potential attacks.
- Descriptions of what respondents imagine the "typical" rape to be like; descriptions of an actual rape they knew about, and if and how they had been affected by it.
- Assessments of the worst aspects of rape, effective prevention strategies, and consequences of rape.
- Assessments of what should be covered in rape laws.
- Assessments of newspaper and television coverage of crime.
- Scales assessing internal-external control dimensions.
- Scales assessing attitudes toward women's roles.

Pretests indicated that respondents talked at great length about rapes they knew about, especially if the respondent was also a victim. Precoded questions seemed inappropriate and in the wrong order. Therefore, we trained interviewers to record the verbatim responses, taking extensive notes as people told their stories. Then, while in the presence of the respondent, interviewers checked the appropriate close-ended responses to a series of questions about the rape. This increased accuracy was not intrusive and gave respondents an opportunity to "let down" after telling their stories.

Notes

CHAPTER 1. LEARNING TO FEAR

1. Brodyaga et al. 1975.
2. Susan Griffin 1979:3. See also Griffin 1977.
3. Griffin 1979.
4. Medea and Thompson 1974.
5. Farberow 1963.
6. Feild 1978; Burt 1980; Latta 1978.
7. Burt 1980.
8. Latta and von Seggern 1978.

CHAPTER 2. THE PERVASIVENESS OF FEMALE FEAR

1. Schutz 1962.
2. Schutz 1971:18.
3. Philosophers, psychoanalysts, and existentialists from Heidegger to Freud and Kierkegaard have focused on fear of death as the "final terror of self-consciousness . . . man's [sic] peculiar and greatest anxiety" (Becker 1973, p. 70).

   Kübler-Ross (1974:20) has described the fear of death as "a fear of a catastrophic force bearing down upon you, and you can't do a thing about it."

   Schutz (1962:228) states that "the whole system of relevances which governs us . . . is founded upon the basic experience of each of us: I know that I shall die and I fear to die. This basic experience we suggest calling the *fundamental anxiety*. It is the primordial anticipation from which all the others originate. From the fundamental anxiety spring the many interrelated systems of hopes and fears, of wants and satisfactions, of chances and risks which incite man . . . to attempt the mastery of the world, to overcome obstacles, to draft projects, to realize them. But the fundamental anxiety itself is merely a correlate of our existence as human beings within the paramount reality of daily life. . . ."

   Schutz (1971:18) further suggests that since daily life is paramount and although supporting data are not available, "it is likely that death is not on our minds much of the time" and asks what it is exactly that people fear about death. He goes on to delineate possible sources of fear:

- Fear of physical suffering (perhaps particularly among the healthy and active).
- Fear of humiliation (being a coward in the face of physical pain or the thought of not existing).
- Interruption of goals (interference with achievements that could commemorate one's existence).
- Impact on survivors.
- Fear of punishment (primary among religious people).
- Fear of not being (leads us to existential anxiety—a deep concern over the meaning of life).

Weisman (1972:14) notes the psychological and physiological symptoms associated with fear of dying:

> Fear of dying is a state of episodic alarm, panic, turmoil. It is associated with excessive autonomic symptoms, and usually conveys a pre-emptive conviction that collapse is at hand. When the fear . . . is intense, reality testing abandons the hapless victim. Familiar cues that indicate a stable world are no longer there. Ordinary objects and events seem strange and threatening; the world, literally, is about to disintegrate. All that is left is an empty feeling of being bereft, confused, alone.

Those writing about fear of death note that it has both destructive and constructive qualities. That is, the fear can be anxiety provoking to the point that individuals experiencing it are unable to cope. On the other hand, the desire to live and to be commemorated can lead one to bravery as well as to producing great works of art and literature.

4. "How safe do you feel or would you feel out alone in your neighborhood at night—very safe, somewhat safe, somewhat unsafe, or very unsafe?" is the most widely used measure of fear. See Fowler and Mangione 1974.

This question is also used by the U.S. Census, and by researchers in the United States and abroad to assess fear of crime among women and men; e.g., Maxfield 1984.

When people respond to this question, it is unclear what their referent point is, that is, what they feel safe or unsafe *from*. Most researchers assume people's greatest fears involve attacks which could result in death, physical pain from injury, or emotional trauma. Garofalo (1979) identified a number of other problems with this measure. First, the question does not mention *crime* as the *source* of feelings of lack of safety, and the meaning of the term "neighborhood" is left to respondents' (undoubtedly varying) interpretations. The amount of time people spend outside alone may differ considerably, affecting responses. The question assumes that "at night" means after dark. Finally, the "do you feel or would you feel" portion of the question mixes actual with hypothetical situations.

Since Fowler and Mangione (1974) identified it as the most frequently used measure of fear of crime and we wanted to gather data that we could compare to that being gathered by others, we used this measure despite its flaws. However, we did omit the "would you feel" portion of the wording in order to focus on women's *actual* experience of fear. Our question was: "How safe do you feel when you are out alone in your neighborhood after dark? Very safe, reasonably safe, somewhat unsafe, or very unsafe?"

5. Skogan and Maxfield 1981.

6. See Gordon and Riger 1978.

7. Comparisons were made between West Philadelphia and South Philadelphia; Wicker Park and Lincoln Park in Chicago; Visitacion Valley and Sunset in San Francisco. Appendix B contains descriptions of the neighborhoods.

8. Neither women nor men worry much about being home alone after dark.

9. Slovic, Fischoff, and Lichtenstein (1980), in a study about the relationship of facts and fears to perceived societal risks, found that three underlying factors describe the dimensions of risk: dread (as defined by feelings of inability to control the severity of the risk), familiarity (as defined by what people generally and scientists know about it), and the number of people involved. They also discuss two other issues which affected their respondents' perceptions: the extent to which the risk was reducible, and the extent to which taking the risk was voluntary. They also found that the greater the perceived risk, the greater the adjustment judged necessary to bring the risk to an acceptable level.

   In terms of the substance of risks, Slovic et al. found crime was among the risks judged to be increasing the most, was the most dreaded, was considered one of the most difficult to reduce, and that taking the risks was nonvoluntary. At the same time, the risks of crime were not judged to be new or unknown (as opposed to nuclear war).

CHAPTER 3. THE REALITIES OF RAPE

1. Seven people died after taking Tylenol capsules which had been laced with cyanide, replaced in bottles, and subsequently sold (in drugstores and supermarkets) to unsuspecting buyers.

2. See also Julia and Herman Schwendinger's (1983) informative discussion of forms of rape: individualistic, sexual extortion, rape in the family, and rape as economic or political policy.

3. U.S. Department of Justice, *Criminal Victimization* 1986.

4. See also Lottes 1988; Kanin 1984 and 1985.

5. Rapaport and Burkhard 1984.

6. Mary Koss 1985 and 1988. See also Thomas J. Meyer 1984.

7. These and other findings about campus date rapes and gang rapes point to the need for new or revised rape-prevention plans since most of those are aimed at preventing stranger rapes. It has become a matter of reeducation, not simply a problem of putting up lights and installing locks.

   Several college campuses (e.g., Duke, Northwestern) now have special orientation programs for first-year students and campuswide programs for all students. These include films, discussions, and the provision of information on rape, sexual harassment, and pornography. See Chapter 10 for more details.

8. U.S. Department of Justice, *Crime in the United States* 1986:6–15.

9. See *Crime in the United States* 1983, 1984, 1985, and 1986.

10. Ibid.

11. See *Crime in the United States* 1986:6–15.

12. E.g.: Reiss 1967; Skogan 1977; Lewis and Maxfield 1980; and Skogan and Gordon 1982.

13. Reiss 1967:7.

14. *Crime and Violence* 1967:25.

15. Skogan and Gordon 1983.

16. Reiss 1967.

17. *Criminal Victimization* 1986. Since 1980, rates of reporting to the police have varied from 48 percent to 61 percent.

    We can only speculate as to why the rate of reporting to victimization surveyors has gone down, since the reports to police (UCR) have gone up. In any case, the reports are now consistent since the victimization survey rates are double the UCR rates, and about half the victims interviewed say they reported to the police.

18. The Chicago-area rates are estimated by the FBI because figures submitted by the Chicago Police Department were not in accordance with UCR guidelines.

19. See *Crime in the United States* 1986.

20. Hough and Mayhew 1983:21. The city-level victimization survey data are available only for 1973 and 1975 as those data have not been collected since then.

21. The national victimization rate was 170 per 100,000 women in 1975. The rate of 140 per 100,000 women is for 1986.

22. Skogan 1977:45.

23. The lack of a direct question about rape in the National Crime Survey is a legacy of the early 1970s when the survey was being designed.

    In addition, both police data and victimization surveys include only violent behavior that fairly closely fits legal definitions of crime. In recent years, feminists have called attention to certain kinds of incidents occurring to women which may be threatening or fear-provoking but are not classified as violent crime, such as obscene telephone calls, sexual harassment at work, or verbal abuse on the street. Although these incidents may generate fear and leave women *feeling* victimized, the National Crime Survey does not ask about them and their prevalence is unknown.

24. Nearly half of the 11 percent revealed their assaults *only* in the in-person interviews; during the telephone surveys they had kept this information to themselves. These data also suggest that rape victims are more likely to discuss their assaults in an in-person interview situation after rapport has been established than during the more impersonal, shorter telephone interview. It also suggests that for some reason victims of sexual assault may have been more likely than nonvictims to agree to be interviewed in person.

25. This calculation does not take account of the decreasing risks as a woman gets older (see Gollin 1980).

26. Diana Russell, telephone communication, July 24, 1981.

27. Chicago *Sun-Times,* July 22–27, 1982.

28. *Crime and Violence* 1967.

29. Shiff 1973, cited in Chappel, Geis, and Geis 1977.

    The British Crime Survey—comparable to the U.S. Victimization Surveys—estimated a rate of 1.6 per 100,000 sexual offenses against women for 1981 and 1.7 per 100,000 for 1982. However, "sexual offenses" included "indecent assault, attempted rape, and rape." The researchers state that the sample of 10,905 on which the estimate was based included only one attempted rape, and no completed rapes.

30. San Francisco *Chronicle,* November 11, 1984, p. 1.

31. Margaret Gordon, Stephanie Riger, Robert LeBailly, and Linda Heath 1980:144–160. The six neighborhoods are Visitacion Valley and Sunset in San Francisco, Wicker Park and Lincoln Park in Chicago, and West and South Philadelphia. See also Lewis and Maxfield 1980.

CHAPTER 4. THE AFTERMATH OF RAPE

1. Burgess and Holmstrom 1974:982.

2. Ibid.:983.

3. Ibid.:985. See also Carter, Prentky, and Burgess 1988.

4. Kilpatrick, Veronen, Resick 1979; Kilpatrick, Resick, and Veronen 1981:111. See also Kilpatrick, Veronen, and Best 1984; and Kilpatrick, et. al. 1985.

5. Feldman-Summers, Gordon, and Meagher 1979.

6. Personal communication, director of Women Organized Against Rape, Philadelphia, June 1981.

7. Holmstrom and Burgess 1978.

8. Ronnie Janoff-Bulman 1979; Katz and Burt 1988.

9. See, for example, Brownmiller 1975.

10. Amir, 1971; Groth 1979.

11. Groth 1979.

12. Groth, personal communication, 1984.

13. Ibid.

14. Groth 1979.

15. See also Carter, Prentky, and Burgess 1988.

CHAPTER 5. SOCIETY'S RESPONSE

1. Durkheim 1982:50–60.

2. See Boulding 1976; and Jeffery 1979 for full treatments of these issues.

3. Jeffery 1979:21.

4. Boulding 1976; Jeffery 1979.

5. See especially Boulding 1976.

6. Smith-Rosenberg 1974:24.

7. Ibid.

8. Lofland 1973:179; Fischer 1981.

9. Lofland 1973.

10. Fischer 1981:308.

11. For example, Gans 1962.

12. Stinchcombe et al. 1980.

13. Hindelang, Gottfredson, and Garofalo 1978; Skogan 1977.

14. Garofalo 1977.

15. Skogan 1978b.

16. Jacob and Lineberry 1981.

17. Daniels 1988.

18. Boulding's term.

19. Kahn-Hut, Daniels, and Colvard 1982.

20. Jeffery 1979.

21. Daniels 1988. See also Lofland 1975.

22. Illich 1982.

23. Ehrensaft 1987.

24. See Kahn-Hut, Daniels, and Colvard 1982 for a collection of essays on this topic.

25. Clark and Lewis 1977:141.

26. Maccoby and Jacklin 1974.

27. Stinchcombe et al. 1980.

28. Summarized in DuBow, McCabe, and Kaplan 1979.

29. For example, Riger, Gordon, and LeBailly 1978.

30. Of the women interviewed in Philadelphia, Chicago, and San Francisco.

31. Cohn, Kidder, and Harvey 1978.

32. Sabini and Silver 1982:51.

33. Caignon and Groves 1987. See also Bart and O'Brien 1985.

34. Lewis and Maxfield 1980.

35. Riger, LeBailly, and Gordon 1981.

36. Skogan and Maxfield 1981.

37. Ibid.

38. Heath, Gordon, and LeBailly 1981.

39. Hindelang, Gottfredson, and Garofalo 1978:255.

40. Furstenberg 1972.

41. Balkin 1979.

42. Riger and Gordon 1981.

CHAPTER 6. VIEWS FROM THE LAW

1. In a few uncommon circumstances, such as cases arising on Indian reservations, it is governed by federal laws.

2. Loh 1981:32.

3. This review relies primarily on the following three sources: "Forcible Rape: An Analysis of the Legal Issues," prepared by the Battelle Institute for the NILCEJ, LEAA (1978); "Man's Trial, Woman's Tribulation: Rape Cases in the Courtroom" by Vivian Berger (1977) in *The Columbia Law Review;* and an article by Wallace Loh (1981) in the *Journal of Social Issues* entitled "Q: What Has Reform of Rape Legislation Wrought? A: Truth in Criminal Labeling."

4. Lord Hale 1847:634.

5. Battelle Institute 1978.

6. See Brownmiller 1975:377.

7. Brownmiller 1975.

8. Berger 1977.

9. Loh 1981:30.

10. Battelle 1978.

11. Margolick 1984. Some sources say twenty-two states. See, for example, Chicago *Tribune,* January 14, 1985, p. 1.

12. Geis 1978.

13. Chicago *Tribune,* January 14, 1985, section 5, p. 1.

14. Husbands can also be charged with rape in France, Germany, the USSR, Czechoslovakia, Poland (since 1932), Sweden, Denmark, and Norway. See Geis 1978b:296–297.

15. Marsh, Geist, and Caplan 1982.

16. For a full evaluation of the impact of the Michigan law, see ibid. See also Largen 1988.

17. Source unknown.

18. Loh 1981:28.

CHAPTER 7. EXPLOITATION OF WOMEN'S FEAR

1. Hughes 1940; Harris 1932.

2. *Crime and Violence* 1967.

3. See Gordon and Heath 1981; and Heath, Gordon, and LeBailly 1981.

4. Ibid.; see also Russell 1975.

5. Craig Klugman, personal communication, May 1980.

6. See Heath and Swim 1984. The articles were coded and verified by independent raters. The variables included locator variables (e.g., magazine name and date of publication) and information variables (e.g., victim aftermath, legal change, rape statistics, and constitutional rights of suspects).

   The data from the six magazines were compiled in graphic and tabular form to facilitate examination of trends. Locator and style variables were cross-tabulated with some information variables to investigate shifts within overall trends, and the original summaries of the articles were examined to clarify patterns within the data.

7. These last two categories were combined since articles that focused on the victim nearly always had clearly stated societal implications, which made these two categories difficult to differentiate.

8. Ann Burgess and Lynda Holmstrom published a book in 1974 identifying and describing what they called the "rape trauma syndrome." By the time their book came out, many scholars and activists were aware of their work and of some of their conclusions after interviews with nearly one hundred rape victims who had had to be hospitalized. Shortly thereafter, in 1975, Susan Brownmiller published her well-known treatise *Against Our Will,* which claimed that through the threat of rape, all men keep all women in a state of fear.

   In 1976, a lot of this activity resulted in the establishment through congressional mandate of the National Center for the Prevention and Control of Rape at the National Institute for Mental Health.

9. The victim in this case was killed in a car crash early in 1987.

10. Clendenin 1984.

11. See also Gordon and Heath 1981.

12. Eysenck and Nias 1978:15.

13. Ibid.:274.

14. See especially research by Edward Donnerstein (University of Wisconsin); Neal Malamuth (UCLA); Murray Strauss (University of New Hampshire); and Dolf Zillman (University of Indiana) and their colleagues, from 1980 to the present.

15. See, for example, Eysenck and Nias 1978.

16. Drafted by Andrea Dworkin and Catherine MacKinnon, 1983.

17. Goleman 1986.

18. For example, see Goffman 1979.

19. These figures, based on interviews with women in San Francisco, Chicago, and Philadelphia, are very similar to those collected for national samples by the Newspaper Advertising Bureau.

20. An important set of studies produced by George Gerbner, Lawrence Gross, and their colleagues at the Annenberg School of Communications at the University of Pennsylvania (1976) indicates that the more prime-time television people watch, the more televised violence they are exposed to, and the more likely it is that their picture of reality will be distorted toward the television portrayals.

21. See also Heath 1984.

22. This finding does not hold across cities; that is, readers' sense of safety is related to the way the newspapers in their own cities portray violent crime.

23. Research on the impact of single messages has demonstrated that it is rare to document significant impact; and current social science methods are not suited to assessing the influence of a series of messages over time, as it is difficult to sort out the effects of such messages from the effects of other events occurring during the same period. Yet the public and many researchers persist in believing that media messages—especially in toto—have significant effect on attitudes and behavior.

24. *Columbia Journalism Review,* May 1984.

CHAPTER 8. COPING STRATEGIES

1. For example, Cobb 1976:311.

2. Skogan and Maxfield 1981.

3. Keppler 1976; Lavrakas and Lewis 1980; Riger and Gordon 1979.

4. Gordon and Riger 1978, 1982; Gordon et al. 1980; Riger and Gordon 1979, 1981; Riger, Gordon, and LeBailly 1978, 1982; Riger, LeBailly, and Gordon 1981; Riger, Rogel, and Gordon 1980.

CHAPTER 9. SHOULD WOMEN FEAR?

1. Brownmiller 1975; Griffin 1979.

2. For example, Burgess and Holmstrom 1974; Holmstrom and Burgess 1978; Katz and Mazur 1979.

3. Berger 1977; Holmstrom and Burgess 1978; Medea and Thompson 1974.

4. Lerner 1980.

5. Ryan 1971.

6. Feild 1978; Jones and Aronson 1973; Krulewitz 1977.

7. Feild 1978; Selby, Calhoun, and Brock 1977.

8. Hindelang and Davis 1977; McDermott 1979; Block and Skogan 1982.

9. Bart 1981; Bart and O'Brien 1985; McIntyre, Myint, and Curtis 1979.

10. Bart 1981; Sanders 1980; see also Carter, Prentky, and Burgess 1988.

11. Janoff-Bulman 1979; Sanders 1980.

12. Block and Skogan 1982. This study excluded persons killed in the course of their attacks.

13. For 1976, for example, the Spearman rank-order correlation was .68; Bowker 1978: 120.

14. Riger, LeBailly, and Gordon 1981.

15. Gordon et al. 1980.

16. Feild 1978; Jones and Aronson 1973; Krulewitz 1977.

17. Lerner 1980.

18. Brownmiller 1975; Malamuth, Haber, and Feshback 1980.

19. See also "Society's Acceptance of 'Legitimate Violence' Might Be Factor in Rape Rate, Study Says," 1987.
    This tolerance for violence was demonstrated by the public's reaction to the Goetz case. Late in December 1984, Bernhard Hugo Goetz shot four black teenagers who tried to rob him on a New York City subway. He disappeared, only later to turn himself in to a New Hampshire police station. By the time he did, he had become something of a national folk hero, with newspaper headlines and radio talk shows providing evidence of strong support for his behavior from all segments of the U.S. population. A *New York Times* headline (January 7, 1985, p. 12) proclaimed, "Angry Citizens in Many Cities Applauding Shootings by Goetz." A TV segment on *Sunday Morning America* was entitled, "We're Mad as Hell About Crime, and We're Not Going to Take It Anymore."

As the *New York Times* article said, "Many people—from Chicago to Hawaii to Canada—have responded vehemently to an event that seems to have embodied their fears and frustrations about crime in their own cities." The only people publicly disagreeing were elected officials and law-enforcement personnel. Even as he condemned it, New York Mayor Ed Koch said he, too, understood the frustration and anger. He cautioned, however, that "vigilantism will not be tolerated in this city."

CHAPTER 10. SOCIETY'S RESPONSIBILITY

1. Wildavsky 1979.

2. Nathan Caplan and Steven Nelson in their 1973 article "On Being Useful" argue that it is easier for psychologists to focus on "person-centered variables" than on "situational" ones which are harder to operationalize and collect valid data on. These authors also argue that it is easier for policymakers to advocate legislation that calls for individuals to change rather than for changes in systems or institutions.

3. Caplan 1978:15.

4. For example, D. Smith 1979.

5. Farberow 1963.

6. See also Cohn, Kidder, and Harvey 1978.

7. Ryan 1971.

8. Pauline Bart, personal communication, 1984.

9. Largen 1976.

10. Caplan and Nelson 1973.

11. Maslach, in Bush and Gordon 1978:113.

12. For example, Latta and von Seggern 1978; Marsh, Geist, and Caplan 1982.

13. See 1984 report of National Advisory Committee on Prevention and Control of Rape to U.S. Secretary of Health and Human Services.

14. New studies are reporting significant percentages of women whose post-rape symptoms increase with time, rather than decreasing. In some instances, after what has appeared to be complete recovery, women suddenly show effects the majority of victims show in the first few weeks or months following an attack.

15. The feminist film *Not a Love Story* depicts the impact of a progression of pornography, violent pornography, and child pornography on society.

16. Chapter 6 is based on Loh 1981; Marsh, Geist, and Caplan 1982; Berger 1977; and others.

17. In one recent case, however, the convicted rapist was given a choice by the judge of castration or thirty years in prison, and chose the former.

18. Marsh, Geist, and Caplan 1982.

19. For examples of scholars, see Marsh, Geist, and Caplan 1982; Caringella-McDonald 1982; for prosecutors, Heiman 1982.

20. See, for example, Bob Greene 1987.

21. Sally Merry 1976.
22. See the series of articles by Gordon and Riger, and Riger and Gordon.
23. Ibid.
24. Bart 1981; Bart and O'Brien 1985.
25. Janoff-Bulman 1979; Katz and Burt 1988.

Appendix B

1. Lewis 1978.
2. Gordon and Riger 1978.
3. Skogan 1978a; Lewis and Salem 1980; Podalevsky and DuBow 1980; Skogan and Maxfield 1981.

References

Abu-Lughod, J. "Engendering knowledge." Paper presented as College of Arts and Sciences Lecture, Northwestern University (January 1981).

Albin, R. S. "Psychological studies of rape." *Signs: Journal of Women in Culture and Society* 3 (1977): 423–435.

Altheide, D. *Creating Reality: How TV Distorts the News.* Beverly Hills: Sage Publications (1974).

Amir, M. *Patterns in Forcible Rape.* Chicago: University of Chicago Press (1971).

Andersen, M. "Rape theories, myth and social change." Review essay, unpublished (1982).

Balkin, S. "Victimization rates, safety and fear of crime." *Social Problems* 26 (1979): 343–358.

Baron, L., and M. Straus. "Legitimate violence and rape: A test of the cultural spillover theory." Unpublished paper (March 1985).

Bart, P. B. "Women who were both raped and avoided being raped." *Journal of Social Issues* 37, 4 (1981): 123–137.

Bart, P. B., and P. H. O'Brien. *Stopping Rape: Successful Survival Strategies.* Elmsford, NY: Pergamon Press (1985).

Battelle Institute. "Forcible rape: An analysis of legal issues." National Institute of Law Enforcement and Criminal Justice, Law Enforcement Assistance Administration (1978).

Baumer, T. L. "Research on fear of crime in the United States." *Victimology: An International Journal* 3 (1978): 253–264.

Becker, E. *The Denial of Death.* New York: Free Press (1973).

Bem, D. J. *Beliefs, Attitudes and Human Affairs.* Monterey, CA: Brooks/Cole (1970).

Berger, V. "Man's trial, woman's tribulation: Rape cases in the courtroom." *Columbia Law Review* 77 (1977): 1–103.

Biderman, A. D., L. A. Johnson, J. McIntyre, and A. W. Weir. *Report on Victimization and Attitudes Toward Law Enforcement.* Washington, DC: Government Printing Office (1967).

Block, R., and W. Skogan. "The dynamics of violence between strangers: Victim resistance and outcomes in rape, assault, and robbery." Center for Urban Affairs and Policy Research, Northwestern University, Evanston, IL (1984).

Blumenthal, M., R. Kahn, F. Andrews, and K. Head. *Justifying Violence: Attitudes of American Men.* Ann Arbor, MI: Institute for Social Research (1982).

Boulding, E. *The Underside of History: A View of Women Through Time.* Boulder, CO: Westview Press (1976).

———. "Women and social violence." *International Social Science Journal* 30, 4 (1978): 801–815.

Bowker, L. H. *Women, Crime, and the Criminal Justice System.* Lexington, MA: D. C. Heath (1978).

———. "The criminal victimization of women." *Victimology: An International Journal* 4 (1979): 371–384.

Brodyaga, L., M. Gates, S. Singer, M. Tucker, and R. White. *Rape and Its Victims: A Report for Citizens, Health Facilities and Criminal Justice Agencies.* Washington, DC: U.S. Government Printing Office (1975).

Brownmiller, S. *Against Our Will: Men, Women and Rape.* New York: Simon & Schuster (1975).

Bulletin, Bureau of Justice Statistics, U.S. Department of Statistics, U.S. Government Printing Office: 0–344–894:QL3 (1981).

Burgess, A. W., and L. L. Holmstrom. *Rape: Victims of Crisis.* Bowie, MD: Brady (1974).

Burt, M. R. "Cultural myths and supports for rape." *Journal of Personality and Social Psychology* 38 (1980): 217–230.

Byers, E. S., A. M. Eastman, and B. G. Nilson. "Relationship between degree of sexual assault, antecedent conditions, and victim-offender relationship." Paper presented at meeting of American Psychological Association, San Francisco (August 1977).

Caignon, D., and G. Groves, eds. *Her Wits About Her: Self-Defense Success Stories by Women.* New York: Harper & Row (1987).

Cannon, W. B. "The James-Lange theory of emotions: A critical examination and an alternative theory." *American Journal of Psychology* 39 (1927): 106–124.

———. *Bodily Changes in Pain, Hunger, Fear and Rage.* 2nd ed. New York: Appleton (1929).

Caplan, N. "Women and policy first: Making rape research pay off." Paper presented at American Psychological Association meeting, Toronto (1978).

Caplan, N., and S. D. Nelson. "On being useful." *American Psychologist* (March 1973): 199–211.

Capuzzo, M. "A sexual battleground: Wife rape—from courtship to courtroom." *Chicago Tribune* Section 5 (January 14, 1985): 1.

Caringella-McDonald, S. "The impetus for change: Reasons and reform in rape legislation." Paper presented at American Society of Criminologists, Toronto (November 4–7, 1982).

Carter, D. L., R. A. Prentky, and A. W. Burgess. "Victim response strategies in sexual assault." In A. W. Burgess, ed., *Rape and Sexual Assault II*. New York and London: Garland Publishing (1988).

Catalano, R. *Health, Behavior and the Community: An Ecological Perspective.* New York: Pergamon Press (1979).

Chapman, J. R., and M. Gates. *The Victimization of Women.* Beverly Hills, CA: Sage Publications (1978).

Chappell, D., and F. Fogarty. "Forcible rape: A literature review and annotated bibliography." Washington, DC: U.S. Department of Justice (1978).

Chappell, D., G. Geis, and F. Fogarty. "Forcible rape: Bibliography." *Journal of Criminal Law and Criminology* 65 (1974): 248–263.

Chappell, D., R. Geis, and G. Geis, eds. *Forcible Rape: The Crime, the Victim, and the Offender.* New York: Columbia University Press (1977).

Clark, L., and D. Lewis. *Rape: The Price of Coercive Sexuality.* Toronto: The Women's Press (1977).

Clark, L. M. G., and S. Armstrong. *A Rape Bibliography. With Special Emphasis on Rape Research in Canada.* Ottawa: Ministry of Supply and Services (1979).

Clark, T. F., and D. Buchner. "Critical issues in the prosecution of rape: A cross jurisdictional study of 17 U.S. cities." Paper presented at American Society of Criminologists, Toronto (November 4–7, 1982).

Clemente, F., and M. B. Kleiman. "Fear of crime in the U.S.: A multivariate analysis." *Social Forces* 56 (1977): 519–531.

Clendenin, D. (reporter for the *New York Times*). Personal communication (November 1984).

Cline, V. B., ed. *Where Do You Draw the Line? An Exploration into Media Violence, Pornography, and Censorship.* Provo, Utah: Brigham Young University Press (1974).

Cobb, S. "Social support as a moderator of life stress." *Psychomatic Medicine* 38 (1976): 300–314.

Cohn, E., L. H. Kidder, and J. Harvey. "Crime prevention vs. victimization prevention: The psychology of two different reactions." *Victimology: An International Journal* 3 (1978): 285–296.

Conklin, J. E. *The Impact of Crime.* New York: Macmillan (1975).

Cook, F. L., W. G. Skogan, T. D. Cook, and G. E. Antunes. *Setting and Reformulating Policy Agendas: The Case of Criminal Victimization of the Elderly.* New York: Oxford University Press (1982).

Crime and Violence. Staff report submitted to the President's National Commission on the Causes and Prevention of Violence (1967).

Daniels, A. K. *Invisible Careers: Women Volunteers Who Become Civic Leaders.* Chicago: University of Chicago Press (1988).

Davis, S. K. "The influence of an untoward public act on conceptions of self." *Symbolic Interaction* 1, 2 (Spring 1978): 106–123.

Dean, C. W., and M. deBruyn-Kops. *The Crime and Consequences of Rape.* Springfield, IL: Charles C. Thomas (1982).

Dodge, R. W., H. Lentzner, and F. Shenk. "Crime in the United States: A report on the National Crime Survey." In W. G. Skogan, ed., *Sample Surveys of the Victims of Crime*. Cambridge, MA: Ballinger (1976).

Donnerstein, E. "Aggressive pornography: Can it influence aggression?" In *Primary Prevention and Pornography*, Vol. 7 (1982).

———. "Erotica and human aggression." In R. Green and E. Donnerstein, eds., *Aggression: Theoretical and Empirical Reviews*. New York: Academic Press (1982).

Drapkin, I., and E. Viano, eds. *Victimology: A New Focus*. Lexington, MA: D. C. Heath (1974).

DuBow, R., E. McCabe, and G. Kaplan. *Reactions to Crime: A Critical Review of the Literature*. Washington, DC: U.S. Department of Justice (1979).

Durkheim, E. *The Rules of Sociological Method*. Trans. W. P. Halls. New York: Free Press (1982).

Dworkin, A., and C. MacKinnon. Antipornography Law Proposed as Amendment to Minneapolis, Minnesota Code of Ordinances, Civil Rights, Title 7, Chapters 139, 141. Hearings, December 12–13, 1983.

Ehrensaft, D. *Parenting Together: Men and Women Sharing the Care of Their Children*. New York: Free Press (1987).

Erskine, H. "The polls: Fear of violence and crime." *Public Opinion Quarterly* 38, 1 (Spring 1974): 131–145.

Eysenck, H. J., and D. K. B. Nias. *Sex, Violence and the Media*. London: Maurice Temple Smith (1978).

Farberow, N. L., ed. *Taboo Topics*. New York: Atherton Press (1963).

Federal Bureau of Investigation. *Crime in the U.S.: Uniform Crime Report*. Washington, DC: U.S. Government Printing Office (1976).

———. *Uniform Crime Reports for the United States*. Washington, DC: U.S. Government Printing Office (1976).

Feild, H. S. "Attitudes toward rape: A comparative analysis of police, rapists, crisis counselors and citizens." *Journal of Personality and Social Psychology* 36 (1978): 156–179.

Feild, H. S., and N. J. Barnett. "Forcible rape, an updated bibliography." *Journal of Criminal Law and Criminology* 68 (1977): 146–159.

Fein, E. B. "Angry citizens in many cities applauding shooting by Goetz." *New York Times* (January 7, 1985): 12.

Fein, J. *Are You a Target?* Belmont, CA: Wadsworth Publishing Co. (1981).

Feldman-Summers, S., P. E. Gordon, and J. R. Meagher. "The impact of rape on sexual satisfaction." *Journal of Abnormal Psychology* 88, 1 (1979): 101–105.

The Figgie Report on Fear of Crime: America Afraid. A-T-O, 4420 Sherwin Road, Willoughby, OH 44094 (1980).

Fischer, C. S. *Networks and Places: Social Relations in the Urban Setting*. New York: Free Press (1977).

———. "The public and private worlds of city life." *American Sociological Review* 46 (1981): 306–316.

Fowler, F. J., and T. W. Mangione. "The nature of fear." Unpublished paper by the Survey Research Program, a facility of the University of Massachusetts-Boston and the Joint Center for Urban Studies of M.I.T. and Harvard University (1974).

Furstenberg, F. F., Jr. "Public reaction to crime in the streets." *American Scholar* 40 (1971): 601–610.

———. "Fear of crime and its effect on citizen behavior." In A. Biderman, ed., *Crime and Justice: A Symposium.* New York: Nailburg (1972).

Gans, H. *Urban Villagers: Group and Class in the Lives of Italian-Americans.* New York: Free Press (1962).

Garofalo, J. *Public Opinion About Crime: The Attitudes of Victims and Non-victims in Selected Cities.* Washington, DC: U.S. Government Printing Office (1977).

———. "Victimization and the fear of crime." *Journal of Research in Crime and Delinquency* 16 (1979): 80–97.

Geis, G. "Forcible rape: An introduction." In D. Chappell, R. Geis, and G. Geis, eds., *Forcible Rape: The Crime, the Victim, and the Offender.* New York: Columbia University Press (1977).

———. "Lord Hale, witches, and rape." *British Journal of Law and Society* 5 (Summer 1978a): 26–44.

———. "Rape in marriage: Law and law reform in England, the United States and Sweden." *Adelaide Law Review* 6, 2 (1978b): 284–303.

Gerbner, G., and L. Gross. "Living with television: The violence profile." *Journal of Communications* 26 (1976): 172–199.

Glazer-Malbin, N., and H. Y. Waehrer, eds. *Woman in a Man-Made World.* New York: Rand McNally (1972).

Goffman, I. *Gender Advertisements.* New York: Harper & Row (1979).

Goleman, D. "Researchers dispute pornography report on link to violence." *New York Times* (May 17, 1986): 1.

Gollin, A. E. "Comment on Johnson's 'On the prevalence of rape in the United States.'" *Signs* 6, 2 (1980): 346–349.

Goode, S. "Where a boyfriend becomes no friend." *Insight* (April 20, 1987): 58–59.

Gordon, M. T. *Involving Paraprofessionals in the Helping Process.* Cambridge, MA: Ballinger (1976).

———. "Services to rape victims, research and contributions of social science." Testimony before House Appropriations Committee, U.S. Congress (June 24, 1981).

———. "Costs of ignoring rape." Expert witness testimony before House Appropriations Committee, U.S. Congress (April 1982).

———. "Foreword." In Marsh, J. C., A. Geist, and N. Caplan, *Rape and the Limits of Law Reform.* Boston: Auburn House (1982).

Gordon, M. T., and L. Heath. "The news business, crime and fear." In D. A. Lewis, ed., *Reactions to Crime.* Beverly Hills, CA: Sage Publications (1981).

Gordon, M. T., and S. Riger. "The fear of rape project." *Victimology: An International Journal* 3 (1978): 346–347.

———. "Attitudes toward rape and adaptive behaviors." Final report submitted to the National Center for Prevention and Control of Rape, NIMH (August 1982).

Gordon, M. T., S. Riger, R. K. LeBailly, and L. Heath. "Crime, women and the quality of urban life." *Signs: Journal of Women in Culture and Society 5* (1980) S144–S160. Reprinted in Stimpson et al., eds., *Women and the American City*. Chicago: University of Chicago Press (1981).

Greene, B. "Media moves on, but pain remains." *Chicago Tribune* Tempo Section (March 18, 1987): 1.

Griffin, S. "Rape: The all-American crime." In D. Chappell, R. Geis, and G. Geis, eds., *Forcible Rape: The Crime, the Victim, and the Offender*. New York: Columbia University Press (1977).

———. *Rape: The Power of Consciousness*. San Francisco: Harper & Row (1979).

Groth, A. N., with H. J. Birnbaum. *Men Who Rape: The Psychology of the Offender*. New York: Plenum Press (1979).

Gurr, T. R. "Crime trends in modern democracies since 1945." *International Annals of Criminology* 16 (1977): 41–85.

Hackler, J. C., K. Ho, and C. Urquhart-Ross. "The willingness to intervene: Differing community characteristics." *Social Problems* 21 (1974): 328–344.

Hale, Lord Chief Justice Matthew. *Pleas of the Crown* (1847).

Harris, F. *Presentation of Crime in Newspapers*. Minneapolis, MN: The Sociological Press (1932).

Heath, L. "Impact of newspaper crime reports on fear of crime: Multimethodological investigations." *Journal of Personality and Social Psychology* 47 (1984): 263–276.

Heath, L., M. T. Gordon, and R. K. LeBailly. "What newspapers tell us (and don't tell us) about rape." *Newspaper Research Journal* 2, 4 (July 1981): 48–55.

Heath, L., and Janet Swim. "Newsworthy aspects of murder and sexual assault." Paper presented at meeting of American Society of Criminology, Cincinnati, OH (November 1984).

Heiman, W. "Public policy issues in the prosecution of sexual assault cases." Paper presented at American Society of Criminologists, Toronto (November 4–7, 1982).

Hindelang, M. J., and B. L. Davis. "Forcible rape in the United States: A statistical profile." In D. Chappell, R. Geis, and G. Geis, eds., *Forcible Rape: The Crime, the Victim, and the Offender*. New York: Columbia University Press (1977).

Hindelang, M. J., M. R. Gottfredson, and J. Garofalo. *Victims of Personal Crime: An Empirical Foundation for a Theory of Personal Victimization*. Cambridge, MA: Ballinger (1978).

Holmstrom, L. L., and A. W. Burgess. *The Victim of Rape: Institutional Reactions*. New York: John Wiley & Sons (1978).

Hough, M., and P. Mayhew. *The British Crime Survey: First Report.* A Home Office Research and Planning Unit Report. London: Her Majesty's Stationery Office (1983).

Hughes, H. *News and the Human Interest Story.* Chicago: University of Chicago Press (1940).

Hursch, C. *The Trouble with Rape.* Chicago: Nelson-Hall (1977).

Illich, I. *Gender.* New York: Pantheon Books (1982).

Jacob, H., and R. Lineberry. "Government responses to crime final report." Evanston, IL: Northwestern University, Center for Urban Affairs and Policy Research, Grant #78-NI-AX-9600 (1981).

James, W. *The Principles of Psychology.* New York: Henry Holt (1890).

Janis, I. L., and S. Feshbach. "Effects of fear-arousing communications." *Journal of Abnormal Psychology* 48 (1953): 78–92.

Janis, I. L., and R. Terwilliger. "An experimental study of psychological resistance to fear-arousing communications." *Journal of Abnormal Psychology* 65 (1962): 403–410.

Janoff-Bulman, R. "Characterological versus behavioral self-blame: Inquiries into depression and rape." *Journal of Personality and Social Psychology* 37 (October 1979): 1798–1809.

Jaycox, V. H. "The elderly's fear of crime: Rational and irrational." *Victimology: An International Journal* 3 (1978): 329–334.

Jeffery, P. *Frogs in a Well: Indian Women in Purdah.* London: Zed Press (1979).

Jones, C., and E. Aronson. "Attribution of fault to a rape victim as a function of responsibility of the victim." *Journal of Personality and Social Psychology* 26 (1973): 415–419.

Kahn-Hut, R., A. K. Daniels, and R. Colvard. *Women and Work: Problems and Perspectives.* New York: Oxford University Press (1982).

Kanin, E. J. "Date rape: Unofficial criminals and victims." *Victimology* 9 (1984): 95–108.

———. "Date rapists: Differential sexual socialization and relative deprivation." *Archives of Sexual Behavior* 14 (1985): 219–231.

Katz, B. L., and M. R. Burt. "Self-blame in recovery from rape: Help or hindrance?" In A. W. Burgess, ed., *Rape and Sexual Assault II.* New York and London: Garland Publishing (1988): 151–168.

Katz, S., and M. A. Mazur. *Understanding the rape victim: A synthesis of research findings.* New York: John Wiley & Sons (1979).

Keppler, H. "Dimensions of reactions to crime: A cluster analysis." Evanston, IL: Center for Urban Affairs and Policy Research, Northwestern University (1976).

Kerlinger, F., and E. Pedhazur. *Multiple Regression in Behavioral Research.* New York: Holt, Rinehart & Winston (1973).

Kidder, L. H., and J. Harvey. "Personal defense for women: Learning to define danger." Paper presented at Eastern Psychological Association meeting (April 1978).

Kilpatrick, D. G., et al. "Mental health correlates of criminal victimization: A random community survey." *Journal of Consulting and Clinical Psychology* 53 (1985): 866–873.

Kilpatrick, D. G., P. A. Resick, and L. J. Veronen. "Effects of a rape experience: A longitudinal study." *Journal of Social Issues* 37 (1981): 105–122.

Kilpatrick, D. G., L. J. Veronen, and C. L. Best. "Factors predicting psychological distress among rape victims." In C. R. Figley, ed., *Trauma and Its Wake: The Study and Treatment of Post-Traumatic Stress Disorders*. New York: Brunner/Mazel (1984): 133–141.

Kilpatrick, D. G., L. J. Veronen, and P. A. Resick. "The aftermath of rape: Recent empirical findings." *American Journal of Orthopsychiatry* 49 (1979): 658–669.

Koss, M. P. "The hidden rape victim: Personality, attitudinal, and situational characteristics." *Psychology of Women Quarterly* 9 (1985): 193–212.

———. "Hidden rape: Sexual aggression and victimization in a national sample in higher education." In A. W. Burgess (ed.) *Rape and Sexual Assault II*. New York and London: Garland Publishing (1988): 3–24.

Krulewitz, J. E. "Sex differences in rape attributions." Paper presented at annual meeting of Midwestern Psychological Association, Chicago (May 1977).

Krupat, E., and W. Guild. "The measurement of community social climate." *Environment and Behavior* 12 (1980): 195–206.

Kübler-Ross, E. *Questions and Answers on Death and Dying*. New York: Macmillan (1974).

Kutschinsky, B. *Pornography and Sex Crimes in Denmark*. A Report to the U.S. Presidential Commission on Obscenity and Pornography (1970).

Largen, M. A. "History of women's movement in changing attitudes, laws, and treatment toward rape victims." In M. J. Walker and S. L. Brodsky, eds., *Sexual Assault: The Victim and the Rapist*. Lexington, MA: Lexington Books (1976).

———. "Rape law reform: An analysis." In A. W. Burgess, ed., *Rape and Sexual Assault II*. New York and London: Garland Publishing (1988): 271–290.

Larwood, L., E. O'Neal, and P. Brennan. "Increasing the physical aggressiveness of women." *Journal of Social Psychology* 101 (1977): 97–101.

Latane, B., and J. M. Darley. *The Unresponsive Bystander*. New York: Meredith Corporation (1970).

Latta, R. M., and B. von Seggern. "Victim or offender: Who's morally responsible for rape?" Paper presented at American Psychological Association convention, Toronto (1978).

Lavrakas, P. J. "Invincibility vs. extreme susceptibility to street crime: Apparent incongruities in perceptions of personal safety." Unpublished working paper, Evanston, IL: Northwestern University, Center for Urban Affairs and Policy Research (June 1979).

Lavrakas, P. J., and D. A. Lewis. "The conceptualization and measurement of citizen crime prevention behaviors." *Journal of Research in Crime Delinquency* 17 (1980): 254–272.

LeBailly, R. K. "Method artifacts in telephone and in-person interviews: An examination of bias and consistency." Evanston, IL: Center for Urban Affairs and Policy Research, Northwestern University (1979).

Lederer, L., ed. *Take Back the Night.* New York: William Morrow & Co. (1980).

Lerner, M. J. *The Belief in a Just World: A Fundamental Delusion.* New York: Plenum (1980).

Lewis, D. A. "The reactions to crime project." *Victimology: An International Journal* 3 (1978): 344–345.

Lewis, D. A., and M. G. Maxfield. "Fear in the neighborhoods: An investigation of the impact of crime." *Journal of Research in Crime and Delinquency* 17 (1980): 160–189.

Lewis, D. A., and G. Salem. "Crime and urban community: Towards a theory of neighborhood security." Unpublished working paper, Evanston, IL: Northwestern University, Center for Urban Affairs and Policy Research (1980).

Lipman-Blumen, J., and J. Bernard. *Sex Roles and Social Policy.* Beverly Hills, CA: Sage Publications (1976).

Lofland, L. H. *A World of Strangers.* New York: Basic Books (1973).

———. "The 'thereness' of women: A selective review of urban sociology." In M. Millman and R. M. Kanter, eds., *Another Voice: Feminist Perspectives on Social Life and Social Sciences.* New York: Anchor Books (1975).

Loh, W. D. "What has reform of rape legislation wrought?" *Journal of Social Issues* 37, 4 (Fall 1981): 28–53.

Lottes, I. L. "Sexual socialization and attitudes toward rape." In A. W. Burgess, ed., *Rape and Sexual Assault II.* New York and London: Garland Publishing (1988).

Lykken, D. T. "A study of anxiety in the sociopathic personality." *Journal of Abnormal and Social Psychology* 55 (1957): 6–10.

Maccoby, E., and C. Jacklin. *The Psychology of Sex Differences.* Stanford, CA: Stanford University Press (1974).

Malamuth, N., and J. Check. "The effects of mass media exposure on acceptance of violence against women: A field experiment." *Journal of Research in Personality* (1982).

Malamuth, N., and E. Donnerstein, eds. *Pornography and Sexual Aggression.* New York: Academic Press (1984).

Malamuth, N. M., S. Haber, and S. Feshback. "Testing hypotheses regarding rape: Exposure to sexual violence, sex differences, and the 'normality' of rapists." *Journal of Research in Personality* 14 (1980): 121–137.

Maltz, M. D. *Evaluation of Crime Control Problems.* Washington, DC: Law Enforcement Assistance Administration (1972).

Margolick, D. "Top court in New York rules men can be charged with rape of wives." *New York Times* (December 21, 1984): 1.

Marsh, J. C., A. Geist, and N. Caplan. *Rape and the Limits of Law Reform.* Boston: Auburn House (1982).

Maslach, C. "The client role in staff burnout." In M. Bush and A. Gordon, eds., *Bureaucracies and People,* Special Issue of *Journal of Social Issues* 34, 4 (January 1978): 111–124.

Maxfield, M. *Fear of Crime in England and Wales.* London: Her Majesty's Stationery Office (1984).

McDermott, M. J. "California rape evidence reform: An analysis of Senate Bill 1678." *Hastings Law Journal* 26 (1975): 1551.

————. *Rape victimization in 26 American cities.* Washington, DC: U.S. Department of Justice (1979).

McIntyre, J. "Public attitudes toward crime and law enforcement." *Annals of the American Academy of Political and Social Science* 41 (1967): 34–36.

McIntyre, J., T. Myint, and L. Curtis. "Sexual assault outcomes: Completed and attempted rapes." Paper presented at annual meeting of American Sociological Association, San Francisco (1979).

McPherson, M. "Realities and perceptions of crime at the neighborhood level." *Victimology: An International Journal* 3 (1978): 319–328.

Medea, A., and K. Thompson. *Against Rape.* New York: Farrar, Straus & Giroux (1974).

Merry, S. E. "The management of danger in a high-crime urban neighborhood." Paper presented at annual meeting of American Anthropological Association (November 1976).

Meyer, M. A. "Economic inequality and the sentencing of sexual assault offenders." Paper presented at American Society of Criminologists, Toronto (November 4–7, 1982).

Meyer, T. J. "Date rape: A serious campus problem that few talk about." *Chronicle of Higher Education* (December 5, 1984).

Millett, K. *Sexual Politics.* Garden City, NY: Doubleday (1970).

National Advertising Bureau. *Readership Studies,* 1979–1984.

National Criminal Justice Reference Service. *Rape.* Washington, DC: U.S. Department of Justice (1981).

Park, R. E. *On Social Control and Collective Behavior.* Chicago: University of Chicago Press (1967).

Park, R. E., and E. W. Burgess. *The City.* Chicago: University of Chicago Press (1925/1967).

Peters, J. "Social, legal, and psychological effects of rape on the victim." *Pennsylvania Medicine* 78 (1975): 34.

Pinkney, A. *The American Way of Violence.* New York: Random House (1972).

Podalevsky, A., and F. DuBow. *Citizens' Participation in Collective Responses to Crime.* Springfield, IL: Charles C. Thomas (1980).

Rapaport, K., and B. R. Burkhardt. "Personality and attitudinal characteristics of sexually coercive college males." *Journal of Abnormal Psychology* 93 (1984): 216–221.

Reiss, A., Jr. "Public perceptions and recollections about crime, law enforcement, and criminal justice." In A. J. Reiss, Jr. (ed.), *Studies in Crime and Law Enforcement in Major Metropolitan Areas.* Vol. 1, Section LL, U.S. President's Commission on Law Enforcement and Administration of Justice Field Survey III. (Washington, DC: U.S. Government Printing Office, 1967).

Riger, S., and P. Galligan. "Women in management: An exploration of competing paradigms." *American Psychologist* 35, 10 (October 1980): 902–910.

Riger, S., and M. T. Gordon. "The structure of rape prevention beliefs." *Personality and Social Psychology Bulletin* 5 (1979): 186–190.

————. "The fear of rape: A study of social control." *Journal of Social Issues* 37, 4 (1981): 71–92.

————. "The impact of crime on urban women." In A. W. Burgess, ed., *Rape and Sexual Assault II.* New York and London: Garland Publishing (1988): 295–312.

Riger, S., M. T. Gordon, and R. K. LeBailly. "Women's fear of crime: From blaming to restricting the victim." *Victimology: An International Journal* 3 (1978): 274–284.

Riger, S., M. T. Gordon, and R. K. LeBailly. "Coping with urban crime: Women's use of precautionary behaviors." *American Journal of Community Psychology* 10 (1982): 369–386.

Riger, S., and P. J. Lavrakas. "Community ties: Patterns of attachment and social interaction in urban neighborhoods." *American Journal of Community Psychology* 9, 1 (1982): 55–66.

Riger, S., R. K. LeBailly, and M. T. Gordon. "Community ties and urbanites' fear of crime: An ecological investigation." *American Journal of Community Psychology* 9, 6 (1981): 653–665.

Riger, S., M. J. Rogel, and M. T. Gordon. "Urban women and the fear of crime." Unpublished working paper. Evanston, IL: Northwestern University, Center for Urban Affairs and Policy Research (1980).

Rose, V. M. "Rape as a social problem: A byproduct of the feminist movement." *Social Problems* 25 (1977): 75–89.

Rothman, S. *Woman's Proper Place.* New York: Basic Books (1978).

Russell, D. E. H. *The Politics of Rape: The Victim's Perspective.* New York: Stein & Day (1975).

————. Personal communication (July 24, 1981).

Ryan, W. *Blaming the Victim.* New York: Vintage Press (1971).

Sabini, J., and M. Silver. *Moralities of Everyday Life.* Oxford, England: Oxford University Press (1982).

Sanders, W. B. *Rape and Woman's Identity.* Beverly Hills, CA: Sage Publications (1980).

Schachter, S. *Emotion, Obesity and Crime.* New York: Academic Press (1971).

Schecter, S. *Women and Male Violence.* Boston: South End Press (1982).

Schiff, A. F. "Rape in foreign countries." *Medical Trial Technique Quarterly* 20 (1973): 66–74.

Schutz, A. *Phaenomenologia, Collected Papers by Alfred Schutz*. The Hague: Martinus Nijhoff (1962).

———. *Collected Papers: Volume I. The Problem of Social Reality*. Ed. Maurice Natanson. The Hague: Martinus Nijhoff (1971).

Schwendinger, J. R., and H. Schwendinger. *Rape and Inequality*. Beverly Hills, CA: Sage Publications (1983).

Schwengles, M., and J. B. Lemert. "Fair warning: A comparison of police and newspaper reports about rape." *Newspaper Research Journal* 7, 3 (1986): 35–42.

Selby, J. W., L. G. Calhoun, and T. A. Brock. "Sex differences in the social perception of rape victims." *Personality and Social Psychology Bulletin* 3 (1977): 412–415.

Skogan, W. G. "Dimension of the dark figure of unreported crime." *Crime and Delinquency* 23 (1977): 41–50.

———. "The Center for Urban Affairs random digit dialing telephone survey." Evanston, IL: Center for Urban Affairs and Policy Research, Northwestern University (1978a).

———. "Crime in contemporary America." In H. Graham and T. R. Gurr, eds., *Violence in America*. 2nd ed. Beverly Hills, CA: Sage Publications (1978b).

———. "Coping with crime: Fear and risk management in urban communities." Paper presented at annual meetings of American Society of Criminology, Dallas (November 1978c).

Skogan, W. G., and A. Gordon. "Detective division reporting practices: A review of the Chicago police crime classification audit." In *Crime in Illinois, 1982* (1983): 166–182.

Skogan, W. G., and M. G. Maxfield. *Coping with Crime: Victimization, Fear and Reactions to Crime in Three American Cities*. Beverly Hills, CA: Sage Publications (1981).

Slovic, P., B. Fischoff, and S. Lichtenstein. "Facts and fears: Understanding perceived risk." In R. Schwing and W. Albers, eds., *Societal Risk Assessment: How Safe Is Enough?* New York: Plenum Press (1980): 181–216.

Smith, D. "A sociology for women." In J. Sherman and E. Beck, *The Prism of Sex: Essays in the Sociology of Knowledge*. Madison, WI: Wisconsin University Press (1979): 135–188.

Smith, M. "Women's fear of violent crime: An exploratory test of a feminist hypothesis." *Journal of Family Violence* (forthcoming).

Smith-Rosenberg, C. "Puberty to menopause: The cycle of femininity in nineteenth-century America." In M. Hartman and L. W. Bannier, eds., *Clio's Consciousness Raised*. New York: Harper Colophon (1974): 23–37.

"Society's acceptance of 'legitimate violence' might be a factor in rape rate, study says." *Miami Herald* (January 9, 1987).

Stimpson, C., E. Dialer, M. Nelson, and K. Yatrakis. *Women and the American City*. Chicago: University of Chicago Press (1980/1981).

Stinchcombe, A. L., R. C. Adams, C. A. Heimer, K. L. Scheppele, T. W. Smith, and G. E. Taylor. *Crime-and-Punishment—Changing Attitudes in America*. San Francisco: Jossey-Bass (1980).

Strauss, M. A., R. J. Gellis, and S. K. Steinmetz. *Behind Closed Doors*. New York: Anchor Books (1980).

Sundeen, R. A., and J. T. Mathieu. "The fear of crime and its consequences among elderly in three urban communities." *Gerontologist* 16 (1976): 211–219.

Tuckman, G. *Making News: A Study in the Construction of Reality*. New York: Free Press (1978).

U.S. Commission on Crime. Task Force Report. Washington, DC: U.S. Government Printing Office (1967).

U.S. Department of Justice. *Criminal Victimization in the United States 1973–78 Trends*. Washington, DC: U.S. Government Printing Office (1980a).

———. *Intimate Victims: A Study of Violence Among Friends and Relatives*. Washington, DC: U.S. Government Printing Office (1980b).

U.S. Department of Justice. Uniform Crime Reports, *Crime in the United States, 1986*. Federal Bureau of Investigation. Washington, DC 20535 (July 25, 1987).

U.S. Department of Justice Statistics. *Criminal Victimization 1986*. Bureau of Justice Statistics. Washington, DC: U.S. Government Printing Office (October 1987).

U.S. Department of Statistics. *Bulletin*, Bureau of Justice Statistics, U.S. Government Printing Office: 0–344–894:QL3 (1981).

Weis, K., and S. S. Borges. "Victimology and rape: The case of the legitimate victim." *Issues in Criminology* 8 (1973): 71–115.

Weisman, A. *On Dying and Denying: A Psychiatric Study of Terminality*. New York: Behavioral Publications (1972).

Wildavsky, A. *Speaking Truth to Power: The Art and Craft of Policy Analysis*. Boston: Little Brown (1979).

Wirth, L. *On Cities and Social Life*. Chicago: University of Chicago Press (1938).

Wolff, K. H., ed. *The Sociology of Georg Simmel*. London: Free Press of Glencoe (1950).

Yin, P. P. "Fear of crime among the elderly: Some issues and suggestions." *Social Problems* 27 (1980): 492–504.

Zillman, D., and J. Bryant. "Effects of massive exposure to pornography." In N. M. Malamuth and E. Donnerstein, eds., *Pornography and Sexual Aggression*. New York: Academic Press (1984): 115–138.

Zillman, D., and J. Wakshlag. "Fear of victimization and the appeal of crime drama." In D. Zillman and J. Bryant, eds., *Selective Exposure to Communication*. Hillsdale, NJ: Erlbaum (in press).

Index